SELECTED MATERIAL FROM

Business Driven Technology

Second Edition

K201: The Computer In Business
Indiana University
Kelley School of Business
Operations and Decision Technologies
Coordinator: Ms. Amy Kinser

Stephen Haag

Paige Baltzan

Amy Phillips
All of Daniels College of Business
University of Denver

 **Learning Solutions**

Boston   Burr Ridge, IL   Dubuque, IA   New York   San Francisco   St. Louis
Bangkok   Bogotá   Caracas   Lisbon   London   Madrid
Mexico City   Milan   New Delhi   Seoul   Singapore   Sydney   Taipei   Toronto

The **McGraw·Hill** Companies

Selected Material from
Business Driven Technology, Second Edition
K201: The Computer In Business
Indiana University
Kelley School of Business
Operations and Decision Technologies
Coordinator: Ms. Amy Kinser

1 2 3 4 5 6 7 8 9 0 PAH PAH 0 9 8 7

ISBN 13: 978-0-697-77766-9
ISBN 10: 0-697-77766-9

Custom Publishing Specialist: Michael Hemmer
Production Editor: Nina Meyer
Printer/Binder: The P.A. Hutchison Company

Contents

1

Business Driven Technology

1.1. Compare management information systems (MIS) and information technology (IT).

1.2. Describe the relationships among people, information technology, and information.

1.3. Identify four different departments in a typical business and explain how technology helps them to work together.

1.4. Compare the four different types of organizational information cultures and decide which culture applies to your school.

Information Technology's Role in Business

Students frequently ask, "Why do we need to study information technology?" The answer is simple: Information technology is everywhere in business. Understanding information technology provides great insight to anyone learning about business.

It is easy to demonstrate information technology's role in business by reviewing a copy of popular business magazines such as *BusinessWeek, Fortune, Business 2.0,* or *Fast Company.* Placing a marker (such as a Post-it Note) on each page that contains a technology-related article or advertisement indicates that information technology is everywhere in business (see Figure 1.1). These are *business* magazines, not *technology* magazines, yet they are filled with technology. Students who understand technology have an advantage in business, and gaining a detailed understanding of information technology is important to all students regardless of their area of expertise.

The magazine articles typically discuss such topics as databases, customer relationship management, Web services, supply chain management, security, ethics, business intelligence, and so on. They also focus on companies such as Siebel, Oracle, Microsoft, and IBM. This text explores these topics in detail, along with reviewing the associated business opportunities and challenges.

FIGURE 1.1

Technology in *BusinessWeek* and *Fortune*

INFORMATION TECHNOLOGY'S IMPACT ON BUSINESS OPERATIONS

Figure 1.2 highlights the business functions receiving the greatest benefit from information technology, along with the common business goals associated with information technology projects according to *CIO* magazine.[2]

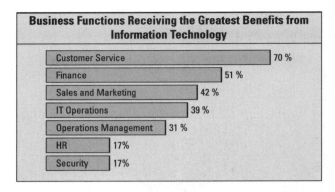

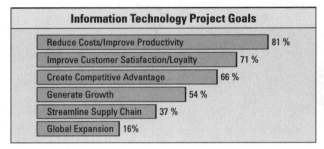

FIGURE 1.2

Business Benefits and
Information Technology
Project Goals

Achieving the results outlined in Figure 1.2, such as reducing costs, improving productivity, and generating growth, is not easy. Implementing a new accounting system or marketing plan is not likely to generate long-term growth or reduce costs across an entire organization. Businesses must undertake enterprisewide initiatives to achieve broad general business goals such as reducing costs. Information technology plays a critical role in deploying such initiatives by facilitating communication and increasing business intelligence. For example, e-mail and cell phones allow people across an organization to communicate in new and innovative ways.

Understanding information technology begins with gaining an understanding of how businesses function and IT's role in creating efficiencies and effectiveness across the organization. Typical businesses operate by functional areas (often called functional silos). Each functional area undertakes a specific core business function (see Figure 1.3).

Functional areas are anything but independent in a business. In fact, functional areas are *interdependent* (see Figure 1.4). Sales must rely on information from operations to understand inventory, place orders, calculate transportation costs, and gain insight into product availability based on production schedules. For an organization to succeed, every department or functional area must work together sharing common information and not be a "silo." Information technology can enable departments to more efficiently and effectively perform their business operations.

Any individual anticipating a successful career in business whether it is in accounting, finance, human resources, or operation management must understand the basics of information technology.

Information Technology Basics

Information technology (IT) is any computer-based tool that people use to work with information and support the information and information-processing needs of an organization. Information technology can be an important enabler of business success and innovation. This is not to say that IT *equals* business success and innovation or that IT *represents* business success and innovation. Information technology is most useful when it leverages the talents of people. Information technology in and of itself is not useful unless the right people know how to use and manage it effectively.

Management information systems is a business function just as marketing, finance, operations, and human resources are business functions. Formally defined, *management information systems (MIS)* is the function that plans for, develops, implements, and maintains IT hardware, software, and applications that people use to support the goals of an organization. To perform the MIS function effectively, almost all organizations today, particularly large and medium-sized ones, have an internal IT department, often called Information Technology (IT), Information Systems (IS), or Management Information Systems (MIS). When beginning to learn about information technology it is important to understand the following:

- Information
- IT resources
- IT cultures

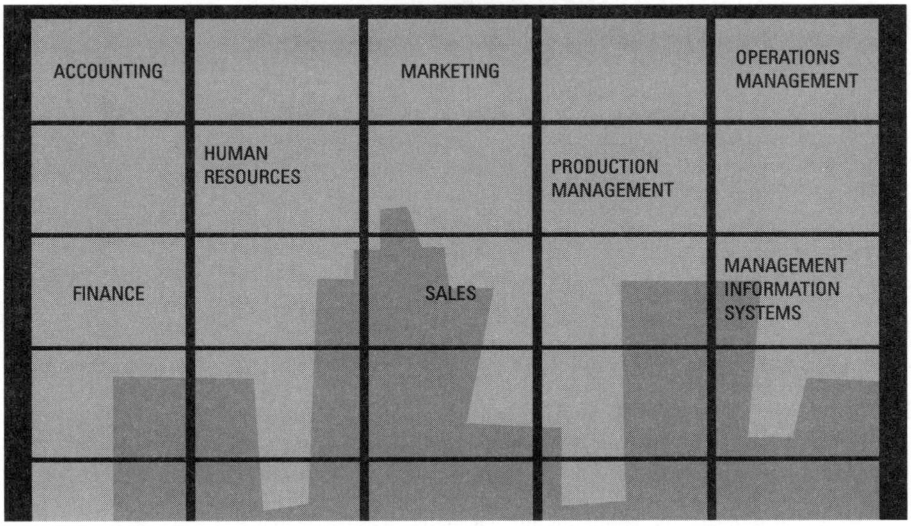

FIGURE 1.3

Departmental Structure of
a Typical Organization

ACCOUNTING		MARKETING		OPERATIONS MANAGEMENT
	HUMAN RESOURCES		PRODUCTION MANAGEMENT	
FINANCE		SALES		MANAGEMENT INFORMATION SYSTEMS

- **Accounting** provides quantitative information about the finances of the business including recording, measuring, and describing financial information.

- **Finance** deals with the strategic financial issues associated with increasing the value of the business, while observing applicable laws and social responsibilities.

- **Human resources (HR)** includes the policies, plans, and procedures for the effective management of employees (human resources).

- **Sales** is the function of selling a good or service and focuses on increasing customer sales, which increases company revenues.

- **Marketing** is the process associated with promoting the sale of goods or services. The marketing department supports the sales department by creating promotions that help sell the company's products.

- **Operations management** (also called **production management**) includes the methods, tasks, and techniques organizations use to produce goods and services. Transportation (also called logistics) is part of operations management.

- **Management information systems (MIS)** is the function that plans for, develops, implements, and maintains IT hardware, software, and the portfolio of applications that people use to support the goals of an organization.

INFORMATION

It is important to distinguish between data and information. *Data* are raw facts that describe the characteristics of an event. Characteristics for a sales event could include the date, item number, item description, quantity ordered, customer name, and shipping details. *Information* is data converted into a meaningful and useful context. Information from sales events could include best-selling item, worst-selling item, best customer, and worst customer.

IT RESOURCES

The plans and goals of the IT department must align with the plans and goals of the organization. Information technology can enable an organization to increase efficiency in manufacturing, retain key customers, seek out new sources of supply, and introduce effective financial management.

FIGURE 1.4

Marketing Working with
Other Organizational
Departments

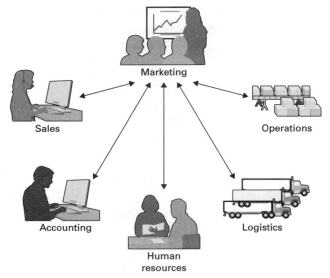

Functional organization—Each functional area has its own systems
and communicates with every other functional area (diagram
displays Marketing communicating with all other functional areas
in the organization).

It is not always easy for managers to make the right choices when using IT to support (and often drive) business initiatives. Most managers understand their business initiatives well, but are often at a loss when it comes to knowing how to use and manage IT effectively in support of those initiatives. Managers who understand what IT is, and what IT can and cannot do, are in the best position for success.

Putting It All Together

In essence,

- *People* use
- *information technology* to work with
- *information* (see Figure 1.5).

Those three key resources—people, information, and information technology (in that order of priority)—are inextricably linked. If one fails, they all fail. Most important, if one fails, then chances are the business will fail.

IT CULTURES

An organization's culture plays a large role in determining how successfully it will share information. Culture will influence the way people use information (their information behavior) and will reflect the importance that company leaders attribute to the use of information in achieving success or avoiding failure. Four common information-sharing cultures exist in organizations today: information-functional, information-sharing, information-inquiring, and information-discovery (see Figure 1.6).[3]

An organization's IT culture can directly affect its ability to compete in the global market. If an organization operates with an information-functional culture it will have a great degree of difficulty operating. Getting products to market quickly and creating a view of its end-to-end (or entire) business from sales to billing will be a challenge. If an organization operates with an information-discovery culture it will

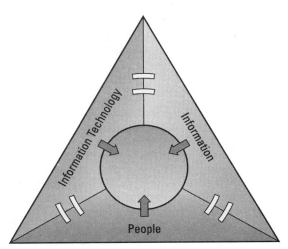

be able to get products to market quickly and easily see a 360-degree view of its entire organization. Employees will be able to use this view to better understand the market and create new products that offer a competitive advantage.

FIGURE 1.6

Different Information Cultures found in Organizations

Organizational Information Cultures	
Information-Functional Culture	Employees use information as a means of exercising influence or power over others. For example, a manager in sales refuses to share information with marketing. This causes marketing to need the sales manager's input each time a new sales strategy is developed.
Information-Sharing Culture	Employees across departments trust each other to use information (especially about problems and failures) to improve performance.
Information-Inquiring Culture	Employees across departments search for information to better understand the future and align themselves with current trends and new directions.
Information-Discovery Culture	Employees across departments are open to new insights about crisis and radical changes and seek ways to create competitive advantages.

OPENING CASE STUDY QUESTIONS

1. Explain how Apple achieved business success through the use of information, information technology, and people.

2. Describe the types of information employees at an Apple store require and compare it to the types of information the executives at Apple's corporate headquarters require. Are there any links between these two types of information?

3. Identify the type of information culture that would have the greatest negative impact on Apple's operations.

In his book, *The World is Flat*, Thomas Friedman describes the unplanned cascade of techno-logical and social shifts that effectively leveled the economic world, and "accidentally made Beijing, Bangalore, and Bethesda next-door neighbors." Chances are good that Bhavya in Bangalore will read your next X-ray, or as Friedman learned first-hand, "Grandma Betty in her bathrobe" will make your JetBlue plane reservation from her Salt Lake City home.

Friedman believes this is Globalization 3.0. "In Globalization 1.0, which began around 1492, the world went from size large to size medium. In Globalization 2.0, the era that introduced us to multinational companies, it went from size medium to size small. And then around 2000 came Globalization 3.0, in which the world went from being small to tiny. There is a difference between being able to make long-distance phone calls cheaper on the Internet and walking around Riyadh with a PDA where you can have all of Google in your pocket. It is a difference in degree that's so enormous it becomes a difference in kind," Friedman states. Figure 1.7 displays Friedman's list of "flatteners."

Friedman says these flatteners converged around the year 2000 and "created a flat world: a global, Web-enabled platform for multiple forms of sharing knowledge and work, irrespec-tive of time, distance, geography, and increasingly, language." At the very moment this plat-form emerged, three huge economies materialized—those of India, China, and the former Soviet Union—"and 3 billion people who were out of the game, walked onto the playing field." A final convergence may determine the fate of the United States in this chapter of globaliza-tion. A "political perfect storm," as Friedman describes it—the dot-com bust, the attacks of 9/11, and the Enron scandal—"distract us completely as a country." Just when we need to face the fact of globalization and the need to compete in a new world, "we're looking totally elsewhere."

FIGURE 1.7

Thomas Friedman's 10 Forces That Flattened the World

1. Fall of the Berlin Wall	The events of November 9, 1989, tilted the worldwide balance of power toward democracies and free markets.
2. Netscape IPO	The August 9, 1995, offering sparked massive investment in fiber-optic cables.
3. Work flow software	The rise of applications from PayPal to VPNs enabled faster, closer coordination among far-flung employees.
4. Open-sourcing	Self-organizing communities, such as Linux, launched a collaborative revolution.
5. Outsourcing	Migrating business functions to India saved money *and* a Third World economy.
6. Offshoring	Contract manufacturing elevated China to economic prominence.
7. Supply-chaining	Robust networks of suppliers, retailers, and customers increased business efficiency.
8. Insourcing	Logistics giants took control of customer supply chains, helping mom-and-pop shops go global.
9. Informing	Power searching allowed everyone to use the Internet as a "personal supply chain of knowledge."
10. Wireless	Wireless technologies pumped up collaboration, making it mobile and personal.

Friedman believes that the next great breakthrough in bioscience could come from a 5-year-old who downloads the human genome in Egypt. Bill Gates's view is similar: "20 years ago, would you rather have been a B-student in Poughkeepsie or a genius in Shanghai? Twenty years ago you'd rather be a B-student in Poughkeepsie. Today, it is not even close. You'd much prefer to be the genius in Shanghai because you can now export your talents anywhere in the world."[4]

Questions

1. Do you agree or disagree with Friedman's assessment that the world is flat? Be sure to justify your answer.
2. What are the potential impacts of a flat world for a student performing a job search?
3. What can students do to prepare themselves for competing in a flat world?
4. Identify a current flattener not mentioned on Friedman's list.

<< BUSINESS PLUG-IN POINTERS

Review the **Business Plug-In B1 "Business Basics"** for an introduction to business fundamentals beginning with the three most common business structures—(1) sole proprietorship, (2) partnership, (3) corporation—and then focusing on the internal operations of a corporation, including accounting, finance, human resources, sales, marketing, operations/ production, and management information systems.

Review the **Business Plug-In B2 "Business Process."** This plug-in dives deeper into the world of business by reviewing business processes, continuous process improvement, business process reengineering, and business process modeling. There are a number of sample business process models diagramming such processes as order entry, online bill payment, e-business processes, and process improvement.

Review the **Business Plug-In B3 "Hardware and Software"** to cover the two basic categories of information technology. Information technology can be composed of the Internet, a personal computer, a cell phone that can access the Web, a personal digital assistant, or presentation software. All of these technologies help to perform specific information processing tasks. This plug-in covers the basics including terminology, business uses, and common characteristics.

Review the **Business Plug-In B4 "Enterprise Architectures,"** which includes the plans for how an organization will build, deploy, use, and share its data, processes, and IT assets. To support the volume and complexity of today's user and application requirements, information technology needs to take a fresh approach to enterprise architectures by constructing smarter, more flexible environments that protect it from system failures and crashes. A solid enterprise architecture can decrease costs, increase

BUSINESS PLUG-IN POINTERS >>

standardization, promote reuse of IT assets, and speed development of new systems. The end result is that the right enterprise architecture can make IT cheaper, strategic, and more responsive.

Review the **Business Plug-In B5 "Networks and Telecommunications"** for a detailed look at telecommunication systems and networks. Businesses around the world are moving to network infrastructure solutions that allow greater choice in how they go to market; the solutions have a global reach. These alternatives include wireless, voice-over Internet protocol (VoIP), and radio-frequency identification (RFID). This plug-in takes a detailed look at key telecommunication, network, and wireless technologies that are integrating businesses around the world.

TECHNOLOGY PLUG-IN POINTER >>

Review the **Technology Plug-In T1 "Personal Productivity Using IT"** for a walk-through on how to take advantage of your computer's many features, including data management, antivirus software, zip files, backup solutions, e-mail etiquette, PC performance, and spam control.

Organizational Structures That Support Strategic Initiatives

5.1. Compare the responsibilities of a chief information officer (CIO), chief technology officer (CTO), chief privacy officer (CPO), chief security officer (CSO), and chief knowledge officer (CKO).

5.2. Explain the gap between IT people and business people and the primary reason this gap exists.

5.3. Define the relationship between security and ethics.

Organizational Structures

Employees across the organization must work closely together to develop strategic initiatives that create competitive advantages. Understanding the basic structure of a typical IT department including titles, roles, and responsibilities will help an organization build a cohesive enterprisewide team.

IT Roles and Responsibilities

Information technology is a relatively new functional area, having been around formally in most organizations only for about 40 years. Job titles, roles, and responsibilities often differ dramatically from organization to organization. Nonetheless, clear trends are developing toward elevating some IT positions within an organization to the strategic level.

Most organizations maintain positions such as chief executive officer (CEO), chief financial officer (CFO), and chief operations officer (COO) at the strategic level. Recently there are more IT-related strategic positions such as chief information officer (CIO), chief technology officer (CTO), chief security officer (CSO), chief privacy officer (CPO), and chief knowledge officer (CKO).

J. Greg Hanson is proud to be the first CIO of the U.S. Senate. Contrary to some perceptions, the technology found in the Senate is quite good, according to Hanson. Hanson's responsibilities include creating the Senate's technology vision, leading the IT department, and deploying the IT infrastructure. Hanson must work with everyone from the 137 network administrators to the senators themselves to ensure that everything is operating smoothly. Hanson is excited to be the first CIO of the U.S. Senate and proud of the sense of honor and responsibility that comes with the job.[30]

The *chief information officer (CIO)* is responsible for (1) overseeing all uses of information technology and (2) ensuring the strategic alignment of IT with business goals and objectives. The CIO often reports directly to the CEO. (See Figure 5.1 for the average CIO compensation.) CIOs must possess a solid and detailed understanding of every aspect of an organization coupled with tremendous insight into the capability of IT. Broad functions of a CIO include:

1. *Manager*—ensure the delivery of all IT projects, on time and within budget.
2. *Leader*—ensure the strategic vision of IT is in line with the strategic vision of the organization.

3. *Communicator*—advocate and communicate the IT strategy by building and maintaining strong executive relationships.

Although CIO is considered a position within IT, CIOs must be concerned with more than just IT. According to a recent survey (see Figure 5.2), most CIOs ranked "enhancing customer satisfaction" ahead of their concerns for any specific aspect of IT. CIOs with the broad business view that customer satisfaction is more crucial and critical than specific aspects of IT should be applauded.[31]

The *chief technology officer (CTO)* is responsible for ensuring the throughput, speed, accuracy, availability, and reliability of an organization's information technology. CTOs are similar to CIOs, except that CIOs take on the additional responsibility for effectiveness of ensuring that IT is aligned with the organization's strategic initiatives. CTOs have direct responsibility for ensuring the *efficiency* of IT systems throughout the organization. Most CTOs possess well-rounded knowledge of all aspects of IT, including hardware, software, and telecommunications.

The *chief security officer (CSO)* is responsible for ensuring the security of IT systems and developing strategies and IT safeguards against attacks from hackers and viruses. The role of a CSO has been elevated in recent years because of the number of attacks from hackers and viruses. Most CSOs possess detailed knowledge of networks and telecommunications because hackers and viruses usually find their way into IT systems through networked computers.

The *chief privacy officer (CPO)* is responsible for ensuring the ethical and legal use of information within an organization. CPOs are the newest senior executive position in IT. Recently, 150 of the Fortune 500 companies added the CPO position to their list of senior executives. Many CPOs are lawyers by training, enabling them to understand the often complex legal issues surrounding the use of information.

The *chief knowledge officer (CKO)* is responsible for collecting, maintaining, and distributing the organization's knowledge. The CKO designs programs and systems that make it easy for people to reuse knowledge. These systems create repositories of organizational documents, methodologies, tools, and practices, and they establish methods for filtering the information. The CKO must continuously encourage employee contributions to keep the systems up-to-date. The CKO can contribute directly to the organization's bottom line by reducing the learning curve for new employees or employees taking on new roles.

In 1998, Danny Shaw became the first CKO at Children's Hospital in Boston. His initial task was to unite information from disparate systems to enable analysis of both the efficiency and effectiveness of the hospital's care. Shaw started by building a series of small, integrated information systems that quickly demonstrated value. He then gradually built on those successes, creating a knowledge-enabled organization one layer at a time. Shaw's information systems have enabled administrative and clinical operational analyses.[32]

All the above IT positions and responsibilities are critical to an organization's success. While many organizations may not have a different individual for each of these positions, they must have leaders taking responsibility for all these areas of concern. The individuals responsible for enterprisewide IT and IT-related issues must provide guidance and support to the organization's employees. Figure 5.3 displays the personal skills pivotal for success in an executive IT role.

Industry	Average CIO Compensation
Wholesale/Retail/Distribution	$243,304
Finance	$210,547
Insurance	$197,697
Manufacturing	$190,250
Medical/Dental/Health Care	$171,032
Government	$118,359
Education	$ 93,750

FIGURE 5.1

Average CIO Compensation by Industry

FIGURE 5.2

What Concerns CIOs the Most?

Percentage	CIO's Concerns
94%	Enhancing customer satisfaction
92	Security
89	Technology evaluation
87	Budgeting
83	Staffing
66	ROI analysis
64	Building new applications
45	Outsourcing hosting

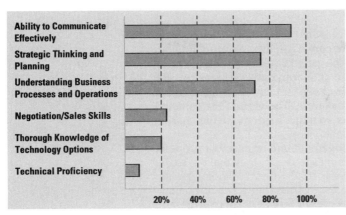

FIGURE 5.3

Skills Pivotal for Success in Executive IT Roles

The Gap Between Business Personnel and IT Personnel

One of the greatest challenges today is effective communication between business personnel and IT personnel. Business personnel possess expertise in functional areas such as marketing, accounting, sales, and so forth. IT personnel have the technological expertise. Unfortunately, a communications gap often exists between the two. Business personnel have their own vocabularies based on their experience and expertise. IT personnel have their own vocabularies consisting of acronyms and technical terms. Effective communication between business and IT personnel should be a two-way street with each side making the effort to better understand the other (including written and oral communication).

IMPROVING COMMUNICATIONS

Business personnel must seek to increase their understanding of IT. Although they do not need to know every technical detail, it will benefit their careers to understand what they can and cannot accomplish using IT. Business managers and leaders should read business-oriented IT magazines, such as *InformationWeek* and *CIO,* to increase their IT knowledge.

At the same time, an organization must develop strategies for integrating its IT personnel into the various business functions. Too often, IT personnel are left out of strategy meetings because of the belief they do not understand the business so they will not add any value. That is a dangerous position to take. IT personnel must understand the business if the organization is going to determine which technologies can benefit (or hurt) the business. With a little effort to communicate IT personnel, by providing information on the functionality available in CRM systems, might add tremendous value to a meeting about how to improve customer service. Working together, business and IT personnel have the potential to create customer-service competitive advantages.

It is the responsibility of the CIO to ensure effective communications between business and IT personnel. While the CIO assumes the responsibility on an enterprisewide level, it is also each employee's responsibility to communicate effectively on a personal level.

Organizational Fundamentals—Ethics and Security

Ethics and security are two fundamental building blocks that organizations must base their businesses on. In recent years, such events as the Enron and Martha Stewart scandals along with 9/11 have shed new light on the meaning of ethics and security. When the behavior of a few individuals can destroy billion-dollar organizations because of a lapse in ethics or security, the value of highly ethical and highly secure organizations should be evident. Review the Ethics and Security plug-ins to gain a detailed understanding of these topics. Due to the importance of these topics, they will be readdressed throughout this text.

ETHICS

Ian Clarke, the inventor of a file-swapping service called Freenet, decided to leave the United States for the United Kingdom, where copyright laws are more lenient. Wayne Rosso, the inventor of a file-sharing service called Grokster, left the United States for Spain, again saying goodbye to tough U.S. copyright protections. File sharing encourages a legal network of shared thinking that can improve drug research, software development, and flow of information. The United States copyright laws, designed decades before the Internet was invented, make file sharing and many other Internet technologies illegal.[33]

The ethical issues surrounding copyright infringement and intellectual property rights are consuming the e-business world. Advances in technology make it easier and easier for people to copy everything from music to pictures. Technology poses new challenges for our *ethics*—the principles and standards that guide our behavior toward other people. Review Figure 5.4 for an overview of concepts, terms, and ethical issues stemming from advances in technology.

In today's electronic world, privacy has become a major ethical issue. *Privacy* is the right to be left alone when you want to be, to have control over your own personal possessions, and to not be observed without your consent. Some of the most problematic decisions organizations face lie in the murky and turbulent waters of privacy. The burden comes from the knowledge that each time employees make a decision regarding issues of privacy, the outcome could sink the company some day.

The Securities and Exchange Commission (SEC) began inquiries into Enron's accounting practices on October 22, 2001. David Duncan, the Arthur Andersen partner in charge of Enron, instructed his team to begin destroying paper and electronic Enron-related records on October 23, 2001. Kimberly Latham, a subordinate to Duncan, sent instructions on October 24, 2001, to her entire team to follow Duncan's orders and even compiled a list of computer files to delete. Arthur Andersen blames Duncan for destroying thousands of Enron-related documents. Duncan blames the Arthur Andersen attorney, Nancy Temple, for sending him a memo instructing him to destroy files. Temple blames Arthur Andersen's document deletion policies.[34]

Regardless of who is to blame, the bigger issue is that the destruction of files after a federal investigation has begun is both unethical and illegal. A direct corporate order to destroy information currently under federal investigation poses a dilemma for any professional. Comply, and you participate in potentially criminal activities; refuse, and you might find yourself looking for a new job.

Privacy is one of the biggest ethical issues facing organizations today. Trust between companies, customers, partners, and suppliers is the support structure of the e-business world. One of the main ingredients in trust is privacy. Widespread fear about privacy continues to be one of the biggest barriers to the growth of e-business. People are concerned their privacy will be violated as a consequence of interactions on the Web. Unless an organization can effectively address this issue of privacy, its customers, partners, and suppliers may lose trust in the organization, which hurts

Intellectual property	Intangible creative work that is embodied in physical form.
Copyright	The legal protection afforded an expression of an idea, such as a song, video game, and some types of proprietary documents.
Fair use doctrine	In certain situations, it is legal to use copyrighted material.
Pirated software	The unauthorized use, duplication, distribution, or sale of copyrighted software.
Counterfeit software	Software that is manufactured to look like the real thing and sold as such.

FIGURE 5.4

Issues Affected by Technology Advances

FIGURE 5.5

Primary Reasons Privacy
Issues Reduce Trust for
E-Business

1. Loss of personal privacy is a top concern for Americans in the 21st century.

2. Among Internet users, 37 percent would be "a lot" more inclined to purchase a product on a Web site that had a privacy policy.

3. Privacy/security is the number one factor that would convert Internet researchers into Internet buyers.

its business. Figure 5.5 displays the results from a *CIO* survey as to how privacy issues reduce trust for e-business.

SECURITY

Organizational information is intellectual capital. Just as organizations protect their assets—keeping their money in an insured bank or providing a safe working environment for employees—they must also protect their intellectual capital. An organization's intellectual capital includes everything from its patents to its transactional and analytical information. With security breaches on the rise and computer hackers everywhere, an organization must put in place strong security measures to survive.

The Health Insurance Portability and Accountability Act (HIPAA) protects the privacy and security of personal health records and has the potential to impact every business in the United States. HIPAA affects all companies that use electronic data interchange (EDI) to communicate personal health records. HIPAA requires health care organizations to develop, implement, and maintain appropriate security measures when sending electronic health information. Most important, these organizations must document and keep current records detailing how they are performing security measures for all transmissions of health information. On April 21, 2005, security rules for HIPAA became enforceable by law.

According to recent Gartner polls, less than 10 percent of all health care organizations have begun to implement the security policies and procedures required by HIPAA. The Health Information Management Society estimates that 70 percent of all health care providers failed to meet the April 2005 deadline for privacy rule compliance. Health care organizations need to start taking HIPAA regulations seriously since noncompliance can result in substantial fines and even imprisonment.[35]

Beyond the health care industry, all businesses must understand the importance of information security, even if it is not enforceable by law. *Information security* is a broad term encompassing the protection of information from accidental or intentional misuse by persons inside or outside an organization. With current advances in technologies and business strategies such as CRM, organizations are able to determine valuable information—such as who are the top 20 percent of their customers who produce 80 percent of their revenues. Most organizations view this type of information as valuable intellectual capital, and they are implementing security measures to prevent the information from walking out the door or falling into the wrong hands.

Adding to the complexity of information security is the fact that organizations must enable employees, customers, and partners to access all sorts of information electronically to be successful. Doing business electronically automatically creates tremendous information security risks for organizations. There are many technical aspects of security, but the biggest information security issue is not technical, but human. Most information security breaches result from people misusing an organization's information either intentionally or inadvertently. For example, many individuals freely give up their passwords or leave them on sticky notes next to their computers, leaving the door wide open to intruders.

Figure 5.6 displays the typical size of an organization's information security budget relative to the organization's overall IT budget from the CSI/FBI 2004 Computer Crime and Security Survey. Forty-six percent of respondents indicated that

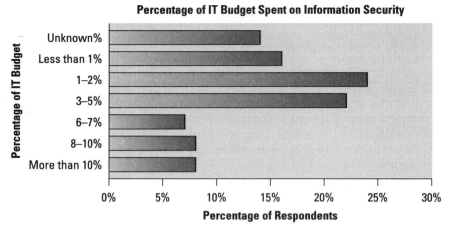

Percentage of IT Budget Spent on Information Security

FIGURE 5.6

Organizational Spending
on Information Security

their organization spent between 1 and 5 percent of the total IT budget on security. Only 16 percent indicated that their organization spent less than 1 percent of the IT budget on security.[36]

Figure 5.7 displays the spending per employee on computer security broken down by both public and private industries. The highest average computer security investment per employee was found in the transportation industry.[37]

Security is perhaps the most fundamental and critical of all the technologies/ disciplines an organization must have squarely in place to execute its business strategy. Without solid security processes and procedures, none of the other technologies can develop business advantages.

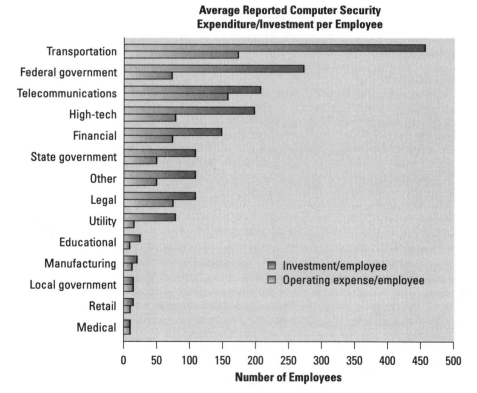

Average Reported Computer Security Expenditure/Investment per Employee

■ Investment/employee
□ Operating expense/employee

FIGURE 5.7

Computer Security
Expenditures/Investments
by Industry

1. Predict what might have happened to Apple if its top executives had not supported investments in IT.

2. Explain why it would be unethical for Apple to allow its customers to download free music from iTunes.

3. Evaluate the effects on Apple's business if it failed to secure its customer information and all of it was accidentally posted to an anonymous Web site.

4. Explain why Apple should have a CIO, CTO, CPO, CSO, and CKO.

Chapter Five Case: Executive Dilemmas in the Information Age

The vast array of business initiatives from supply chain management, customer relationship management, business process reengineering, and enterprise resource planning makes it clear that information technology has evolved beyond the role of mere infrastructure to the support of business strategy. Today, in more and more industries, IT is the business strategy and is quickly becoming a survival issue.

Board and executive team agendas are increasingly peppered with, or even hijacked by, a growing range of IT issues from compliance to ethics and security. In most companies today, computers are key business tools. They generate, process, and store the majority of critical business information. Executives must understand how IT can affect a business by successfully addressing a wide range of needs—from large electronic discovery projects to the online review of document collections by geographically dispersed teams. A few examples of executive IT issues follow.

Stolen Proprietary Information

A computer company investigated to determine if an executive who accepted a job with a competitor stole proprietary information. The hard drive from the executive's laptop and desktop machine were forensically imaged. The analysis established that the night before the executive left, he downloaded all of the company's process specifications and distributor agreements, which he then zipped and e-mailed to the competitor. Additionally, reconstruction of deleted files located e-mails between the executive and the competitor discussing his intent to provide the proprietary information if he was offered additional options in the new company.

Sexual Harassment

A woman employed by a large defense contractor accused her supervisor of sexual harassment. The woman was fired from her job for poor performance and subsequently sued her ex-boss and the former employer.

A computer company was retained by the plaintiff's attorneys to investigate allegations of the former supervisor's harassing behavior. After making a forensic image backup of the ex-boss's hard drive, the forensic company was able to recover deleted electronic messages that showed the ex-boss had a history of propositioning women under his supervision for "special favors." A situation that might have been mired in a "he said/she said" controversy was quickly resolved; the woman got her job back, and the real culprit was terminated.

Stolen Trade Secrets

The board of directors of a technical research company demoted the company's founder and CEO. The executive, disgruntled because of his demotion, was later terminated. It was subsequently determined that the executive had planned to quit about the same time he was fired and establish a competitive company. Upon his termination, the executive took home two computers; he returned them to the company four days later, along with another company computer that he had previously used at home. Suspicious that critical information had been taken, the company's attorneys sent the computers to a computer forensic company for examination.

After making a forensic image backup of the hard drives, the forensic analysis identified a file directory that had been deleted during the aforementioned four-day period that had the same name as the competing company the executive had established. A specific search of the deleted files in this directory identified the executive's "to do list" file. This file indicated the executive planned to copy the company's database (valued at $100 million) for his personal use. Another item specified the executive was to "learn how to destroy evidence on a computer."

The computer forensic company's examination also proved that the executive had been communicating with other competing companies to establish alliances, in violation of the executive's nondisclosure agreement with the company. It was also shown that numerous key company files were located on removable computer storage media that had not been turned over by the executive to the company. [38]

Questions

1. Explain why understanding technology, especially in the areas of security and ethics, is important for a CEO. How do CEO's actions affect the organizational culture?
2. Identify why executives in nontechnological industries need to worry about technology and its potential business ramifications.
3. Describe why continuously learning about technology allows an executive to better analyze threats and opportunities.
4. Identify three things that a CTO, CPO, or CSO could do to prevent the above issues.

<< BUSINESS PLUG-IN POINTERS

Review the Business Plug-In B6 "Information Security" for an overview of security issues and features including information security policies and plans, hackers, viruses, public key encryption, digital certificates, digital signatures, firewalls, and authentication, authorization, and detection and response technologies.

Review the Business Plug-In B7 "Ethics" for an overview of privacy laws, ethical computer use policy, Internet use policy, information privacy policy, acceptable use policy, e-mail privacy policy, anti-spam policy, monitoring technologies, and monitoring polices.

15 Creating Collaborative Partnerships

15.1. Identify the different ways in which companies collaborate using technology.

15.2. Compare the different categories of collaboration technologies.

15.3. Define the fundamental concepts of a knowledge management system.

15.4. Provide an example of a content management system along with its business purpose.

15.5. Evaluate the advantages of using a workflow management system.

15.6. Explain how groupware can benefit a business.

Teams, Partnerships, and Alliances

To be successful—and avoid being eliminated by the competition—an organization must constantly undertake new initiatives, address both minor and major problems, and capitalize on significant opportunities. To support these activities, an organization often will create and utilize teams, partnerships, and alliances because the expertise needed is beyond the scope of a single individual or organization. These teams, partnerships, and alliances can be formed internally among a company's employees or externally with other organizations (see Figure 15.1).

Businesses of all sizes and in all markets have witnessed the benefits of leveraging their IT assets to create competitive advantage. Whereas information technology efforts in the past were aimed at increasing operational efficiency, the advent and proliferation of network-based computing (the Internet being the most visible, but not only, example) has enabled organizations to build systems with which all sorts of communities can interact. The ultimate result will allow organizations to do business with customers, business partners, suppliers, governments and regulatory agencies, and any other community relevant to their particular operation or activity.

FIGURE 15.1

Teams, Partnerships, and Alliances Within and External to an Organization

In the same way that organizations use internal teams, they are increasingly forming alliances and partnerships with other organizations. The **core competency** of an organization is its key strength, a business function that it does better than any of its competitors. Apple Computer is highly regarded for its strength in product design, while Accenture's core competency is the design and installation of information systems. A **core competency strategy** is one in which an organization chooses to focus specifically on what it does best (its core competency) and forms partnerships and alliances with other specialist organizations to handle nonstrategic business processes. Strategic alliances enable businesses to gain competitive advantages through access to a partner's resources, including markets, technologies, and people. Teaming up with another business adds complementary resources and capabilities, enabling participants to grow and expand more quickly and efficiently, especially fast-growing companies that rely heavily on outsourcing many areas of their business to extend their technical and operational resources. In the outsourcing process, they save time and boost productivity by not having to develop their own systems from scratch. They are then free to concentrate on innovation and their core business.

Information technology makes such business partnerships and alliances easier to establish and manage. An **information partnership** occurs when two or more organizations cooperate by integrating their IT systems, thereby providing customers with the best of what each can offer. The advent of the Internet has greatly increased the opportunity for IT-enabled business partnerships and alliances. Amazon developed a profitable business segment by providing e-business outsourcing services to other retailers that use Amazon's Web site software. Some well-known retailers partnering with Amazon include Marshall Fields, Office Depot, and Target.[17]

Collaboration Systems

Heineken USA has shortened its inventory cycle time for beer production and distribution from three months to four weeks. By using its collaborative system to forecast demand and expedite shipping, the company has dramatically cut inventory levels and shipping costs while increasing sales.

Over the past few years most business processes have changed on various dimensions (e.g., flexibility, interconnectivity, coordination style, autonomy) because of market conditions and organizational models. Frequently, information is located within physically separated systems as more and more organizations spread their reach globally. This creates a need for a software infrastructure that enables collaboration systems.

A **collaboration system** is an IT-based set of tools that supports the work of teams by facilitating the sharing and flow of information. Collaboration solves specific business tasks such as telecommuting, online meetings, deploying applications, and remote project and sales management (see Figure 15.2).

Collaboration systems allow people, teams, and organizations to leverage and build upon the ideas and talents of staff, suppliers, customers, and business partners. It involves a unique set of business challenges that:

- Include complex interactions between people who may be in different locations and desire to work across function and discipline areas.

- Require flexibility in work process and the ability to involve others quickly and easily.

- Call for creating and sharing information rapidly and effortlessly within a team.

Most organizations collaborate with other companies in some capacity. Consider the supplier-customer relationship, which can be thought of in terms of a continuous life cycle of engagement, transaction, fulfillment, and service activities. Rarely do companies excel in all four life cycle areas, either from a business process

FIGURE 15.2

Collaborative Business
Areas

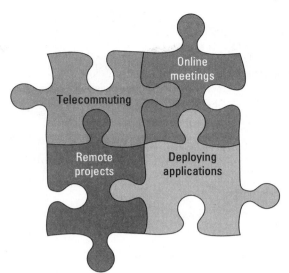

or from a technology-enabled aspect. Successful organizations identify and invest in their core competencies, and outsource or collaborate for those competencies that are not core to them. Collaboration systems fall into one of two categories:

1. **Unstructured collaboration** (sometimes referred to as **information collaboration**) includes document exchange, shared whiteboards, discussion forums, and e-mail. These functions can improve personal productivity, reducing the time spent searching for information or chasing answers.

2. **Structured collaboration** (or **process collaboration**) involves shared participation in business processes, such as workflow, in which knowledge is hard-coded as rules. This is beneficial in terms of improving automation and the routing of information.

Regardless of location or format—be it unstructured or structured—relevant accurate information must be readily and consistently available to those who need it anytime, anywhere, and on any device. The integration of IT systems enables an organization to provide employees, partners, customers, and suppliers with the ability to access, find, analyze, manage, and collaborate on content. The collaboration can be done across a wide variety of formats, languages, and platforms. Figure 15.3 illustrates many of the typical collaborative functions within most organizations.

Lockheed Martin Aeronautics Company's ability to share complex project information across an extended supply chain in real time was key in its successful bid of a $19 billion Department of Defense (DoD) contract to build 21 supersonic stealth fighters. New government procurement rules require defense contractors to communicate effectively to ensure that deadlines are met, costs are controlled, and projects are managed throughout the life cycle of the contract.[18]

In anticipation of the contract, the Fort Worth, Texas, unit of Lockheed Martin Corporation developed a real-time collaboration system that can tie together its partners, suppliers, and DoD customers via the Internet. The platform lets participants collectively work on product design and engineering tasks as well as supply chain and life cycle management issues. Lockheed will host all transactions and own the project information. The platform will let DoD and Lockheed project managers track the daily progress of the project in real time. This is the first major DoD project with such a requirement. The contract, awarded to the Lockheed unit and partners Northrop Grumman Corp. and BAE Systems, is the first installment in

Function	Collaborator(s)	Business Function(s)
Planning and forecasting	Supplier, Customer	Real-time information sharing (forecast information and sales information)
Product design	Supplier, Customer	Document exchange, computer-aided design (CAD)
Strategic sourcing	Supplier	Negotiation, supplier performance management
Component compatibility testing	Supplier	Component compatibility
Pricing	Supplier, Customer	Pricing in supply chain
Marketing	Supplier, Customer	Joint/coop marketing campaigns, branding
Sales	Customer	Shared leads, presentations, configuration and quotes
Make-to-order	Customer	Requirements, capabilities, contract terms
Order processing	Supplier, Customer	Order solution
Fulfillment: Logistics and service	Supplier, Customer	Coordination of distribution
International trade logistics	Customer	Document exchange, import/export documents
Payment	Customer	Order receipt, invoicing
Customer service/support	Supplier, Customer	Shared/split customer support

FIGURE 15.3

Typical Collaborative
Business Functions

what could amount to a $200 billion program for 3,000 jet fighters over 40 years. The strengths of the collaboration process lie with the integration of many systems, namely:

- Knowledge management systems
- Content management systems
- Workflow management systems
- Groupware systems

Knowledge Management

Knowledge management (KM) involves capturing, classifying, evaluating, retrieving, and sharing information assets in a way that provides context for effective decisions and actions. It is best to think of KM in the broadest context. Succinctly put, KM is the process through which organizations generate value from their intellectual and knowledge-based assets. Most often, generating value from such assets involves codifying what employees, partners, and customers know, and sharing that information among employees, departments, and even with other companies to devise best practices. It is important to note that the definition says nothing about technology; while KM is often facilitated by IT, technology by itself is not KM.

Think of a golf caddie as a simplified example of a knowledge worker. Good caddies do more than carry clubs and track down wayward balls. When asked, a good caddie will give advice to golfers, such as, "The wind makes the ninth hole play 15 yards longer." Accurate advice may lead to a bigger tip at the end of the day. The golfer, having derived a benefit from the caddie's advice, may be more likely to play that course again. If a good caddie is willing to share what he knows with other caddies, then they all may eventually earn bigger tips. How would KM work to make this happen? The caddie master may decide to reward caddies for sharing their knowledge by offering them credits for pro shop merchandise. Once the best advice is collected, the course manager would publish the information in notebooks (or make it available on PDAs) and distribute them to all the caddies. The end result of a well-designed KM program is that everyone wins. In this case, caddies get bigger tips and deals on merchandise, golfers play better because they benefit from the collective experience of caddies, and the course owners win because better scores lead to repeat business.

KM IN BUSINESS

KM has assumed greater urgency in American business over the past few years as millions of baby boomers prepare to retire. When they punch out for the last time, the knowledge they gleaned about their jobs, companies, and industries during their long careers will walk out with them—unless companies take measures to retain their insights. In addition, CIOs who have entered into outsourcing agreements must address the thorny issue of transferring the knowledge of their full-time staff members, who are losing their jobs because of an outsourcing deal, to the outsourcer's employees.

Knowledge Management Systems

Knowledge can be a real competitive advantage for an organization. Information technology can distribute an organization's knowledge base by interconnecting people and digitally gathering their expertise. The primary objective of knowledge management is to be sure that a company's knowledge of facts, sources of information, and solutions are readily available to all employees whenever it is needed.

Such knowledge management requires that organizations go well beyond providing information contained in spreadsheets, databases, and documents. It must include expert information that typically resides in people's heads. A *knowledge management system (KMS)* supports the capturing, organization, and dissemination of knowledge (i.e., know-how) throughout an organization. It is up to the organization to determine what information qualifies as knowledge.

EXPLICIT AND TACIT KNOWLEDGE

Not all information is valuable. Individual companies must determine what information qualifies as intellectual and knowledge-based assets. In general, intellectual and knowledge-based assets fall into one of two categories: explicit or tacit. As a rule, *explicit knowledge* consists of anything that can be documented, archived, and codified, often with the help of IT. Examples of explicit knowledge are assets such as patents, trademarks, business plans, marketing research, and customer lists.

Tacit knowledge is the knowledge contained in people's heads. The challenge inherent in tacit knowledge is figuring out how to recognize, generate, share, and manage knowledge that resides in people's heads. While information technology in the form of e-mail, instant messaging, and related technologies can help facilitate the dissemination of tacit knowledge, identifying it in the first place can be a major obstacle. Shadowing and joint problem solving are two best practices for transferring or re-creating tacit knowledge inside an organization.

Shadowing

With **shadowing**, less experienced staff observe more experienced staff to learn how their more experienced counterparts approach their work. Dorothy Leonard and Walter Swap, two knowledge management experts, stress the importance of having the protégé discuss his or her observations with the expert to deepen the dialog and crystallize the knowledge transfer.

Joint Problem Solving

Another sound approach is **joint problem solving** by expert and novice. Because people are often unaware of how they approach problems or do their work and therefore cannot automatically generate step-by-step instructions for doing whatever they do, having a novice and expert work together on a project will bring the expert's approach to light. The difference between shadowing and joint problem solving is that shadowing is more passive. With joint problem solving, the expert and the novice work hand in hand on a task.[19]

Information is of little use unless it is analyzed and made available to the right people, at the right place, and at the right time. To get the most value from intellectual assets, knowledge must be shared. An effective KMS system should help do one or more of the following:

- Foster innovation by encouraging the free flow of ideas.
- Improve customer service by streamlining response time.
- Boost revenues by getting products and services to market faster.
- Enhance employee retention rates by recognizing the value of employees' knowledge.
- Streamline operations and reduce costs by eliminating redundant or unnecessary processes.

A creative approach to knowledge management can result in improved efficiency, higher productivity, and increased revenues in practically any business function. Figure 15.4 indicates the reasons organizations launch KMS.

Software is helping ChevronTexaco Corporation improve how it manages the assets in oil fields by enabling employees in multiple disciplines to easily access and share the information they need to make decisions. ChevronTexaco teams of 10 to 30 people are responsible for managing the assets, such as the drilling equipment, pipelines, and facilities, for a particular oil field. Within each team, earth scientists and various engineers with expertise in production, reservoir, and facilities work together to keep the oil field up and running. Each member of the asset team needs to

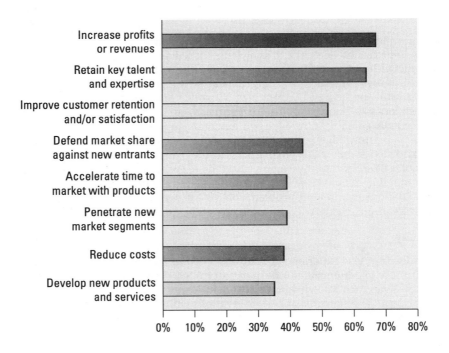

communicate with other members to make decisions based on the collection and analysis of huge amounts of information from various departments. Individual team members can look at information from the perspective of their own department.

This has helped ChevronTexaco achieve a 30 percent productivity gain, a 50 percent improvement in safety performance, and more than $2 billion in operating cost reductions. Through KMSs, ChevronTexaco has restructured its gasoline retailing business and now drills oil and gas wells faster and cheaper.[20]

Not every organization matches ChevronTexaco's success with KM. Numerous KM projects have failed over the past few years, generating an unwillingness to undertake—or even address—KM issues among many organizations. However, KM is an effective tool if it is tied directly to discrete business needs and opportunities. Beginning with targeted projects that deliver value quickly, companies can achieve the success that has proved elusive with many big-bang approaches. Successful KM projects typically focus on creating value in a specific process area, or even just for a certain type of transaction. Companies should start with one job at a time—preferably the most knowledge-oriented one—and build KM into a job function in a way that actually helps employees do their work better and faster, then expand to the next most knowledge-intensive job, and so on. Celebrating even small success with KM will help build a base of credibility and support for future KM projects.

KM TECHNOLOGIES

KM is not a purely technology-based concept. Organizations that implement a centralized database system, electronic message board, Web portal, or any other collaborative tool in the hope that they have established a KMS are wasting both their time and money.

Although tools don't make a KMS, such a system does need tools, from standard, off-the-shelf e-mail packages to sophisticated collaboration tools designed specifically to support community building and identity. Generally, KMS tools fall into one or more of the following categories:

- Knowledge repositories (databases).
- Expertise tools.
- E-learning applications.
- Discussion and chat technologies.
- Search and data mining tools.

KM AND SOCIAL NETWORKING

Companies that have been frustrated by traditional KM efforts are increasingly looking for ways to find out how knowledge flows through their organization, and social networking analysis can show them just that. *Social networking analysis (SNA)* is a process of mapping a group's contacts (whether personal or professional) to identify who knows whom and who works with whom. In enterprises, it provides a clear picture of how far-flung employees and divisions work together and can help identify key experts in the organization who possess the knowledge needed to, say, solve a complicated programming problem or launch a new product.

M&M maker Mars used SNA to identify how knowledge flows through its organizations, who holds influence, who gives the best advice, and how employees share information. The Canadian government's central IT unit used SNA to establish which skills it needed to retain and develop, and to determine who, among the 40 percent of the workforce that was due to retire within five years, had the most important knowledge and experience to begin transferring to others.[21]

SNA is not a replacement for traditional KM tools such as knowledge databases or portals, but it can provide companies with a starting point for how best to proceed with KM initiatives. As a component to a larger KM strategy, SNA can help companies identify key leaders and then set up a mechanism, such as communities of practice, so that those leaders can pass on their knowledge to colleagues. To identify experts in their organizations, companies can use software programs that track e-mail and other kinds of electronic communication.[22]

Content Management Systems

A *content management system* provides tools to manage the creation, storage, editing, and publication of information in a collaborative environment. As a Web site grows in size and complexity, the business must establish procedures to ensure that things run smoothly. At a certain point, it makes sense to automate this process and use a content management system to manage this effectively. The content management system marketplace is complex, incorporating document management, digital asset management, and Web content management. Figure 15.5 highlights the three primary types of content management systems. Figure 15.6 lists the major content management system vendors.

Content management software is helping BMW Group Switzerland accelerate personalized, real-time information about products, services, prices, and events to its dealers countrywide. BMW uses a process that allows dealers to specify what information is seen by which employee, as well as to deliver marketing materials solely to members of the sales department, and technical specifications and support documents only to mechanics. That enhanced personalization eliminates the chance that information is sent to the wrong dealership or to the wrong individual, which provides higher quality customer service. The content management software also enables nontechnical employees to create pages using predefined layout templates, simplifying the Web publishing process. More than 500 people use the solution daily, and all employees are able to publish information without calling on IT specialists, while maintaining the look and feel of the BMW brand.[23]

Workflow Management Systems

A *workflow* defines all the steps or business rules, from beginning to end, required for a business process. Therefore, *workflow management systems* facilitate the automation and management of business processes and control the movement of

FIGURE 15.5

Common Types of Content Management Systems

Common Types of Content Management Systems	
Document management system (DMS)	DMS—Supports the electronic capturing, storage, distribution, archiving, and accessing of documents. A DMS optimizes the use of documents within an organization independent of any publishing medium (for example, the Web). A DMS provides a document repository with information about other information. The system tracks the editorial history of each document and its relationships with other documents. A variety of search and navigation methods are available to make document retrieval easy. A DMS manages highly structured and regulated content, such as pharmaceutical documentation.
Digital asset management (DAM) system	DAM—Though similar to document management, DAM generally works with binary rather than text files, such as multimedia file types. DAM places emphasis on allowing file manipulation and conversion, for example, converting GIF files to JPEG.
Web content management (WCM) system	WCM—Adds an additional layer to document and digital asset management that enables publishing content both to intranets and to public Web sites. In addition to maintaining the content itself, WCM systems often integrate content with online processes like e-business systems.

Vendors	Strengths	Weaknesses	Costs
Documentum www.documentum.com	Document and digital asset management	Personalization features not as strong as competitors	Major components start at less than $100,000
FatWire www.fatwire.com	Web content management	May not scale to support thousands of users	SPARK, $25,000; Update Engine, $70,000 and up
InterWoven www.interwoven.com	Collaboration, enterprise content management	Requires significant customization	InterWoven 5 Platform, $50,000; average cost for a new customer, $250,000
Percussion www.percussion.com	Web content management	May not scale to support thousands of users	Rhythmyx Content Manager, about $150,000
Stellent www.stellent.com	Document conversion to Web-ready formats	Engineering for very large implementations with thousands of users	Content and Collaboration Servers, $50,000 to $250,000 each
Vignette www.vignette.com	Personalization	Document management and library services are not as robust as others	V6 Multisite Content Manager, $200,000 and up; V6 Content Suite, $450,000 and up

FIGURE 15.6

Major Content
Management System
Vendors

work through the business process. Work activities can be performed in series or in parallel and involve people and automated computer systems. In addition, many workflow management systems allow the opportunity to measure and analyze the execution of the process because workflow systems allow the flow of work between individuals and/or departments to be defined and tracked. Workflow software helps automate a range of business tasks and electronically route the right information to the right people at the right time. Users are notified of pending work, and managers can observe status and route approvals through the system quickly.

There are two primary types of workflow systems: messaging-based and database-based. *Messaging-based workflow systems* send work assignments through an e-mail system. The workflow system automatically tracks the order for the work to be assigned and, each time a step is completed, the system automatically sends the work to the next individual in line. For example, each time a team member completes a piece of the project, the system would automatically send the document to the next team member.

Database-based workflow systems store documents in a central location and automatically ask the team members to access the document when it is their turn to edit the document. Project documentation is stored in a central location and team members are notified by the system when it is their turn to log in and work on their portion of the project.

Either type of workflow system helps to present information in a unified format, improves teamwork by providing automated process support, and allows team members to communicate and collaborate within a unified environment. Figure 15.7 lists some typical features associated with workflow management systems.

New York City was experiencing a record number of claims, ranging from injuries resulting from slips on sidewalks to medical malpractice at city hospitals. The city processes over 30,000 claims and incurs $250 million in claim costs annually. Claims are generally filed with the Comptroller's Office, which investigates them and offers to settle meritorious claims. The New York City Comptroller's Office, with the assistance of its consultants Xerox and Universal Systems Inc., utilized a workflow management system to enhance revenues and decrease operating costs. With the implementation of the Omnibus Automated Image Storage Information System (OAISIS) for processing contracts and claims, New York City will save over $20 million. Numerous city organizations were involved in the workflow management system, including: Bureau

Workflow Feature	Description
Process definition tool	A graphical or textual tool for defining a business process. Each activity within the process is associated with a person or a computer application. Rules are created to determine how the activities progress across the workflow and which controls are in place to govern each activity.
Simulation, prototyping, and piloting	Some systems allow workflow simulation or create prototype and/or pilot versions of a particular workflow to test systems on a limited basis before going into production.
Task initiation and control	The business process defined above is initiated and the appropriate resources (either human and/or IT related) are scheduled and/or engaged to complete each activity as the process progresses.
Rules-based decision making	Rules are created for each step to determine how workflow-related information is to be processed, routed, tracked, and controlled. As an example, one rule might generate e-mail notifications when a condition has been met. Another rule might implement conditional routing of documents and tasks based on the content of fields.
Document routing	In simple systems, this is accomplished by passing a file or folder from one recipient to another (e.g., an e-mail attachment). In sophisticated systems, document routing is completed by checking the documents in and out of a central repository. Both systems might allow for "redlining" of the documents so that each person in the process can add their own comments without affecting the original document.
Applications to view and manipulate information	Word-processors, spreadsheets, and production systems are used to allow workers to create, update, and view information.
Work list	Current tasks are quickly identified along with such things as a due date, goal date, and priority by using work lists. In some systems, an anticipated workload is displayed as well. These systems analyze where jobs are in the workflow and how long each step should take, and then estimate when various tasks will reach a worker's desk.
Task automation	Computerized tasks are automatically invoked. These might include such things as letter writing, e-mail notices, or execution of production systems. Task automation often requires customization of the basic workflow product.
Event notification	Employees can be notified when certain milestones occur or when workload increases.
Process monitoring	The workflow system can provide an organization with valuable information on current workload, future workload, bottlenecks (current or potential), turn-around time, or missed deadlines.
Tracking and logging of activities	Information about each step can be logged. This might include such things as start and completion times, worker(s) assigned to the task, and key status fields. Later, this information can be used to analyze the process or to provide evidence that certain tasks were in fact completed.

FIGURE 15.7

Workflow Management
System Features

of Law and Adjustment; Office of Contracts/Administration; Management and Accounting Systems; and Bureau of Information Systems.

In supporting all these NYC organizations, the system performs many functions that were previously labor-intensive and detracted from the quality and efficiency of investigations. The workflow management system screens claims to determine accordance with statutory requirements. Acknowledgment letters are generated automatically, with little or no resource allocation involved in assignment of claims or routing of claims to specific work locations. Status letters are automatically generated by the system for certain claim types, thus allowing the Comptroller's Office to keep claimants informed two months, five months, and one year from the date of their filing. All this is done automatically by the workflow management system.

Workflow management systems allow management to schedule individual systematic claim reviews without disrupting the investigation. Management can also see the entire claim process graphically and determine bottlenecks. Deployment of additional resources to needed areas occurs without a management analysis of a particular process problem.

Groupware Systems

Groupware is software that supports team interaction and dynamics including calendaring, scheduling, and videoconferencing. Organizations can use this technology to communicate, cooperate, coordinate, solve problems, compete, or negotiate. While traditional technologies like the telephone qualify as groupware, the term refers to a specific class of technologies relying on modern computer networks, such as e-mail, newsgroups, videophones, and chat rooms. Groupware systems fall along two primary categories (see Figure 15.8):

1. Users of the groupware are working together at the same time (real-time or synchronous groupware) or different times (asynchronous groupware).

2. Users are working together in the same place (colocated or face-to-face) or in different places (non-colocated or distance).

The groupware concept integrates various systems and functionalities into a common set of services or a single (client) application. In addition, groupware can represent a wide range of systems and methods of integration. Figure 15.9 displays the advantages groupware systems offer an organization over single-user systems.

Lotus Notes is one of the world's leading software solutions for collaboration that combines messaging, groupware, and the Internet. The structure of Notes allows it to track, route, and manage documents. Systems that lend themselves to Notes involve tracking, routing, approval, document management, and organization.

Toyota developed an intranet system to promote information sharing within the company and to raise productivity. Unfortunately, the company's conventional e-mail system became overloaded, generating problems. Users did not receive incoming

	Same time "Synchronous"	Different time "Asynchronous"
Same place "Colocated"	Presentation support	Shared computers
Different place "Distance"	Videophones, Chat	E-mail, Workflow

FIGURE 15.8

Groupware Systems

Groupware System Advantages
Facilitating communication (faster, easier, clearer, more persuasive)
Enabling telecommuting
Reducing travel costs
Sharing expertise
Forming groups with common interests where it would not be possible to gather a sufficient number of people face-to-face
Saving time and cost in coordinating group work
Facilitating group problem solving

FIGURE 15.9

Groupware Advantages

messages and were not able to send messages. Individual departments had introduced their own e-mail systems, which were not always compatible. Messages to other mail systems, including those outside the company, experienced delays. To deal with these difficulties, Toyota's information systems department reviewed the e-mail system and restructured it so that e-mail, now recognized as an important communication tool, is utilized more effectively in business transactions.[24]

Collaboration Trends

E-mail is by far the dominant collaboration application, but real-time collaboration tools like instant messaging are creating a new communication dynamic within organizations. ***Instant messaging*** (sometimes called ***IM*** or ***IMing***) is a type of communications service that enables someone to create a kind of private chat room with another individual in order to communicate in real time over the Internet. In 1992, AOL deployed IM to the consumer market, allowing users to communicate with other IMers through a buddy list. Most of the popular instant messaging programs provide a variety of features, such as:

- Web links: Share links to favorite Web sites.
- Images: Look at an image stored on someone else's computer.
- Sounds: Play sounds.
- Files: Share files by sending them directly to another IMer.
- Talk: Use the Internet instead of a phone to talk.
- Streaming content: Receive real-time or near-real-time stock quotes and news.
- Instant messages: Receive immediate text messages.

Commercial vendors such as AOL and Microsoft offer free instant messaging tools. Real-time collaboration, such as instant messaging, live Web conferencing, and screen or document sharing, creates an environment for decision making. AOL, Microsoft's MSN, and Yahoo! have begun to sell enterprise versions of their instant messaging services that match the capabilities of business-oriented products like IBM's Lotus Sametime. Figure 15.10 demonstrates the IM application presence within IT systems.

IBM Lotus software has released new versions of its real-time collaboration platform, IBM Lotus Instant Messaging and IBM Lotus Web Conferencing, plus its mobile counterpart, IBM Lotus Instant Messaging Everyplace. These built-for-business products let an organization offer presence awareness, secure instant messaging, and Web conferencing. The products give employees instant access to colleagues and company information regardless of time, place, or device.

FIGURE 15.10

Instant Messaging Application

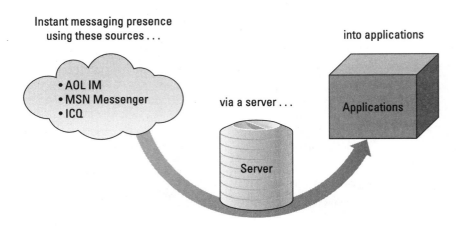

Instant messaging presence using these sources . . .

- AOL IM
- MSN Messenger
- ICQ

via a server . . .

Server

into applications

Applications

The bigger issue in collaboration for organizations is cultural. Collaboration brings teams of people together from different regions, departments, and even companies—people who bring different skills, perceptions, and capabilities. A formal collaboration strategy helps create the right environment as well as the right systems for team members.

1. Identify which systems eBay could use to collaborate internally.

2. Explain which Internet technologies have facilitated the way in which eBay collaborates with both its customers and business partners.

3. List the four collaboration systems discussed in this chapter and rank them in order of importance to eBay's business.

4. Describe how eBay could leverage the power of a knowledge management system for its employees and for its customers.

Chapter Fifteen Case: DreamWorks Animation Collaboration

Hewlett-Packard (HP) and DreamWorks Animation SKG were the first to introduce a collaboration studio for simulating face-to-face business meetings across long distances. Vyomesh Joshi, executive vice president at HP, and Jeffrey Katzenberg, CEO of DreamWorks, officially unveiled the HP Halo Collaboration Studio in New York City in 2005. Halo enables people in different locations to communicate in a vivid, face-to-face environment in real time. Whether across a country or across the ocean, users can see and hear one another's physical and emotional reactions to conversation and information.

By giving participants the remarkable sense that they are in the same room, the Halo Collaboration Studio is already transforming the way businesses such as PepsiCo, Advanced Micro Devices, and DreamWorks communicate across the globe. Halo significantly increases team effectiveness, provides faster decision-making capabilities, and decreases the need for travel.

"The HP Halo Collaboration Studio enables remote teams to work together in a setting so lifelike that participants feel as though they are in the same room," said Joshi. "To create this experience, HP is harnessing its expertise in color science, imaging, and networking in this new category of innovation. It is something we believe will not only disrupt the traditional videoconferencing market, but will also change the way people work in a global market."

Early in the production of the animated film *Shrek 2*, DreamWorks realized a significant return on investment using the Halo technology. By connecting its California teams in Glendale and Redwood City, DreamWorks was able to speed up many aspects of the production.

"In 2002, while we were producing *Shrek 2*, we realized that DreamWorks needed face-to-face collaboration between key creative talent in different locations," said Katzenberg. "We weren't satisfied with the available videoconferencing systems, so we designed a collaboration solution that would fulfill our needs. HP took the system and turned it into Halo, which is now the only solution on the market that allows this kind of effective communication."

Halo Connection

To connect via Halo, organizations purchase at least two Halo rooms set up for six people each. Three plasma displays in each room enable participants to see those they are collaborating with in life-size images. The rooms come equipped with studio-quality audio and lighting, and participants use a simple on-screen user interface to begin collaborating with just a few mouse clicks.

An intricate software control system ensures Halo rooms work easily and seamlessly together. The control system also provides precise image and color calibration, so participants see each other as they appear in real life. A dedicated HP Halo Video Exchange Network provides a high-bandwidth experience with imperceptible delays between Halo studios worldwide.

To ensure a 24x7 connection and eliminate the need for enterprises to manage the operation and maintenance of a Halo room, services offered include network operations and management, remote diagnostics and calibration, concierge, equipment warranty, and ongoing service and repair.

Participants can easily share documents and data directly from their notebook PCs with individuals in other rooms using a collaboration screen mounted above the plasma displays. The rooms also contain a high-magnification camera that enables individuals to zoom in on objects on a table, revealing the finest of details and color shading, and a phone that opens a conference call line to those not in one of the Halo rooms.

"We believe there is a personal connection that comes with Halo that just clearly doesn't come from any other kind of technology we've used in the past," said Steve Reinemund, CEO of PepsiCo. "Halo is one of the best investments we've made to improve the effectiveness of our business and work/life balance for our people."[25]

Questions

1. How can companies use Halo to increase their business efficiency?
2. Explain how a company like PepsiCo can use Halo to gain a competitive advantage in its industry.
3. How can knowledge management be increased by using a product such as Halo?
4. Why would a company like DreamWorks, that is not IT focused, be interested in collaboration technology?

PLUG-IN

B1

Business Basics

1. Define the three common business forms.
2. List and describe the seven departments commonly found in most organizations.
3. Describe a transaction and its importance to the accounting department.
4. Identify the four primary financial statements used by most organizations.
5. Define the relationship between sales and marketing, along with a brief discussion of the marketing mix.
6. Define business process reengineering and explain how an organization can use it to transform its business.

Introduction

A sign posted beside a road in Colorado states, "Failing to plan is planning to fail." Playnix Toys posted the sign after successfully completing its 20th year in the toy business in Colorado. The company's mission is to provide a superior selection of high-end toys for children of all ages. When the company began, it generated interest by using unique marketing strategies and promotions. The toy business has a lot of tough competition. Large chain stores such as Wal-Mart and Target offer toys at deep discount prices. Finding the right strategy to remain competitive is difficult in this industry, as FAO Schwarz discovered when it filed for bankruptcy after 143 years in the toy business.[1]

This plug-in introduces basic business fundamentals beginning with the three most common business structures—sole proprietorship, partnership, and corporation. It then focuses on the internal operations of a corporation including accounting, finance, human resources, sales, marketing, operations/production, and management information systems.

Types of Business

Businesses come in all shapes and sizes and exist to sell products or perform services. Businesses make profits or incur losses. A **profit** occurs when businesses sell products or services for more than they cost to produce. A **loss** occurs when businesses sell products or services for less then they cost to produce. Businesses typically organize in one of the following types:

1. Sole proprietorship
2. Partnership
3. Corporation

SOLE PROPRIETORSHIP

The *sole proprietorship* is a business form in which a single person is the sole owner and is personally responsible for all the profits and losses of the business. The sole proprietorship is the quickest and easiest way to set up a business operation. No prerequisites or specific costs are associated with starting a sole proprietorship. A simple business license costing around $25 from the local county clerk is all that is required to start a sole proprietorship. The person who starts the sole proprietorship is the sole owner.

PARTNERSHIP

Partnerships are similar to sole proprietorships, except that this legal structure allows for more than one owner. Each partner is personally responsible for all the profits and losses of the business. Similar to the sole proprietorship, starting a partnership is a relatively easy process since there are no prerequisites or specific costs required. When starting a partnership, it is wise to have a lawyer draft a partnership agreement. A *partnership agreement* is a legal agreement between two or more business partners that outlines core business issues. Partnership agreements typically include:

■ Amount of capital each partner expects to contribute. *Capital* represents money whose purpose is to make more money, for example, the money used to buy a rental property or a business.
■ Duties and responsibilities expected from each partner.
■ Expectations for sharing profits and losses.
■ Partner's salary requirements.
■ Methods for conflict resolution.
■ Methods for dissolving the partnership.

Limited Partnership

A *limited partnership* is much like a general partnership except for one important fundamental difference; the law protects the limited partner from being responsible for all of the partnership's losses. The limited partner's legal liability in the business is limited to the amount of his or her investment. The limited partnership enables this special type of investor to share in the partnership profits without being exposed to its losses in the event the company goes out of business. However, this protection exists only as long as the limited partner does not play an active role in the operation of the business.

CORPORATION

The corporation is the most sophisticated form of business entity and the most common among large companies. The *corporation* (also called *organization*, *enterprise*, or *business*) is an artificially created legal entity that exists separate and apart from those individuals who created it and carry on its operations. In a corporation, the business entity is separate from the business owners. *Shareholder* is another term for business owners. An important advantage of using a corporation as a business form is that it offers the shareholders limited liability. *Limited liability*

means that the shareholders are not personally liable for the losses incurred by the corporation. In most instances, financial losses incurred by a corporation are limited to the assets owned by the corporation. Shareholders' personal assets, such as their homes or investments, cannot be claimed to pay off debt or losses incurred by the corporation.

There are two general types of corporations—for profit and not for profit. *For profit corporations* primarily focus on making money and all profits and losses are shared by the business owners. *Not for profit* (or *nonprofit*) *corporations* usually exist to accomplish some charitable, humanitarian, or educational purpose, and the profits and losses are not shared by the business owners. Donations to nonprofit businesses may be tax deductible for the donor. Typical examples include hospitals, colleges, universities, and foundations.

Eleanor Josaitis is a tiny 72-year-old woman who co-founded the Detroit civil-rights group Focus: HOPE. Focus: HOPE, founded in 1968, began as a food program serving pregnant women, new mothers, and their children. Josaitis has built the nonprofit organization from a basement operation run by a handful of friends into a sprawling 40-acre campus in Detroit that now employs over 500 people, boasts more than 50,000 volunteers and donors, and has helped over 30,000 people become gainfully employed.

Josaitis and her team developed a technical school to help job seekers gain certifications in IT support. They operate a machinists' training program that funnels people into the employment pipeline at local automotive companies. The organization also teams up with local universities to help disadvantaged students receive college educations, and it runs a child care center to make sure all these opportunities are available to working and single parents. Josaitis states that the most courageous act she has performed in her life occurred 36 years ago when she turned off her television, got up off the couch, and decided to do something. "You have to have the guts to try something, because you won't change a thing by sitting in front of the TV with the clicker in your hand," Josaitis said.[2]

Forming a corporation typically costs several hundred dollars in fees, and the owners must file a charter within the respective state. The charter typically includes:

- Purpose of the intended corporation.
- Names and addresses of the incorporators.
- Amount and types of stock the corporation will be authorized to issue.
- Rights and privileges of the shareholders.

FIGURE B1.1

Reasons Businesses Choose to Incorporate

Reasons Businesses Choose to Incorporate	
Limited liability	In most instances, financial losses or judgments against the corporation are limited to the assets owned by the corporation.
Unlimited life	Unlike sole proprietorships and partnerships, the life of the corporation is not dependent on the life of a particular individual or individuals. It can continue indefinitely until it accomplishes its objective, merges with another business, or goes bankrupt. Unless stated otherwise, it could go on indefinitely.
Transferability of shares	It is easy to sell, transfer, or give the ownership interest in a corporation to another person. The process of divesting sole proprietorships or partnerships can be cumbersome and costly. Property has to be re-titled, new deeds drawn, and other administrative steps taken any time the slightest change of ownership occurs. With a corporation, all of the individual owners' rights and privileges are represented by the shares of stock they own. Corporations can quickly transfer ownership by simply having the shareholders endorse the back of each stock certificate to another party.
Ability to raise investment capital	It is easy to attract new investors into a corporate entity because of limited liability and the easy transferability of ownership.

	Sole Proprietorship	Partnership	Corporation
Licensing	Local license, $25–$100	Partnership agreement, legal fees	Articles of incorporation through the Secretary of State
Income	Business flows directly into personal income	Distributions taken by partners, as agreed by partners	Business and personal earnings separate, depending on corporate structure
Liability	Owner is liable	Owners are liable	Only business is liable

FIGURE B1.2

Comparison of Business
Structures

The most common reason for incurring the cost of setting up a corporation is the recognition that the shareholder is not legally liable for the actions of the corporation. Figure B1.1 displays the primary reasons businesses choose to incorporate.

The Limited Liability Corporation (LLC)

The *limited liability corporation (LLC)* is a hybrid entity that has the legal protections of a corporation and the ability to be taxed (one time) as a partnership. A company can form an LLC for any lawful business as long as the nature of the business is not banking, insurance, and certain professional service operations. By simply filing articles of organization with the respective state agency, an LLC takes on a separate identity similar to a corporation, but without the tax problems of the corporation. Figure B1.2 summarizes the primary differences between the three most common business structures.

Internal Operations of a Corporation

The majority of corporations use different specialized departments to perform the unique operations required to run the business. These departments commonly include accounting, finance, human resources, sales, marketing, operations/production, and management information systems (see Figure B1.3).

Accounting

The *accounting department* provides quantitative information about the finances of the business including recording, measuring, and describing financial information. People tend to use the terms *accounting* and *bookkeeping* synonymously;

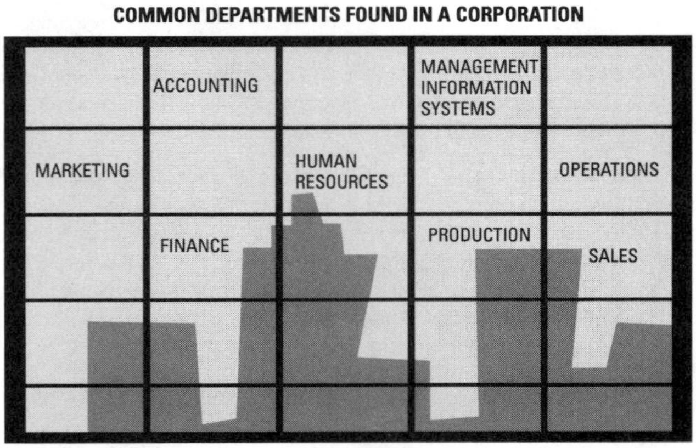

COMMON DEPARTMENTS FOUND IN A CORPORATION

FIGURE B1.3

Departmental Structure of
a Typical Organization

however, the two are different. **Bookkeeping** is the actual recording of the business's transactions, without any analysis of the information. **Accounting** analyzes the transactional information of the business so the owners and investors can make sound economic decisions.

The two primary types of accounting are financial and managerial. **Financial accounting** involves preparing financial reports that provide information about the business's performance to external parties such as investors, creditors, and tax authorities. Financial accounting must follow strict guidelines known as Generally Accepted Accounting Principles (GAAP) guidelines. **Managerial accounting** involves analyzing business operations for internal decision making and does not have to follow any rules issued by standard-setting bodies such as GAAP.

FINANCIAL STATEMENTS

All businesses operate using the same basic element, the transaction. A **transaction** is an exchange or transfer of goods, services, or funds involving two or more people. Each time a transaction occurs a source document captures all of the key data involved with the transaction. The **source document** describes the basic transaction data such as its date, purpose, and amount and includes cash receipts, canceled checks, invoices, customer refunds, employee time sheet, etc. The source document is the beginning step in the accounting process and serves as evidence that the transaction occurred. **Financial statements** are the written records of the financial status of the business that allow interested parties to evaluate the profitability and solvency of the business. **Solvency** represents the ability of the business to pay its bills and service its debt. The financial statements are the final product of the accountant's analysis of the business transactions. Preparing the financial statements is a major undertaking and requires a significant amount of effort. Financial statements must be understandable, timely, relevant, fair, and objective in order to be useful. The four primary financial statements include:

- Balance sheet.
- Income statement.
- Statement of owner's equity.
- Statement of cash flows.

Balance Sheet

The **balance sheet** gives an accounting picture of property owned by a company and of claims against the property on a specific date. The balance sheet is based on the fundamental accounting principle that assets = liabilities + owner's equity. An **asset** is anything owned that has value or earning power. A **liability** is an obligation to make financial payments. **Owner's equity** is the portion of a company belonging to the owners. The left (debit) side of a balance sheet states assets. The right (credit) side shows liabilities and owners' equity. The two sides must be equal (balance). The balance sheet is like a snapshot of the position of an individual or business at one point in time (see Figure B1.4).

Income Statement

The **income statement** (also referred to as **earnings report, operating statement,** and **profit-and-loss (P&L) statement**) reports operating results (revenues minus expenses) for a given time period ending at a specified date. **Revenue** refers to the amount earned resulting from the delivery or manufacture of a product or from the rendering of a service. Revenue can include sales from a product or an amount received for performing a service. **Expenses** refer to the costs incurred in operating and maintaining a business. The income statement reports a company's **net income**, or the amount of money remaining after paying taxes (see Figure B1.5).

ASSETS		LIABILITIES	
Current Assets		**Current Liabilities**	
Cash	$ 250,000	Accounts Payable	$ 150,000
Securities	$ 30,000	Loans (due < 1 year)	$ 750,000
Accounts Receivable	$ 1,500,000	Taxes	$ 200,000
Inventory	$ 2,920,000		
		Long-term Liabilities	
Fixed Assets	$ 7,500,000	Loans (due > 1 year)	$ 2,500,000
		Total Liabilities	$ 3,600,000
		Owner's Equity	$ 8,600,000
Total Assets	**$12,200,000**	**Total Liabilities + Owner's Equity**	**$12,200,000**

ASSETS = LIABILITIES + OWNER'S EQUITY

FIGURE B1.4

Balance Sheet Example

Income Statement	
Revenue (Sales)	$60,000,000
Cost of Goods Sold	$30,000,000
Gross Profit	$30,000,000
(Sales – Cost of Goods Sold)	
Operating Expenses	$7,000,000
Profit Before Taxes	$23,000,000
(Gross Profit – Operating Expenses)	
Taxes	$18,000,000
Net Profit (or Loss)	**$5,000,000**

FIGURE B1.5

Income Statement Example

Statement of Owner's Equity

The *statement of owner's equity* (also called the *statement of retained earnings* or *equity statement*) tracks and communicates changes in the shareholder's earnings. Profitable organizations typically pay the shareholders dividends. *Dividends* are a distribution of earnings to shareholders.

Statement of Cash Flows

Cash flow represents the money an investment produces after subtracting cash expenses from income. The *statement of cash flows* summarizes sources and uses of cash, indicates whether enough cash is available to carry on routine operations, and offers an analysis of all business transactions, reporting where the firm obtained its cash and how it chose to allocate the cash. The cash flow statement shows where money comes from, how the company is going to spend it, and when the company will require additional cash. Companies typically project cash flow statements on a monthly basis for the current year and a quarterly basis for the next two to five years. A *financial quarter* indicates a three-month period (four quarters per year). Cash flow statements become less valid over time since numerous assumptions are required to project into the future.

When it comes to decreasing expenses and managing a company's cash flow, managers need to look at all costs. Ben Worthen, executive vice president and CIO of Manufacturers Bank in Los Angeles, states that everyone notices the million-dollar negotiation; however, a couple of thousand dollars here and there are just as important. When attempting to cut costs, Worthen listed every contract the bank had. He saved $5,000 by renegotiating a contract with the vendor who watered the plants, a vendor that most employees did not even know existed. He also saved $50,000 by renegotiating the contract with the bank's cleaning agency. "You need to think of everything when cutting costs," Worthen said. "$5,000 buys three or four laptops for salespersons."[3]

Finance

Finance deals with the strategic financial issues associated with increasing the value of the business while observing applicable laws and social responsibilities. Financial decisions include such things as:

- How the company should raise and spend its capital.
- Where the company should invest its money.
- What portion of profits will be paid to shareholders in the form of dividends.
- Should the company merge with or acquire another business.

Financial decisions are short term (usually up to one year), medium term (one to seven years), or long term (more than seven years). The typical forms of financing include loans (debt or equity) or grants. Financing may be required for immediate use in business operations or for an investment.

FINANCIAL ANALYSIS

Different financial ratios are used to evaluate a company's performance. Companies can gain additional insight into their performance by comparing financial ratios against other companies in their industry. A few of the more common financial ratios include:

- **Internal rate of return (IRR)**—the rate at which the net present value of an investment equals zero.
- **Return on investment (ROI)**—indicates the earning power of a project and is measured by dividing the benefits of a project by the investment.
- **Cash flow analysis**—a means to conduct a periodic check on the company's financial health. A projected cash flow statement estimates what the stream of money will be in coming months or years, based on a history of sales and expenses. A monthly cash flow statement reveals the current state of affairs. The ability to perform a cash flow analysis is an essential skill for every business owner; it can be the difference between being able to open a business and being able to stay in business.
- **Break-even analysis**—a way to determine the volume of business required to make a profit at the current prices charged for the products or services. For example, if a promotional mailing costs $1,000 and each item generates $50 in revenue, the company must generate 20 sales to break even and cover the cost of the mailing. The *break-even point* is the point at which revenues equal costs. The point is located by performing a break-even analysis. All sales over the break-even point produce profits; any drop in sales below that point will produce losses (see Figure B1.6).

Human Resources

Human resources (HR) includes the policies, plans, and procedures for the effective management of employees (human resources). HR typically focuses on the following:

- Employee recruitment.
- Employee selection.

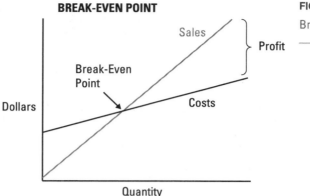

FIGURE B1.6

Break-Even Analysis

- Employee training and development.
- Employee appraisals, evaluations, and rewards.
- Employee communications.

The primary goal of HR is to instill employee commitment by creating an environment of shared values, innovation, flexibility, and empowerment. Most organizations recognize that focusing on strong HR practices that foster employee growth and satisfaction can significantly contribute to achieving business success. The most obvious way HR practices create business success is through quality employee selection. Hiring the right employee who suits the company's culture is difficult. Organizations create employee value by implementing employment practices such as training, skill development, and rewards. An organization that focuses on HR creates valuable employees with strategic business competencies.

MANAGEMENT TECHNIQUES

There may be no such thing as a best practice for managing people. Numerous management techniques are used by all different types of managers in a variety of industries. For example, Sears and Nordstrom are legends in the retailing industry; however, their approaches to HR are completely different. Sears is one of the pioneering companies in the science of employee selection, relying on some of the most sophisticated selection tests in American industry. Sears employees receive extensive training in company practices; management tracks employee attitudes and morale through frequent and rigorous employee surveys. The company provides its sales representatives, who work on salary rather than commission, with intensive training in Sears' products, the company's operating systems, and sales techniques.

Nordstrom operates with virtually no formal personnel practices. Its hiring is decentralized, using no formal selection tests. Managers look for applicants with experience in customer contact, but the main desirable quality appears to be pleasant personalities and motivation. The company has only one rule in its personnel handbook: "Use your best judgment at all times." Individual salesclerks virtually run their areas as private stores. Nordstrom maintains a continuous stream of programs to motivate employees to provide intensive service, but it offers very little training. Its commission-based payroll system makes it possible for salesclerks to earn sizable incomes. Nordstrom sales personnel are ranked within each department according to their monthly sales; the most successful are promoted (almost all managers are promoted from within the company) and the least successful are terminated.[4]

Sears and Nordstrom are both highly successful retailers, yet they operate using widely different recruitment policies. One of the biggest success factors for any business is the company's management and personnel. Employees must possess certain critical skills for the company to succeed. The HR department takes on the important task of hiring, training, evaluating, rewarding, and terminating employees. Effective HR goes far beyond executing a standard set of policies and procedures; it requires questioning and understanding the relationships between choices in managing people, the strategies and goals of the organization, and the possibilities presented by the external environment. Today's competitive environment features rapid technological change, increasingly global markets, and a diverse workforce comprising not just men and women with different sorts of career objectives, but also potential workers from diverse cultural and ethnic backgrounds. HR must ensure that the choices made in managing people are made sensibly and with clear purposes in mind.

Sales

Sales is the function of selling a good or service and focuses on increasing customer sales, which increases company revenues. A salesperson has the main activity of selling a product or service. Many industries require a license before a salesperson can sell the products, such as real estate, insurance, and securities.

A common view of the sales department is to see the salespersons only concerned with making the sale now, without any regard to the cost of the sale to the business. This is called the hard sell, where the salesperson heavily pushes a product (even when the customer does not want the product) and where price cuts are given even if they cause financial losses for the company. A broader view of the sales department sees it as taking on the task of building strong customer relationships where the primary emphasis is on securing new customers and keeping current customers satisfied. Many sales departments are currently focusing on building strong customer relationships.

THE SALES PROCESS

FIGURE B1.7

The Sales Process

Figure B1.7 depicts the typical sales process, which begins with an opportunity and ends with billing the customer for the sale. An opportunity is a name of a potential customer who might be interested in making a purchase (opportunities are also

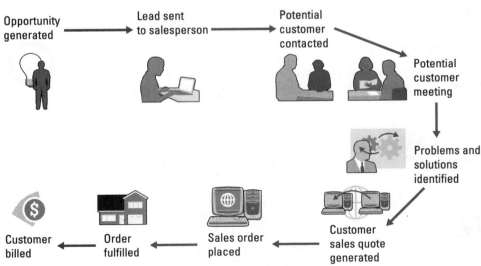

Sales Process

called leads). The company finds opportunities from a variety of sources such as mailing lists and customer inquiries. The name is sent to a salesperson who contacts the potential customer and sets up a meeting to discuss the products. During the meeting, all problems and issues are identified and resolved, and the salesperson generates a quote for the customer. If the customer decides to accept the quote, a sales order is placed. The company fulfills the order and delivers the product, and the process ends when the customer is billed.

MARKET SHARE

Sales figures offer a good indication of how well a company is performing. For example, high sales volumes typically indicate that a company is performing well. However, they do not always indicate how a firm is performing relative to its competitors. For example, changes in sales might simply reflect shifts in market size or in economic conditions. A sales increase might occur because the market increased in size, not because the company is performing better.

Measuring the proportion of the market that a firm captures is one way to measure a firm's performance relative to its competitors. This proportion is the firm's *market share* and is calculated by dividing the firm's sales by the total market sales for the entire industry. For example, if a firm's total sales (revenues) were $2 million and the sales for the entire industry were $10 million, the firm would have captured 20 percent of the total market, or have a 20 percent market share.

Many video game products launch with great enthusiasm and die a quick death such as Sega's GameGear and DreamCast, Atari's Lynx, and Nintendo's Virtual Boy. Video game consoles die quickly when only a limited number of game publishers sign up to supply games for the particular product. Producing video game products is a tough competitive business in a finicky market.

Sony recently released its first hand-held video game player, the PSP (for PlayStation Portable). The current market leader is Nintendo's GameBoy, which uses pricey cartridges for games. Instead of pricey cartridges, the PSP plays inexpensive mini disks to bring PlayStation2-quality graphics to the relatively primitive hand-held market. When Sony announced the PSP, game publishers raced to get a piece of the action, and Sony had 89 companies contracted to build games within a few weeks. In contrast, when Nokia launched its N-Gage game device, it struggled to land five game publishers. Electronic Arts, the world's biggest game publisher, has already committed to developing almost a dozen PSP games and has declared that the PSP will be the biggest driver of growth in the video game market for the next five years. For a new video game product heading into an uncertain and high-stakes market, that is the ultimate vote of confidence.[5]

Reasons to Increase Market Share

Many organizations seek to increase their market share because many individuals assimilate market share with profitability. Figure B1.8 indicates the primary reasons organizations seek to increase their market share.

Reasons to Increase Market Share
Economies of scale—An organization can develop a cost advantage by selling additional products or higher volumes.
Sales growth in a stagnant industry—If an industry stops growing, an organization can increase its sales by increasing its market share.
Reputation—A successful organization with a solid reputation can use its clout to its advantage.
Increased bargaining power—Larger organizations have an advantage in negotiating with suppliers and distributors.

FIGURE B1.8

Reasons to Increase Market Share

Ways to Increase Market Share

A primary way to increase market share is by changing one of the following variables: product, price, place, or promotion (see Figure B1.9). It is common to refer to these four variables as the marketing mix, discussed in detail below.

Reasons Not to Increase Market Share

Surprisingly, it is not always a good idea to increase an organization's market share. Figure B1.10 offers a few reasons why increasing an organization's market share can actually decrease an organization's revenues.

Marketing

Marketing is the process associated with promoting the sale of goods or services. The marketing department supports the sales department by creating promotions that help sell the company's products. *Marketing communications* seek to build product or service awareness and to educate potential consumers on the product or service.

Jenny Ming, president of Old Navy, a division of Gap Inc., believes that unique marketing ideas for Old Navy's original designs heavily contributed to the success of the $6.5 billion brand. Ideas come from anywhere, and Ming found one of the company's most successful products when she was dropping her daughter off at school. It was pajama day at school, and all of the girls were wearing pajama bottoms with a tank top. Ming began wondering why they even created and sold pajama tops; nobody seemed to wear them. The company, having problems selling pajama sets, quickly introduced "just bottoms," a line of pajama bottoms selling at $15. A full pajama set cost $25. Along with the bottoms, the company offered tank tops in different colors so the customer could mix and match the items. The company built a huge business from the "just bottoms" line. Ming encourages her staff to look for marketing and product opportunities everywhere, even in the most unlikely of places.[6]

FIGURE B1.9

Ways to Increase Market Share

Ways to Increase Market Share
Product—An organization can change product attributes to provide more value to the customer. Improving product quality is one example.
Price—An organization can decrease a product's price to increase sales. This strategy will not work if competitors are willing to match discounts.
Place (Distribution)—An organization can add new distribution channels. This allows the organization to increase the size of its market, which should increase sales.
Promotion—An organization can increase spending on product advertising, which should increase sales. This strategy will not work if competitors also increase advertising.

FIGURE B1.10

Reasons Not to Increase Market Share

Reasons Not to Increase Market Share
If an organization is near its production capacity and it experiences an increase in market share, it could cause the organization's supply to fall below its demand. Not being able to deliver products to meet demand could damage the organization's reputation.
Profits could decrease if an organization gains market share by offering deep discounts or by increasing the amount of money it spends on advertising.
If the organization is not prepared to handle the new growth, it could begin to offer shoddy products or less attentive customer service. This could result in the loss of its professional reputation and valuable customers.

MARKETING MIX

The classic components of marketing include the four Ps in the marketing mix: product, price, place, and promotion. The *marketing mix* includes the variables that marketing managers can control in order to best satisfy customers in the target market (see Figure B1.11). The organization attempts to generate a positive response in the target market by blending these four marketing mix variables in an optimal manner.

Figure B1.12 summarizes the primary attributes involved with each decision made in the marketing mix.

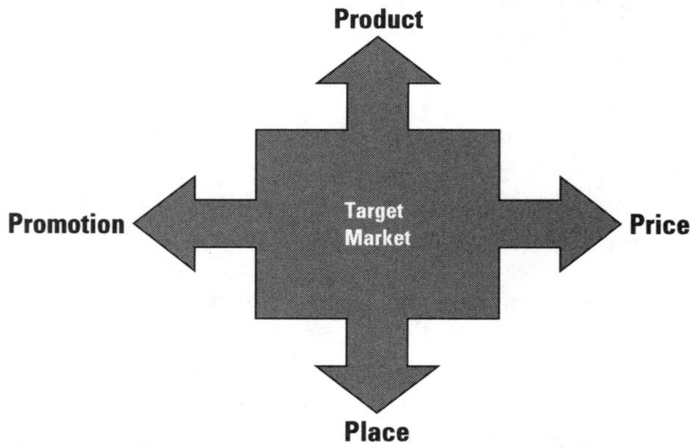

FIGURE B1.11
The Marketing Mix

1. **Product** – the physical product or service offered to the consumer. Product decisions include function, appearance, packaging, service, warranty, etc.

2. **Price** – takes into account profit margins and competitor pricing. Pricing includes list price, discounts, financing, and other options such as leasing.

3. **Place** (distribution) – associated with channels of distribution that serve as the means for getting the product to the target customers. Attributes involved in place decisions include market coverage, channel member selection, logistics, and levels of service.

4. **Promotion** – related to the communication and selling to potential consumers. An organization can perform a break-even analysis when making promotion decisions. If an organization knows the value of each customer, it can determine whether additional customers are worth the coast of acquisition. Attributes involved in promotion decisions involve advertising, public relations, media types, etc.

Product	Price	Place (Distribution)	Promotion
Quality	Discount	Channel	Advertising
Brand	Financing	Market	Sales
Appearance	Lease	Location	Public relations
Package		Logistics	Marketing message
Function		Service Level	Media type
Warranty			Budget
Service/Support			

FIGURE B1.12

Common Attributes Involved with Each P in the Marketing Mix

CUSTOMER SEGMENTATION

Market segmentation is the division of a market into similar groups of customers. It is not always optimal for an organization to offer the same marketing mix to vastly different customers. Market segmentation makes it possible for organizations to tailor the marketing mix for specific target markets, hence better satisfying its customer needs. Not all attributes of the marketing mix need to be changed for each market segment. For example, one market segment might require a discounted price, while another market segment might require better customer service. An organization uses marketing research, market trends, and managerial judgment when deciding the optimal way to segment a market. Market segmentation typically includes:

- **Geographic segmentation**—based on regional variables such as region, climate, population density, and population growth rate.
- **Demographic segmentation**—based on variables such as age, gender, ethnicity, education, occupation, income, and family status.
- **Psychographic segmentation**—based on variables such as values, attitudes, and lifestyles.
- **Behavioral segmentation**—based on variables such as usage rate, usage patterns, price sensitivity, and brand loyalty.

THE PRODUCT LIFE CYCLE

The *product life cycle* includes the four phases a product progresses through during its life cycle including introduction, growth, maturity, and decline. An organization's marketing of a product will change depending on its stage in the product life cycle. An organization can plot a product's profits as a function of the product life cycle (see Figure B1.13).

Joanne Bischmann, vice president, Harley-Davidson Inc., is still awed by the lengths customers will go to display their commitment to Harley-Davidson products. Recently, she saw a man who had tattooed a portrait of the four founding fathers along with their 100th anniversary logo on his back. When Bischmann was hired, her manager told her the following, "This will be the best job you're ever going to have because it isn't just about working at a company that makes motorcycles. The founding fathers actually seep out of the walls here." After 15 years with the company, Bischmann agrees with that statement. She always receives calls asking for the Harley-Davidson manual on how to keep customers passionate. Unfortunately, there is no manual. According to Bischmann, Harley-Davidson is a brand that none can own individually; it is more like a tribe, and its members carry on its traditions so it will be here for future generations.[7]

Operations/Production

Operations management (also called *production management*) includes the methods, tasks, and techniques organizations use to produce goods and services. The operations department oversees the transformation of input resources (i.e., labor, materials, and machines) into output resources (i.e., products and services). The operations department is critical because it manages the physical processes by which companies take in raw materials, convert them into products, and distribute them to customers. The operations department generally ranks high in the responsibilities of general management.

BUSINESS PROCESS REENGINEERING

A *business process* is a standardized set of activities that accomplishes a specific task, such as processing a customer's order. *Business process reengineering (BPR)* is the analysis and redesign of workflow within and between enterprises. In

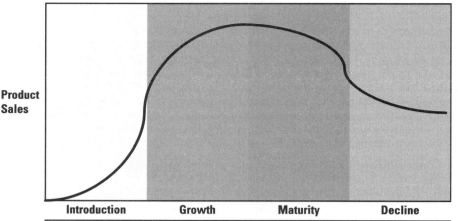

Product Sales

| Introduction | Growth | Maturity | Decline |

- **Introduction Stage**—The organization seeks to build product awareness and develop the product's market. The organization will use the marketing mix to help impact the target market. Product branding and quality level are established.

- **Growth Stage**—The organization seeks to build brand preference and increase market share. The organization maintains or increases the quality of the product and might add additional features or better customer service. The organization typically enjoys increases in demand with little competition allowing the price to remain constant.

- **Maturity Stage**—The strong growth in sales diminishes. Competition begins to appear with similar products. The primary objective at this point is to defend market share while maximizing profits. Some companies enhance product features to differentiate the product in the market.

- **Decline Stage**—Sales begin to decline. At this point, the organization has several options. It can maintain the product, possibly rejuvenating it by adding new features and finding new uses. It can reduce costs and continue to offer it, possibly to a loyal niche segment. It can discontinue the product, liquidating remaining inventory or selling it to another firm that is willing to continue the product.

business process reengineering, the project team starts with a clean sheet of paper and redesigns the process to increase efficiency and effectiveness. The project team does not take anything for granted and questions all the aspects of the process and the business. The reengineering project team obtains dramatic process improvement by redesigning processes that cross departments.

Most of the major opportunities for process improvement exist in cross-departmental processes. Information technology usually plays a key role in process improvement by making possible a radically faster and almost paperless process. However, IT is only an enabling factor. A classic reengineering project example is the accounts payable process at Ford. Through BPR, Ford reduced the number of people required to perform the process from 500 to 125.[8]

TRANSFORMING CORPORATIONS

Complete transformation of an organization, or an entire industry, is the ultimate goal of successful business process reengineering. Figure B1.14 displays a matrix that has project scope on one axis and project speed on the other. For a project with a relatively narrow scope where the speed is fast, reengineering occurs. Fast speed with broad scope may be a turnaround situation requiring downsizing and tough decision making. A project with a relatively slow speed and narrow scope results in continuous improvement. In the upper right-hand corner of Figure B1.14, where the project scope is broad and the time frame for achieving that change is longer, the term *transformation* is appropriate.

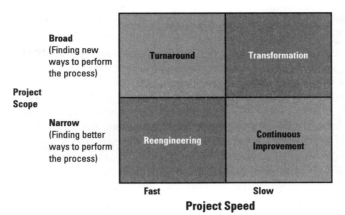

Progressive Insurance offers a great example of a corporation that transformed its entire industry by reengineering the insurance claims process. Progressive Insurance has seen phenomenal growth in an otherwise staid auto insurance market. Progressive's growth came not through acquisitions or mergers—the stuff that puts CEOs on the front page of *The Wall Street Journal*—but through substantial innovations in everyday operations. Progressive reengineered the insurance claim process. When a customer has an auto accident, Progressive representatives are on hand 24 hours a day to take the call and schedule a claims adjustor. The claims adjustor works out of a mobile van, enabling a nine-hour turnaround rather than the industry-standard of 10 to 17 days. The Progressive adjustor prepares an estimate on the spot and will, in most cases, write the customer a check immediately and even offer a ride home.

What provoked this innovation? Progressive says it was the strong connection it has to its customers, its willingness to listen to customers' frustrations, and the common sense to act on those frustrations by changing the core of its business operations. As a result of customer feedback, the company did not merely tweak the details of the claims adjustment process. It dramatically rewrote the process, resulting in significant cost savings for the company. More important, however, the hassle-free claims process keeps customers happy and loyal, reducing the significant burden of constantly replacing lapsed customers with new ones.[9]

Management Information Systems

Information technology (IT) is any computer-based tool that people use to work with information and support the information and information-processing needs of an organization. Information technology is a broad subject concerned with technology and other aspects of managing and processing information, especially in large organizations. In particular, IT deals with the use of electronic computers and computer software to convert, store, protect, process, transmit, and retrieve information. For that reason, computer professionals are often called IT specialists, and the division that deals with software technology is often called the IT department.

Management information systems is a business function just as marketing, finance, operations, and human resources management are business functions. Formally defined, *management information systems (MIS)* is the function that plans for, develops, implements, and maintains IT hardware, software, and applications that people use to support the goals of an organization. Other names for MIS include information services (IS), management information services (MIS), or managed service provider (MSP). In business, MIS supports business processes and operations, decision making, and competitive strategies. MIS involves collecting, recording, storing, and basic processing of information including:

- Accounting records such as sales, purchase, investment, and payroll information, processed into financial statements such as income statements, balance sheets, ledgers, management reports, and so on.

- Operations records such as inventory, work-in-process, equipment repair and maintenance, supply chain, and other production/operations information, processed into production schedules, production controllers, inventory systems, and production monitoring systems.

- Human resources records such as personnel, salary, and employment history information, processed into employee expense reports and performance-based reports.

- Marketing records such as customer profiles, customer purchase histories, marketing research, advertising, and other marketing information, processed into advertising reports, marketing plans, and sales activity reports.

- Strategic records such as business intelligence, competitor analysis, industry analysis, corporate objectives, and other strategic information, processed into industry trends reports, market share reports, mission statements, and portfolio models.

The bottom line is that management information systems use all of the above to implement, control, and monitor plans, strategies, tactics, new products, new business models, or new business ventures. Unit 1 covers IT and MIS in detail.

The study of business begins with understanding the different types of businesses including a sole proprietorship, partnership, or a corporation. Figure B1.15 highlights seven departments found in a typical business.

All of these departments must be able to execute activities specific to their business function and also be able to work with the other departments to create synergies throughout the entire business.

- **Accounting** provides quantitative information about the finances of the business including recording, measuring, and describing financial information.

- **Finance** deals with the strategic financial issues associated with increasing the value of the business, while observing applicable laws and social responsibilities.

- **Human resources (HR)** includes the policies, plans, and procedures for the effective management of employees (human resources).

- **Sales** is the function of selling a good or service and focuses on increasing customer sales, which increases company revenues.

- **Marketing** is the process associated with promoting the sale of goods or services. The marketing department supports the sales department by creating promotions that help sell the company's products.

- **Operations management** (also called **production management**) includes the methods, tasks, and techniques organizations use to produce goods and services. Transportation (also called logistics) is part of operations management.

- **Management information systems (MIS)** is the function that plans for, develops, implements, and maintains IT hardware, software, and applications that people use to support the goals of an organization.

FIGURE B1.15

Common Departments in a Business

Accounting, 240
Accounting department, 239
Asset, 240
Balance sheet, 240
Bookkeeping, 240
Break-even point, 242
Business process, 248
Business process
    reengineering (BPR), 248
Capital, 237
Corporation (also called,
    organization, enterprise, or
    business), 237
Dividend, 241
Expense, 240
Finance, 242
Financial accounting, 240
Financial quarter, 241
Financial statement, 240
For profit corporation, 238
Human resources (HR), 242
Income statement (also
    referred to as earnings
    report, operating statement,

and profit-and-loss (P&L)
    statement), 240
Information technology (IT), 250
Liability, 240
Limited liability, 237
Limited liability corporation
    (LLC), 239
Limited partnership, 237
Loss, 236
Management information
    systems (MIS), 250
Managerial accounting, 240
Marketing, 246
Marketing communication, 246
Marketing mix, 247
Market segmentation, 248
Market share, 245
Net income, 240
Not for profit (or nonprofit)
    corporation, 238
Operations management (also
    called production
    management), 248
Owner's equity, 240

Partnership, 237
Partnership agreement, 237
Product life cycle, 248
Profit, 236
Revenue, 240
Sales, 244
Shareholder, 237
Sole proprietorship, 237
Solvency, 240
Source document, 240
Statement of cash flow, 241
Statement of owner's equity
    (also called the statement of
    retained earnings or equity
    statement), 241
Transaction, 240

* CLOSING CASE ONE

Battle of the Toys—FAO Schwarz Is Back!

German immigrant Frederick Schwarz established FAO Schwarz, a premier seller of fine toys, in 1862. After moving between several store locations in Manhattan, the growing company settled at 745 Fifth Avenue in 1931. FAO Schwarz soon became a toy institution, despite the impending Depression.

Unfortunately, the New York institution closed its doors in 2004 after its owner, FAO Inc., filed for bankruptcy twice in 2003. The company ran into trouble because it could not compete with the deep discounts offered on toys at chain stores like Wal-Mart and Target. All the stores in the FAO chain were closed.

Some people believe that FAO Schwarz was its own worst enemy. The company sold Sesame Street figures for $9 while the same figure at a discount store went for less than $3.

In 2004, the New York investment firm D. E. Shaw & Co. bought the rights to the FAO Schwarz name and reopened the Manhattan and Las Vegas stores. The grand reopening of the New York store occurred on November 25, 2004, during the Macy's Thanksgiving Day parade. It appears that the company has learned from its previous mistakes and is moving forward with a new business strategy of offering high-end, hard-to-find toys and products along with outstanding customer service.

Jerry Welch, FAO chief executive officer, states the company based its new business strategy on offering customers—local, visitors, and Internet—a unique shopping experience in which they can spend thousands of dollars or just twenty, but still purchase an exclusive item.

The store no longer carries any items from top toymakers Hasbro Inc. or Lego. The only toys it carries from Mattel Inc. are Hot Wheels and limited-edition Barbie dolls, starting at $130 for the Bridal Barbie dressed in a Badgley Mischka designer wedding gown and chandelier earrings. A few of the items the store is offering include:

- $20 made-to-order Hot Wheels car that a child can custom design via a computer.
- $50,000 miniature Ferrari with a full leather interior, fiberglass body, three-speed transmission, and working sound system that travels up to 24 kilometers an hour and is not recommended for children six and under.
- $15,000 stuffed elephant.
- $150,000 6.7-meter-long piano keyboard, which premiered in the Tom Hanks movie *Big*.
- Baby dolls that are arranged in incubators and sold by staff wearing nurses' uniforms.

Welch said, "FAO is a 142-year-old brand that, because of our location on Fifth Avenue, people all over the world know. So we start out with great recognition and what we've done here is pull together something that you just can't find anywhere else in the world. Everything here is made by small, unique manufacturers from all over the world." Welch is confident the stores will be richly profitable for its new owners because they have stopped offering mainstream products found in rival stores to generate sales volume. The new owners have returned to a business strategy focusing on quality and exclusivity that were the hallmark of the original store.

The Future of the Toy Store Playing Field

Toys 'R' Us began slashing prices during the 2004 holiday season in a last-ditch effort to fight off intense price competition from big discounters like Wal-Mart and Target. Toys 'R' Us CEO John Eyler stated the company would not be outdone on pricing, during the holiday sales rush, though he cautioned he was not planning to engage in a price war. There have been several reports that the company might leave the toy business to focus on its more profitable Babies 'R' Us unit. Toys 'R' Us lost $25 million for the three months ended in October 2004. The company lost $46 million in the same period the year earlier. The decrease in losses can be attributed to a big cost-cutting effort.

Kurt Barnard of Barnard's Retail Trend Report stated that Toys 'R' Us is destined for oblivion—it cannot stand up to the discounters. Toymakers like Mattel and Hasbro, whose profits have also suffered from Wal-Mart's market power, have given Toys 'R' Us a hand by offering it 21 exclusive items not available at other stores.

Toy manufacturers fear that greater monopoly power from Wal-Mart will force them to slash their profit margins. Wal-Mart carries fewer items than toy stores like Toys 'R' Us, which could lead to fewer choices for consumers.

FAO's new owners believe that Wal-Mart cannot compare with the atmosphere now offered at FAO Schwarz, a true toy heaven. The company is hoping that its new business strategy will allow it to move beyond the battle of the toy stores. Toys 'R' Us and Disney Stores will need to find new ways to compete with discounters like Wal-Mart and Target.[10]

Questions

1. Why did FAO Inc. have to declare bankruptcy?
2. Describe the issues with FAO's original business model.
3. Identify the toy retailer's new business model. Do you believe it will keep the new company in business? Why or why not?
4. What strategy can Toys 'R' Us follow that will help it compete with big discount chains like Wal-Mart and Target?

Innovative Managers	
Jeffrey Immelt, General Electric (GE)	■ Repositioned GE's portfolio with major acquisitions in health care, entertainment, and commercial finance ■ Created a more diverse, global, and customer-driven culture
Steven Reinemund, PepsiCo	■ Developed strong and diverse leadership that helped PepsiCo tap new markets ■ Attained consistent double-digit growth through product innovation and smart marketing
Steven Spielberg, Jeffrey Katzenberg, and David Geffen, DreamWorks SKG	■ Computer-animated *Shrek 2* set a record with a gross of $437 million ■ IPO pulled in $812 million
Robert Nardelli, Home Depot	■ Turned a $46 billion company focused on big stores into a $70 billion chain with urban, suburban, and international outlets ■ Drive for efficiency, such as centralizing purchasing and investing in technology, pushed margins above 30 percent
John Henry, Boston Red Sox	■ Broke the most fabled curse in sports, when the Boston Red Sox won the team's first World Championship since 1918 ■ Sold out all 81 home games for the first time in team history
Phil Knight, Nike	■ Transformed a volatile, fad-driven marketing and design icon into a more shareholder-friendly company

FIGURE B1.16

Innovative Business Managers

_____

Innovative Business Managers

BusinessWeek magazine recognized several innovative managers who have demonstrated talent, vision, and the ability to identify excellent opportunities (see Figure B1.16).

Jeffrey Immelt, General Electric (GE)

When Jeffrey Immelt took over as CEO of General Electric, he had big shoes to fill. The former CEO, Jack Welch, had left an unprecedented record as one of the top CEOs of all time. Immelt proved his ability to run the company by creating a customer-driven global culture that spawns innovation and embraces technology. The company was forecasting earnings to increase 17 percent in 2005.

Steven Reinemund, PepsiCo

Steven Reinemund has turned PepsiCo into a $27 billion food and beverage giant. "To be a leader in consumer products, it's critical to have leaders who represent the population we serve," states Reinemund, who created a diverse leadership group that defines the strategic vision for the company. Reinemund also takes a major role in mentoring and teaching his employees and demands that all senior executives do the same. The payoff: consistent double-digit earnings and solid sales at a time when many of the company's staple products—potato chips and soft drinks—are under attack for fears about childhood obesity and health concerns.

Steven Spielberg, Jeffrey Katzenberg, and David Geffen, DreamWorks

The DreamWorks studio, founded 10 years ago by Steven Spielberg, Jeffrey Katzenberg, and David Geffen, suffered through its share of early bombs. Finally, the studio discovered a green ogre named Shrek and quickly became the hottest studio this side of Pixar Animation. Dream-Works Animation turned a $187 million loss in 2003 into a $196 million profit in 2004, with revenues of $1.1 billion. DreamWorks plans to release two animation films per year, each taking almost four years to produce.

Robert Nardelli, Home Depot

Robert Nardelli took several risks when he became CEO of Home Depot. First, he allocated $14 billion into upgrading merchandise, renovating outdated stores, and investing in new technology such as self-checkout lanes and cordless scan guns. Second, Nardelli expanded into Mexico, China, and other regions, tapping the growing homeowner market. Finally, Nardelli bet big on carrying products for aging baby boomers who wanted to spruce up their empty nests. The moves are paying off. The company sits on $3.4 billion in cash. With 2005 revenues headed to $80 billion, Home Depot is the number two U.S. retailer after Wal-Mart.

John Henry, Boston Red Sox

John Henry earned his fortune in the global futures market by developing a proprietary futures-trading system that consistently produced double-digit returns. Henry's new system, Sabermet-rics, helped him reverse the most fabled curse in sports history by leading the Boston Red Sox to the team's first World Championship since 1918. Sabermetrics mines baseball statistics to find undervalued players while avoiding long contracts for aging stars whose performance is likely to decline. With the help of Sabermetrics, Henry built one of the most effective teams in baseball.

Philip Knight, Nike

Philip Knight, who got his start by selling Japanese sneakers from the trunk of his car, built the $12 billion sports behemoth Nike. Knight and his team transformed high-performance sports equipment into high-fashion gear and forever changed the rules of sports marketing with huge endorsement contracts and in-your-face advertising. Then, just as suddenly, Nike lost focus. In early 2000, kids stopped craving the latest sneaker, the company's image took a huge hit from its labor practices, sales slumped, and costs soared.

Thus began Knight's second act. He revamped management and brought in key outsiders to oversee finances and apparel lines. Knight devoted more energy to developing new information systems. Today, Nike's earnings are less volatile and less fad-driven. In 2004, Nike's earnings increased $1 billion.[11]

Questions

1. Choose one of the companies listed above and explain how it has achieved business success.

2. Why is it important for all of DreamWorks' functional business areas to work together? Provide an example of what might happen if the DreamWorks marketing department failed to work with its sales department.

3. Why is marketing important to an organization like the Boston Red Sox? Explain where Major League Baseball is in the product life cycle.

4. Which types of financial statements are most important to Home Depot's business?

5. Identify the marketing mix and why customer segmentation is critical to PepsiCo's business strategy.

6. Explain business process reengineering and how a company like GE can use it to improve operations.

1. **Setting Up a Business**

   Your friend, Lindsay Harvey, is going to start her own chocolate shop, called Chocolate-By-Design. Lindsay is an expert candy maker and one of the city's top pastry chefs. Lindsay has come to you for advice on what type of business Chocolate-By-Design should be—a sole proprietorship, partnership, or corporation. Create a report comparing the three different types of businesses, along with your recommendation for Chocolate-By-Design's business structure.

2. **Guest Lecturing on Business**

   As a recent college graduate, your favorite professor, Dr. Henning, has asked you to come back and guest lecture at his introduction to business course. Create a presentation defining the different departments in a typical business, what roles each play, and why it is important that they all work together.

3. **Expanding Markets**

   J. R. Cash created a small business selling handmade cowboy boots, and within a year his business is booming. J. R. currently builds all of the boots in his store and takes orders over the phone and from walk-in customers. There is currently a three-month waiting list for boots. J. R. is not sure how to grow his business and has come to you for advice. Describe the reasons and ways some businesses increase market share and why J. R. might choose not to increase his market share.

4. **Segmenting Customers**

   Due to your vast marketing experience, you have been hired by a new company, Sugar, to perform a strategic analysis on chewing gum. The company wants to understand the many market segments for the different brands, flavors, sizes, and colors of gum. Create an analysis of the different market segments for chewing gum. What market segment would you recommend Sugar pursue?

5. **Product Life Cycle**

   An associate, Carl Grotenhuis, has developed a new brand of laundry detergent called Clean. Carl wants your opinion on his potential to enter and dominate the laundry detergent market. Using the product life cycle create a recommendation for Carl's new product.

6. **Redesigning a Business**

   Tom Walton is the new CEO for Lakeside, a large cereal manufacturing company. Tom's predecessor had run the company for 50 years and did little in terms of process improvement; in fact, his motto was "if it isn't broke, why fix it." Tom wants to take advantage of technology to create new processes for the entire company. He believes that improving operations will increase efficiency and lower costs.

   Tom has a major hurdle to overcome before he can begin revamping the company— its employees. Many of the employees have worked at the company for decades and are comfortable with the motto "if it isn't broke, why fix it." Develop a plan Tom can use to communicate to his employees the potential value gained from business process reengineering.

Business Process

LEARNING OUTCOMES

1. Describe business processes and their importance to an organization.
2. Differentiate between customer facing processes and business facing processes.
3. Compare the continuous process improvement model and business process reengineering.
4. Describe the importance of business process modeling (or mapping) and business process models.
5. Explain business process management along with the reason for its importance to an organization.

Introduction

The benefits of business process improvement vary, but a rough rule of thumb is that it will, at a minimum, double the gains of a project by streamlining outdated practices, enhancing efficiency, promoting compliance and standardization, and making an organization more agile. Business process improvement involves three key steps:

1. Measure what matters to most customers.
2. Monitor the performance of key business processes.
3. Assign accountability for process improvement.

Comprehensive business process management systems help organizations model and define complete business processes, implement those processes integrated with existing systems, and provide business leaders with the ability to analyze, manage, and improve the execution of processes in real time.

Examining Business Processes

Waiting in line at a grocery store is a great example of the need for process improvement. In this case, the "process" is called checkout, and the purpose is to pay for and bag groceries. The process begins when a customer steps into line and ends when the customer receives the receipt and leaves the store. The *process* steps are the activities the customer and store personnel do to complete the transaction. A **business process** is a standardized set of activities that accomplish a specific task, such as processing a customer's order. Business processes transform a set of inputs into a set of outputs (goods or services) for another person or process by using people and tools. This simple example describes a customer checkout process. Imagine other business processes: developing new products, building a new home, ordering clothes from mail-order companies, requesting new telephone service from a telephone company, administering Social Security payments, and so on.

Examining business processes helps an organization determine bottlenecks and identify outdated, duplicate, and smooth running processes. To stay competitive, organizations must optimize and automate their business processes. To identify which business processes need to be optimized, the organization must clearly understand its business processes, which typically have the following important characteristics:

- The processes have internal and external users.
- A process is cross-departmental. Departments are functional towers of expertise, but processes cut across departments.
- The processes occur across organizations.
- The processes are based on how work is done in the organization.
- Every process should be documented and fully understood by everyone participating in the process.
- Processes should be modeled to promote complete understanding.

A business process can be viewed as a "value chain." By contributing to the creation or delivery of a product or service, each step in a process should add value to the preceding step. For example, one step in the product development process consists of conducting market acceptance tests. This step adds value by ensuring that the product meets the needs of the market before the product or service is finalized. A tremendous amount of learning and improvement can result from the documentation and examination of the input-output linkages. However, between every input and every output is a process. Knowledge and improvement can only be completed by peeling the layers of the onion and examining the processes through which inputs are converted into outputs. Figure B2.1 displays several sample business processes.

Some processes (such as a programming process) may be contained wholly within a single department. However, most processes (such as ordering a product) are cross-departmental, spanning the entire organization. Figure B2.2 displays the different categories of cross-departmental business processes. **Customer facing processes** result in a product or service that is received by an organization's external customer. **Business facing processes** are invisible to the external customer but essential to the effective management of the business and include goal setting, day-to-day planning, performance feedback, rewards, and resource allocation.

UNDERSTANDING THE IMPORTANCE OF BUSINESS PROCESSES

Organizations are only as effective as their business processes. Developing logical business processes can help an organization achieve its goals. For example, an automobile manufacturer might have a goal to reduce the time it takes to deliver a car to a customer. The automobile manufacturer cannot hope to meet this goal with an inefficient ordering process or a convoluted distribution process. Sales representatives might be making mistakes when completing order forms, data-entry clerks might not accurately code order information, and dock crews might be inefficiently loading cars onto trucks. All of these errors increase the time it will take to get the

Sample Business
Processes

Sample Business Processes

ACCOUNTING BUSINESS PROCESSES
- Accounts payable
- Accounts receivable
- Bad/NSF checks
- Bank account reconciliation
- Cash receipts
- Check requests
- Check signing authority
- Depreciation
- Invoice billings
- Petty cash
- Month-end closing procedures

CUSTOMER SERVICE BUSINESS PROCESSES
- Customer satisfaction survey
- Customer service contact/complaint handling
- Guarantee customer service satisfaction
- Postsale customer follow-up
- Warranty and service policies

ENVIRONMENTAL BUSINESS PROCESSES
- Environmental protection
- Hazardous waste management
- Air/water/soil resource management

FINANCE BUSINESS PROCESSES
- Account collection
- Bank loan applications
- Banking policy and relations
- Business plans and forecasts
- Customer credit approval and credit terms
- Exercise of incentive stock options
- Property tax assessments
- Release of financial or confidential information
- Stock transactions
- Weekly financial and six-week cash flow reports

HUMAN RESOURCES BUSINESS PROCESSES
- Board of directors and shareholders meetings, minutes, and protocol
- Disabilities employment policies
- Drug-free workplace employment policies
- Employee hiring policies
- Employee orientation
- Family and medical leave act
- Files and records management
- Health care benefits
- Paid and unpaid time off
- Pay and payroll matters
- Performance appraisals and salary adjustments
- Resignations and terminations
- Sexual harassment policies
- Training/tuition reimbursement
- Travel and entertainment
- Workplace rules and guidelines
- Workplace safety

Sample Business Processes
MANAGEMENT INFORMATION SYSTEMS BUSINESS PROCESSES ■ Disaster recovery procedures ■ Backup/recovery procedures ■ Service agreements, emergency services, and community resources ■ Emergency notification procedures ■ Office and department recovery ■ User workstation standards ■ Use of personal software ■ Computer security incident reporting ■ Control of computer virus programs ■ Computer user/staff training plan ■ Internet use policy ■ E-mail policy ■ Computer support center
MANUFACTURING BUSINESS PROCESSES ■ Assembly manuals ■ Bill of materials ■ Calibration for testing and measuring equipment ■ FDA inspections ■ Manufacturing change orders ■ Master parts list and files ■ Serial number designation ■ Quality control for finished goods ■ Quality assurance audit procedure
SALES AND MARKETING BUSINESS PROCESSES ■ Collection of sales tax ■ Copyrights and trademarks ■ Marketing plans model number ■ Designation public relations ■ Return of goods from customers ■ Sales leads ■ Sales order entry ■ Sales training ■ Trade shows
SHIPPING, PURCHASING, AND INVENTORY CONTROL BUSINESS PROCESSES ■ Packing, storage, and distribution ■ Physical inventory procedures ■ Purchasing procedures ■ Receiving, inspection, and stocking of parts and materials ■ Shipping and freight claims ■ Vendor selection, files, and inspections

FIGURE B2.1

(Continued)

car to the customer. Improving any one of these business processes can have a significant effect on the total distribution process, made up of the order entry, production scheduling, and transportation processes.

IBM Business Consulting Services helped Bank of America's card services division identify $40 million of simplification and cost savings projects over two years by improving business processes to identify opportunities, eliminate redundancies, consolidate systems/applications, and remove duplicate processes. Within the card services and e-commerce division were several fragmented strategies and IT architectures. These were consolidated and simplified to streamline the business area and provide better and faster response to customer demand.

The scope of the IT strategy and architecture business process realignment project included all consumer card segments (including military, school, airlines, etc.), ATM cards and services, and e-commerce.[1]

Customer Facing Processes	Industry-Specific Customer Facing Processes	Business Facing Processes
Marketing and sales	Banking—loan processing	Strategic planning
Product development	Insurance—claims processing	Tactical planning
Service development	Government—grant allocation	Budgeting
Manufacturing	Retail—merchandise return	Training
Distribution	Restaurant—food preparation	Purchasing
Billing	Airline—baggage handling	
Order processing	Hotel—reservation handling	
Customer service		

Business Process Improvement

Improving business processes is paramount for businesses to stay competitive in today's marketplace. Over the past 10 to 15 years, companies have been forced to improve their business processes because customers are demanding better products and services; if they do not receive what they want from one supplier, they have many others to choose from (hence the competitive issue for businesses). Figure B2.3 displays several opportunities for business process improvement.

Many organizations began business process improvement with a continuous improvement model. A **continuous process improvement model** attempts to understand and measure the current process, and make performance improvements accordingly. Figure B2.4 illustrates the basic steps for continuous process improvement. Organizations begin by documenting what they do today, establish some way to measure the process based on what customers want, perform the process, measure the results, and then identify improvement opportunities based on the collected information. The next step is to implement process improvements, and then measure the performance of the new process. This loop repeats over and over again and is called continuous process improvement. It might also be called business process improvement or functional process improvement.

This method for improving business processes is effective to obtain gradual, incremental improvement. However, several factors have accelerated the need to improve business processes. The most obvious is technology. New technologies (like the Internet and wireless) rapidly bring new capabilities to businesses, thereby raising the competitive bar and the need to improve business processes dramatically.

Another apparent trend is the opening of world markets and increased free trade. Such changes bring more companies into the marketplace, adding to the competition. In today's marketplace, major changes are required just to stay in

Business Process Improvement Examples
Eliminate duplicate activities
Combine related activities
Eliminate multiple reviews and approvals
Eliminate inspections
Simplify processes
Reduce batch sizes
Process in parallel
Implement demand pull
Outsource inefficient activities
Eliminate movement of work
Organize multifunctional teams
Design cellular workplaces
Centralize/decentralize

the game. As a result, companies have requested methods for faster business process improvement. Also, companies want breakthrough performance changes, not just incremental changes, and they want it now. Because the rate of change has increased for everyone, few businesses can afford a slow change process. One approach for rapid change and dramatic improvement is business process reengineering (BPR).

BUSINESS PROCESS REENGINEERING (BPR)

An organization must continuously revise and reexamine its decisions, goals, and targets to improve its performance. A bank may have many activities, such as investing, credit cards, loans, and so on, and it may be involved in cross-selling (e.g., insurance) with other preferred vendors in the market. If the credit card department is not functioning in an efficient manner, the bank might reengineer the credit card business process. This activity, ***business process reengineering (BPR),*** is the analysis and redesign of workflow within and between enterprises. BPR relies on a different school of thought than continuous process improvement. *In the extreme,* BPR assumes the current process is irrelevant, does not work, or is broken and must be overhauled from scratch. Such a clean slate enables business process designers to disassociate themselves from today's process and focus on a new process. It is like the designers projecting themselves into the future and asking: What should the process look like? What do customers want it to look like? What do other employees want it to look like? How do best-in-class companies do it? How can new technology facilitate the process?

Figure B2.5 displays the basic steps in a business process reengineering effort. It begins with defining the scope and objectives of the reengineering project, then goes through a learning process (with customers, employees, competitors, noncompetitors, and new technology). Given this knowledge base, the designers can create a vision for the future and design new business processes by creating a plan of action based on the gap between current processes, technologies, structures, and process vision. It is then a matter of implementing the chosen solution. The Department of Defense (DoD) is an expert at reengineering business process. Figure B2.6 highlights the Department of Defense's best-in-class suggestions for a managerial approach to a reengineering effort.

Business Process Design

After choosing the method of business process improvement that is appropriate for the organization, the process designers must determine the most efficient way to begin revamping the processes. To determine whether each process is appropriately structured, organizations should create a cross-functional team to build process models that display input-output relationships among process-dependent operations and departments. They should create business process models documenting a step-by-step process sequence for the activities that are required to convert inputs to outputs for the specific process.

Business process modeling (or ***mapping***) is the activity of creating a detailed flow chart or process map of a work process showing its inputs, tasks, and activities, in a structured sequence. A ***business process model*** is a graphic description of a process, showing the sequence of process tasks, which is developed for a specific

Managerial Approach to Reengineering Projects
1. **Define the scope.** Define functional objectives; determine the management strategy to be followed in streamlining and standardizing processes; and establish the process, data, and information systems baselines from which to begin process improvement.
2. **Analyze.** Analyze business processes to eliminate non-value-added processes; simplify and streamline processes of little value; and identify more effective and efficient alternatives to the process, data, and system baselines.
3. **Evaluate.** Conduct a preliminary, functional, economic analysis to evaluate alternatives to baseline processes and select a preferred course of action.
4. **Plan.** Develop detailed statements of requirements, baseline impacts, costs, benefits, and schedules to implement the planned course of action.
5. **Approve.** Finalize the functional economic analysis using information from the planning data, and present to senior management for approval to proceed with the proposed process improvements and any associated data or system changes.
6. **Execute.** Execute the approved process and data changes, and provide functional management oversight of any associated information system changes.

purpose and from a selected viewpoint. A set of one or more process models details the many functions of a system or subject area with graphics and text and its purpose is to:

- Expose process detail gradually and in a controlled manner.
- Encourage conciseness and accuracy in describing the process model.
- Focus attention on the process model interfaces.
- Provide a powerful process analysis and consistent design vocabulary.

A process model typically displays activities as boxes and uses arrows to represent data and interfaces. Process modeling usually begins with a functional process representation of *what* the process problem is or an As-Is process model. *As-Is process models* represent the current state of the operation that has been mapped, without any specific improvements or changes to existing processes. The next step is to build a To-Be process model that displays *how* the process problem will be solved or implemented. *To-Be process models* show the results of applying change improvement opportunities to the current (As-Is) process model. This approach ensures that the process is fully and clearly understood before the details of a process solution are decided. The To-Be process model shows *how* the *what* is to be realized. Figure B2.7 displays the As-Is and To-Be process models for ordering a hamburger.

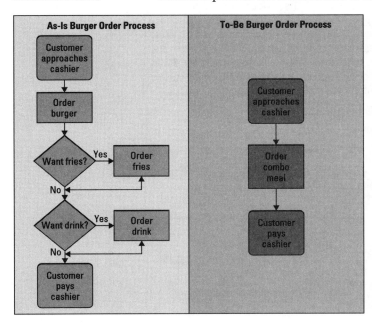

Analyzing As-Is business process models leads to success in business process reengineering since these diagrams are very powerful in visualizing the activities, processes, and data flow of an organization. As-Is and To-Be process models are integral in process reengineering projects. Figure B2.8 illustrates an As-Is process

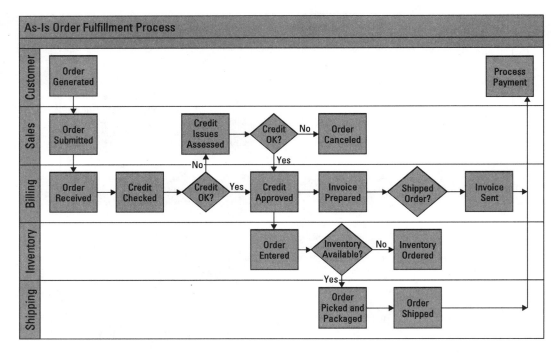

FIGURE B2.8

As-Is Process Model for Order Entry

model of an order-filling process developed by a process modeling team representing all departments that contribute to the process. The process modeling team traces the process of converting the input (orders) through all the intervening steps until the final required output (payment) is produced. The map shows how all departments are involved as the order is processed.

It is easy to become bogged down in excessive detail when creating an As-Is process model. The objective is to aggressively eliminate, simplify, or improve the To-Be processes. Successful process improvement efforts result in positive answers to the key process design or improvement question: Is this the most efficient and effective process for accomplishing the process goals? This process modeling structure allows the team to identify all the critical interfaces, overlay the time to complete various processes, start to define the opportunities for process simulation, and identify disconnects (illogical, missing, or extraneous steps) in the processes. Figure B2.9 displays sample disconnects in the order filling process in Figure B2.8.

The team then creates a To-Be process model, which reflects a disconnect-free order fulfillment process (see Figure B2.10). Disconnects fixed by the new process include

- Direct order entry by sales, eliminating sales administration.
- Parallel order processing and credit checking.
- Elimination of multiple order-entry and order-logging steps.

Issues in the As-Is Order Process Model
■ Sales representatives take too long to submit orders.
■ There are too many process steps.
■ Sales administration slows down the process by batch-processing orders.
■ Credit checking is performed for both old and new customers.
■ Credit checking holds up the process because it is done before (rather than concurrently with) order picking.

FIGURE B2.9

Issues in the As-Is Process Model for Order Entry

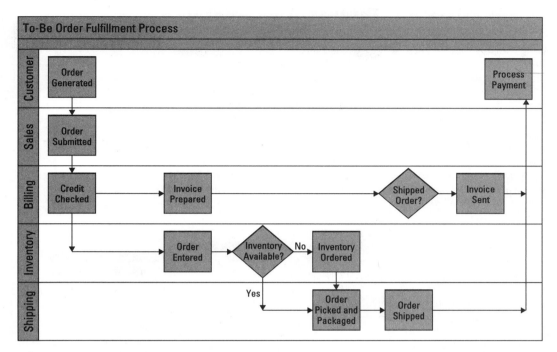

To-Be Order Fulfillment Process

Customer: Order Generated → Process Payment

Sales: Order Submitted

Billing: Credit Checked → Invoice Prepared → Shipped Order? → Invoice Sent

Inventory: Order Entered → Inventory Available? —No→ Inventory Ordered / Yes

Shipping: Order Picked and Packaged → Order Shipped

FIGURE B2.10

To-Be Process Model
for Order Entry

The consulting firm KPMG Peat Marwick uses process modeling as part of its business reengineering practice. Recently the firm helped a large financial services company slash costs and improve productivity in its Manufactured Housing Finance Division. Turnaround time for loan approval was reduced by half, using 40 percent fewer staff members.

Modeling helped the team analyze the complex aspects of the project. "In parts of the loan origination process, a lot of things happen in a short period of time," according to team leader Bob Karrick of KPMG. "During data capture, information is pulled from a number of different sources, and the person doing the risk assessment has to make judgment calls at different points throughout the process. There is often a need to stop, raise questions, make follow-up calls, and so on and then continue with the process modeling effort. Modeling allows us to do a thorough analysis that takes into account all these decision points and variables."[2]

SELECTING A PROCESS TO REENGINEER

An organization can reengineer its cross-departmental business processes or an individual department's business processes according to its needs. When selecting a business process to reengineer, wise organizations will focus on those core processes that are critical to their performance, rather than marginal processes that have little impact. Reengineering practitioners can use several criteria to determine the importance of the process:

- Is the process broken?
- Is it feasible that reengineering of this process will succeed?
- Does it have a high impact on the agency's strategic direction?
- Does it significantly impact customer satisfaction?
- Is it antiquated?
- Does it fall far below best-in-class?
- Is it crucial for productivity improvement?
- Will savings from automation be clearly visible?
- Is the return on investment from implementation high and preferably immediate?

Business Process Management (BPM)

A key advantage of technology is its ability to improve business processes. Working faster and smarter has become a necessity for companies. Initial emphasis was given to areas such as production, accounting, procurement, and logistics. The next big areas to discover technology's value in business process were sales and marketing automation, customer relationship management, and supplier relationship management. Some of these processes involve several departments of the company and some are the result of real-time interaction of the company with its suppliers, customers, and other business partners. The latest area to discover the power of technology in automating and reengineering business process is business process management. ***Business process management (BPM)*** integrates all of an organization's business process to make individual processes more efficient. BPM can be used to solve a single glitch or to create one unifying system to consolidate a myriad of processes.

Many organizations are unhappy with their current mix of software applications and dealing with business processes that are subject to constant change. These organizations are turning to BPM systems that can flexibly automate their processes and glue their enterprise applications together. Figure B2.11 displays the key reasons organizations are embracing BPM technologies.

BPM technologies effectively track and orchestrate the business process. BPM can automate tasks involving information from multiple systems, with rules to define the sequence in which the tasks are performed as well as responsibilities, conditions, and other aspects of the process (see Figure B2.12 for BPM benefits). BPM not only allows a business process to be executed more efficiently, but it also provides the tools to measure performance and identify opportunities for improvement—as well as to easily make changes in processes to act upon those opportunities such as:

- Bringing processes, people, and information together.
- Identifying the business processes is relatively easy. Breaking down the barriers between business areas and finding owners for the processes are difficult.
- Managing business processes within the enterprise and outside the enterprise with suppliers, business partners, and customers.
- Looking at automation horizontally instead of vertically.

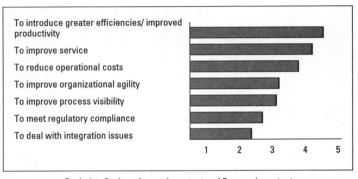

Scale 1 to 5 where 1 = not important and 5 = very important

FIGURE B2.11

Key Reasons for BPM

FIGURE B2.12

Benefits of BPM

IS BPM FOR BUSINESS OR IT?

A good BPM solution requires two great parts to work together as one. Since BPM solutions cross application and system boundaries, they often need to be sanctioned and implemented by the IT organization, while at the same time BPM products are business tools that business managers need to own. Therefore, confusion often arises in companies as to whether business or IT managers should be responsible for driving the selection of a new BPM solution.

The key requirement for BPM's success in an organization is the understanding that it is a collaboration of business and IT, and thus both parties need to be involved in evaluating, selecting, and implementing a BPM solution. IT managers need to understand the business drivers behind the processes, and business managers need to understand the

BPM Benefits
■ Update processes in real time
■ Reduce overhead expenses
■ Automate key decisions
■ Reduce process maintenance cost
■ Reduce operating cost
■ Improve productivity
■ Improve process cycle time
■ Improve forecasting
■ Improve customer service

impact the BPM solution may have on the infrastructure. Generally, companies that have successfully deployed BPM solutions are those whose business and IT groups have worked together as a cohesive team.

All companies can benefit from a better understanding of their key business processes, analyzing them for areas of improvement and implementing improvements. BPM applications have been successfully developed to improve complex business issues of some medium- to large-sized companies. Like many large-scale implementation projects, BPM solutions are most successful in companies with a good understanding of their technology landscape and management willing to approach business in a new way. BPM solutions are truly driven by the business process and the company's owners.

Effective BPM solutions allow business owners to manage many aspects of the technology through business rules they develop and maintain. Companies that cannot support or manage cultural and organizational changes may lack positive BPM results.

BPM TOOLS

Business process management tools are used to create an application that is helpful in designing business process models and also helpful in simulating, optimizing, monitoring, and maintaining various processes that occur within an organization. Many tasks are involved in achieving a goal, and these tasks are done either manually or with the help of software systems. For example, if an organization needs to buy a software application that costs $6 million, then a request has to be approved by several authorities and managers. The request approval may be done manually. However, when a person applies for a loan of $300,000, several internal and external business processes are triggered to find out details about that person before approving the loan. For these activities, BPM tool creates an application that coordinates the manual and automated tasks. Figure B2.13 displays several popular BPM tools.

Tool Name	Company Name
BPM Suite	Ultimus
Process Suite	Staffware
Business Manager	Savvion
Pega Rules Process Commander	PegaSystem
E Work Vision	MetaStorm
Team Works	Lombardi Software
Intalio	Intalio
Bizflow	Handysoft
FugeoBPM	Fugeo
Business Process Manager	Filenet

FIGURE B2.13

Popular BPM Tools

BPM RISKS AND REWARDS

If an organization is considering BPM, it must be aware of the risks involved in implementing these systems. One factor that commonly derails a BPM project has nothing to do with technology and everything to do with people. BPM projects involve cultural and organizational changes that companies must make to support the new management approach required for success. Where 10 area leaders once controlled 10 pieces of an end-to-end process, there is now a new group involved in implementing a BPM solution across all these areas. Suddenly the span of control is consolidated and all are accountable to the whole process, not just one piece of the puzzle.

The added benefit of BPM is not only a technology solution, but also a business solution. BPM is a new business architecture and approach to managing the process and enabling proactive, continuous improvement. The new organizational structure and roles created to support BPM help maximize the continuous benefits to ensure success.

An IT director from a large financial services company gave this feedback when asked about his experience in using a BPM solution to improve the company's

Critical Success Factors for BPM Projects
1. Understand reengineering.
■ Understand business process fundamentals.
■ Know what reengineering is.
■ Differentiate and integrate process improvement approaches.
2. Build a business and political case.
■ Have necessary and sufficient business (mission delivery) reasons for reengineering.
■ Have the organizational commitment and capacity to initiate and sustain reengineering.
■ Secure and sustain political support for reengineering projects.
3. Adopt a process management approach.
■ Understand the organizational mandate and set mission-strategic directions and goals cascading to process-specific goals and decision making across and down the organization.
■ Define, model, and prioritize business processes important for mission performance.
■ Practice hands-on senior management ownership of process improvement through personal involvement, responsibility, and decision making.
■ Adjust organizational structure to better support process management initiatives.
■ Create an assessment program to evaluate process management.
4. Measure and track performance continuously.
■ Create organizational understanding of the value of measurement and how it will be used.
■ Tie performance management to customer and stakeholder current and future expectations.
5. Practice change management and provide central support.
■ Develop human resource management strategies to support reengineering.
■ Build information resources management strategies and a technology framework to support process change.
■ Create a central support group to assist and integrate reengineering efforts and other improvement efforts across the organization.
■ Create an overarching and project-specific internal and external communication and education program.
6. Manage reengineering projects for results.
■ Have a clear criterion to select what should be reengineered.
■ Place the project at the right level with a defined reengineering team purpose and goals.
■ Use a well-trained, diversified, expert team to ensure optimum project performance.
■ Follow a structured, disciplined approach for reengineering.

application help desk process. "Before BPM, the company's application help desk was a manual process, filled with inefficiencies, human error, and no personal accountability. In addition, the old process provided no visibility into the process. There was absolutely no way to track requests, since it was all manual. Business user satisfaction with the process was extremely low. A BPM solution provided a way for the company to automate, execute, manage, and monitor the process in real time. The biggest technical challenge in implementation was ensuring that the user group was self-sufficient. While the company recognized that the IT organization is needed, it wanted to be able to maintain and implement any necessary process changes with little reliance on IT. It views process management as empowering the business users to maintain, control, and monitor the process. BPM goes a long way to enable this process."[3]

CRITICAL SUCCESS FACTORS

In a publication for the National Academy of Public Administration, Dr. Sharon L. Caudle identified six critical success factors that ensure government BPM initiatives achieve the desired results (see Figure B2.14).

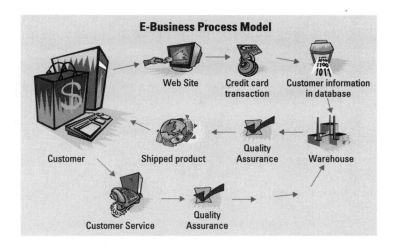

Business Process Modeling Examples

A picture is worth a thousand words. Just ask Wayne Kendrick, a system analyst for Mobil Oil Corporation in Dallas, Texas. Kendrick, whose work involves planning and designing complex processes, was scheduled to make a presentation to familiarize top management with a number of projects his group was working on. "I was given 10 minutes for my presentation, and I had 20 to 30 pages of detailed documentation to present. Obviously, I could not get through it all in the time allocated." Kendrick turned to business process models to help communicate his projects. "I think people can relate to pictures better than words," Kendrick said. He applied his thinking to his presentation by using Microsoft's Visio to create business process models and graphs to represent the original 30 pages of text. "It was an effective way to get people interested in my projects and to quickly see the importance of each project," he stated. The process models worked and Kendrick received immediate approval to proceed with all of his projects. Figures B2.15 through B2.21 offer examples of business process models.[4]

FIGURE B2.16

Online Banking Business
Process Model

Online Banking Business Process

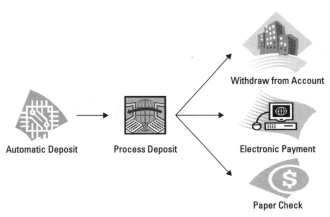

Order Business Process
Call Center
Customer
Warehouse Server
Online Order
FEDERAL EXPRESS
Item Shipped
Inventory Check
Item in stock
Yes
No
Item Packed
Process Payment
Customer Notified of Backorder

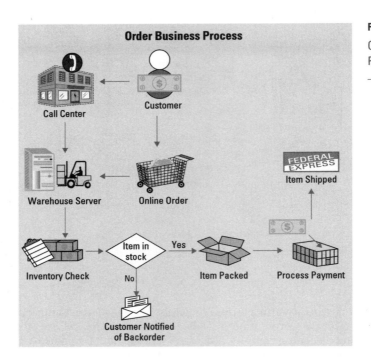

FIGURE B2.17

Customer Order Business Process Model

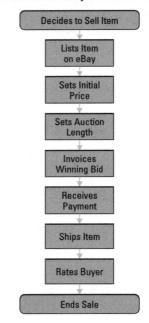

Purchase an Item on eBay Business Process
Decides to Purchase Item
Reviews Auction Listing
Places Bid
Wins Bid
Receives Invoice
Pays Invoice
Receives Item
Rates Seller
Ends Sale

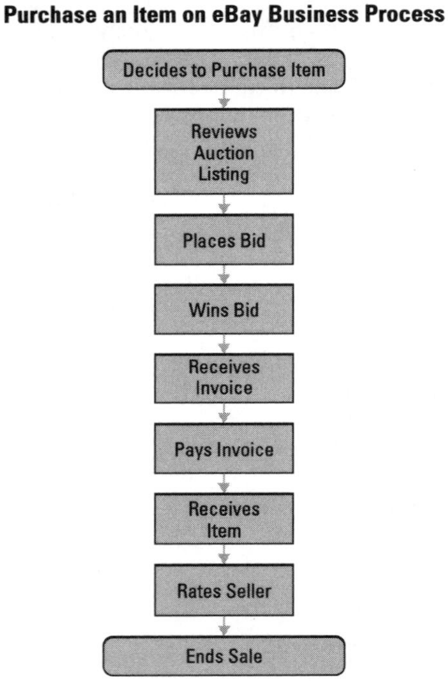

FIGURE B2.18

eBay Buyer Business Process Model

Sell an Item on eBay Business Process
Decides to Sell Item
Lists Item on eBay
Sets Initial Price
Sets Auction Length
Invoices Winning Bid
Receives Payment
Ships Item
Rates Buyer
Ends Sale

FIGURE B2.19

eBay Seller Business Process Model

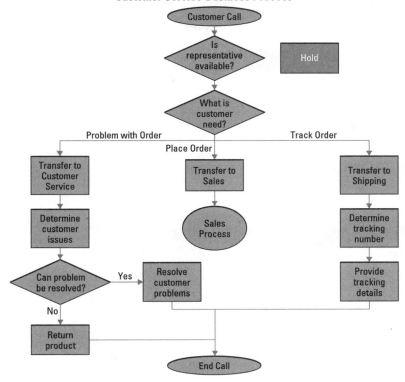

Customer Service Business Process

Process Improvement Model

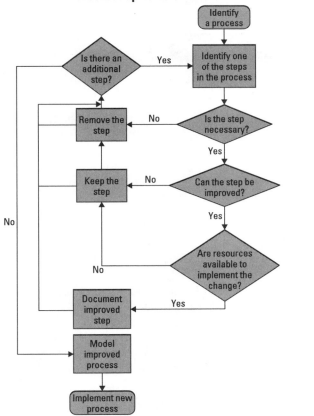

Investment in continuous process improvement, business process reengineering, or business process management is the same as any other technology-related investment. Planning the project properly, setting clear goals, educating those people who have to change their mind-set once the system is implemented, and retaining strong management support will help with a successful implementation generating a solid return on investment.

Organizations must go beyond the basics when implementing business process improvement and realize that it is not a one-time project. Management and improvement of end-to-end business processes is difficult and requires more than a simple, one-time effort. Continuously monitoring and improving core business processes will guarantee performance improvements across an organization.

★ KEY TERMS

As-Is process model, 264
Business facing process, 259
Business process, 259
Business process management (BPM), 267
Business process management tool, 268

Business process model, 263
Business process modeling (or mapping), 263
Business process reengineering (BPR), 263

Continuous process improvement model, 262
Customer facing process, 259
To-Be process model, 264

★ CLOSING CASE ONE

Streamlining Processes at Adidas

The Adidas name resonates with athletes and retail consumers worldwide. Registered as a company in 1949, the company differentiated itself during the 1960s by supporting all athletes who were committed to raising performance levels, including athletes in what some considered fringe sports such as high jumping. During a banner year in 1996, the "three stripes company" equipped 6,000 Olympic athletes from 33 countries. Those athletes won 220 medals, including 70 gold, and helped increase immediate apparel sales by 50 percent.

In 1997, Adidas acquired the Salomon Group, which included the Salomon, Taylor Made, and Bonfire brands. Today, Adidas-Salomon strives to be the global leader in the sporting goods industry with a wide range of products that promote a passion for competition and a sports-oriented lifestyle. Its strategy is simple: continuously strengthen its brands and products to improve its competitive position and financial performance.

Adidas-Salomon competes in an environment as relentless as that of the Olympics. Staying in the forefront requires the support of world-class technology. Over the past 15 years, Adidas-Salomon transformed itself from a manufacturing organization to a global sports brand manager with 14,000 employees located around the world. Previously, Adidas-Salomon operated in a decentralized manner, and each operating unit chose software that suited its geography and internal preferences. The company believed that implementing and creating common processes, especially in its sales organization, would help it establish global direction. With common processes, the company could streamline and automate its business operations—improving flexibility, scalability, and visibility across the extended enterprise. Overall, system integration would translate into faster time to market, higher revenue, and lower costs.

Adidas-Salomon reviewed its IT systems and associated information. One finding was that the company needed to develop a better solution for business process integration and establish an easy way to automate new applications throughout the enterprise. Such an infrastructure required Adidas-Salomon to impose a common business process platform that would allow the company's operating units to remain flexible in meeting their own particular needs and goals.

Adidas-Salomon identified several major business requirements for the project. First, it wanted to automate business events and reduce the manual effort required to exchange data between internal and external parties. Second, Adidas-Salomon needed to develop a cost-effective solution that would be simple to use, maintain, and update in the future. Last, the company wanted to enable real-time data exchange among the key Adidas-Salomon business processes.

"We considered many metrics, and it was clear that TIBCO Software had the breadth and depth of product offering backed by a strong reputation," said Garry Semetka, head of development and integration services in global application development at Adidas-Salomon. With its desired infrastructure in place, Adidas-Salomon standardized on TIBCO products and moved toward real-time business process management of its internal supply chain. The company now publishes and makes the most of events when they occur on key systems, giving the most current, valuable information to business processes and decision makers.[5]

Questions

1. Describe business processes and their importance for Adidas-Salomon.
2. Identify a few examples of customer facing processes and business facing processes at Adidas-Salomon.
3. How could Adidas-Salomon use continuous process improvement and business process reengineering to remain competitive?
4. How can a business process management tool help Adidas-Salomon remain at the top of its game?

 CLOSING CASE TWO

3Com Optimizes Product Promotion Processes

Product promotions, such as rebates or subsidized promotional items, can serve as excellent marketing and sales tools to drive increased revenues by providing incentives for customers to purchase select items. However, when you are a leading global networking provider like 3Com that serves thousands of channel partners and customers, such promotions must be easily managed and executed.

To gain better control over the creation and execution of its product promotions, 3Com used Savvion's business process automation and management platform to build a Web-based system that streamlines the approval and management workflow of product promotions offered to distributors and resellers. "We needed to ensure that our product promotions were attractive to our channel partners while also being manageable in terms of execution," said Ari Bose, CIO at 3Com. "Using Savvion BusinessManager, we were able to quickly put a process in place that speeds approval and enhances awareness of product promotions to generate opportunities for increased revenue."

Promoting Effective Promotions

The Savvion BusinessManager-based promotions system provides significant time and cost savings by replacing former inefficient and uncontrollable e-mail processes. Instead of informally sending promotion ideas around for approval, employees now use the automated system as a centralized location to manage the workflow involved in proposing new promotions and ensuring all needed approvals are in place before promotion details are shared on the 3Com partner and reseller Web site.

The promotions system automatically routes proposed promotions to each department that is required to sign off on the promotion, including marketing, promotions communications, and claims administration. The streamlined system also immediately notifies all key parties once new promotions are approved, increasing visibility and revenue opportunities through improved communication with 3Com sales representatives, distributors, and resellers.

Adding Muscle to Management

An important feature of the new system is the automatic auditing of each step taken. The company can easily establish an audit trail, increasing accountability as approvals are given. The structured process also ensures that approved promotions are manageable from an administrative perspective.

In addition, the system tracks promotion fulfillment, enforcing associated terms and conditions such as purchasing limits or available supplies—tracking that was previously almost impossible to do, creating numerous management headaches. The promotions system is also integrated with another BusinessManager-developed process that generates special price quotes (SPQs) for 3Com channel partners, creating built-in checks and balances to prevent the approval of an SPQ while a promotion is being offered for the same product.

The system also provides extensive reporting capabilities that 3Com now uses to gain a better understanding of all offered promotions, authorizations, and potential financial impacts. These online reports replace manually created Excel spreadsheets, enabling departments to generate reports on the fly for enhanced strategic planning.

Bottom-Line Benefits

Greater visibility of product promotions is yielding significant opportunities for increased revenue at 3Com. Sales representatives are immediately notified when promotions are approved, improving internal communications and enabling representatives to share promotion details with resellers and distributors more quickly to foster increased sales. Other business benefits delivered by the automated promotions system include the following:

- Real-time monitoring features enable 3Com employees to check the status of a promotion's approval at any time.
- Greater efficiency in the approval cycle and streamlined communications increase employee productivity, providing significant time and cost savings.
- Claims processing is also more effective because of the structured approval process, delivering additional savings.
- Increased visibility enables 3Com to reduce reserve spending by having a clearer idea of channel response to each promotion.
- Order and efficiency come to previously chaotic manual processes.[6]

Questions

1. Describe business processes and their importance to 3Com's business model.
2. How can 3Com use continuous process improvement to become more efficient?
3. How can 3Com use business process reengineering to become more efficient?

4. Describe the importance of business process modeling (or mapping) and business process models for 3Com.

5. How did 3Com use business process management software to revamp its business?

★ MAKING BUSINESS DECISIONS

1. **Discovering Reengineering Opportunities**

In an effort to increase efficiency, your college has hired you to analyze its current business processes for registering for classes. Analyze the current business processes from paying tuition to registering for classes and determine which steps in the process are:

- Broken
- Redundant
- Antiquated

Be sure to define how you would reengineer the processes for efficiency.

2. **Modeling a Business Process**

Do you hate waiting in line at the grocery store? Do you find it frustrating when you go to the movie store and cannot find the movie you wanted to rent? Do you get annoyed when the pizza delivery person brings you the wrong order? This is your chance to reengineer the annoying process that drives you craze. Choose a problem you are currently experiencing and reengineer the process to make it more efficient. Be sure to provide an As-Is and To-Be process model.

3. **Revamping Business Processes**

The following is the sales order business process for MusicMan. Draw the As-Is process model based on the following narrative:

1. A customer submits an order for goods to MusicMan, a music retailer, through an on-line mechanism such as a browser-based order form. The customer supplies his or her name, the appropriate e-mail address, the state to which the order will be shipped, the desired items (IDs and names), and the requested quantities.

2. The order is received by a processing system, which reads the data and appends an ID number to the order.

3. The order is forwarded to a customer service representative, who checks the customer's credit information.

4. If the credit check fails, the customer service representative is assigned the task of notifying the customer to obtain correct credit information, and the process becomes manual from this point on.

5. If the credit check passes, the system checks a database for the current inventory of the ordered item, according to the item ID, and it compares the quantity of items available with the quantity requested.

6. If the amount of stock is not sufficient to accommodate the order, the order is placed on hold until new inventory arrives. When the system receives notice of new incoming inventory, it repeats step 5 until it can verify that the inventory is sufficient to process the order.

7. If the inventory is sufficient, the order is forwarded simultaneously to a shipping agent who arranges shipment and an accounting agent who instructs the system to generate an invoice for the order.

8. If the system encounters an error in processing the input necessary to calculate the total price for the invoice, including state sales tax, the accounting agent who initiated the billing process is notified and prompted to provide the correct information.

9. The system calculates the total price of the order.

10. The system confirms that the order has been shipped and notifies the customer via e-mail.

11. At any point in the transaction before shipping, the order can be canceled by notification from the customer.

4. Revamping Accounts

The accounting department at your company deals with the processing of critical documents. These documents must arrive at their intended destination in a secure and efficient manner. Such documents include invoices, purchase orders, statements, purchase requisitions, financial statements, sales orders, and quotes.

The current processing of documents is done manually, which causes a negative ripple effect. Documents tend to be misplaced or delayed through the mailing process. Unsecured documents are vulnerable to people making changes or seeing confidential documents. In addition, the accounting department incurs costs such as preprinted forms, inefficient distribution, and storage. Explain BPM and how it can be used to revamp the accounting department.

B3

Hardware and Software

LEARNING OUTCOMES

1. Describe the six major categories of hardware and provide an example of each.
2. Identify the different computer categories and explain their potential business uses.
3. Explain the difference between primary and secondary storage.
4. List the common input, output, storage, and communication devices.
5. Describe the eight categories of computers by size.
6. Define the relationship between operating system software and utility software.

Introduction

Managers need to determine what types of hardware and software will satisfy their current and future business needs, the right time to buy the equipment, and how to protect their IT investments. This does not imply that managers need to be experts in all areas of technology; however, building a basic understanding of hardware and software can help them make the right IT investment choices.

Information technology (IT) is any computer-based tool that people use to work with information and support the information and information-processing needs of an organization. Information technology can be composed of the Internet, a personal computer, a cell phone that can access the Web, a personal digital assistant, or presentation software. All of these technologies help to perform specific information processing tasks. There are two basic categories of information technology: hardware and software. *Hardware* consists of the physical devices associated with a computer system. *Software* is the set of instructions that the hardware executes to carry out specific tasks. Software, such as Microsoft Excel, and various hardware devices, such as a keyboard and a monitor, interact to create a spreadsheet or a graph. This plug-in covers the basics of computer hardware and software including terminology, business uses, and common characteristics.

Hardware Basics

In many industries, exploiting computer hardware is key to gaining a competitive advantage. Frito-Lay gained a competitive advantage by using hand-held devices to

Six Hardware Components	
Central processing unit (CPU)	The actual hardware that interprets and executes the program (software) instructions and coordinates how all the other hardware devices work together.
Primary storage	The computer's main memory, which consists of the random access memory (RAM), cache memory, and the read-only memory (ROM) that is directly accessible to the central processing unit (CPU).
Secondary storage	Equipment designed to store large volumes of data for long-term storage (e.g., diskette, hard drive, memory card, CD).
Input devices	Equipment used to capture information and commands (e.g., keyboard, scanner).
Output devices	Equipment used to see, hear, or otherwise accept the results of information processing requests (e.g., monitor, printer).
Communication devices	Equipment used to send information and receive it from one location to another (e.g., modem).

FIGURE B3.1

Hardware Components of a Computer System

track the strategic placement and sale of items in convenience stores. Sales representatives could track sale price, competitor information, the number of items sold, and item location in the store all from their hand-held device.[1]

A ***computer*** is an electronic device operating under the control of instructions stored in its own memory that can accept, manipulate, and store data. A computer system consists of six hardware components (see Figure B3.1). Figure B3.2 displays how these components work together to form a computer system.

CENTRAL PROCESSING UNIT

The dominant manufacturers of CPUs today include Intel (with its Celeron and Pentium lines for personal computers) and Advanced Micro Devices (AMD) (with its Athlon series). AMD was initially dismissed as a company that simply cloned current chips, producing processors that mimic the features and capabilities of those from industry leader Intel. However, over the past few years, AMD has begun introducing innovative CPUs that are forcing Intel into the unfamiliar position of reacting to competition. AMD led the way in transforming the processor market by creating chips that handle 64-bits of data at a time, up

from 32-bits. It also broke new territory when it became the first provider of dual-core processors for the server market. Hector Ruiz, chairman and CEO of AMD, stated, "In our position there is only one thing we can do: Stay close to our customers and end users, understand what they need and want, and then simply out-innovate the competition. Innovation is at the center of our ability to succeed. We cannot win by just copying the competition."[2]

The ***central processing unit (CPU)*** (or ***microprocessor***) is the actual hardware that interprets and executes the program (software) instructions and coordinates how all the other hardware devices work together. The CPU is built on a small flake of silicon and can contain the equivalent of several million transistors. CPUs are unquestionably one of the 20th century's greatest technological advances.

A CPU contains two primary parts: control unit and arithmetic/logic unit. The ***control unit*** interprets software instructions and literally tells the other hardware

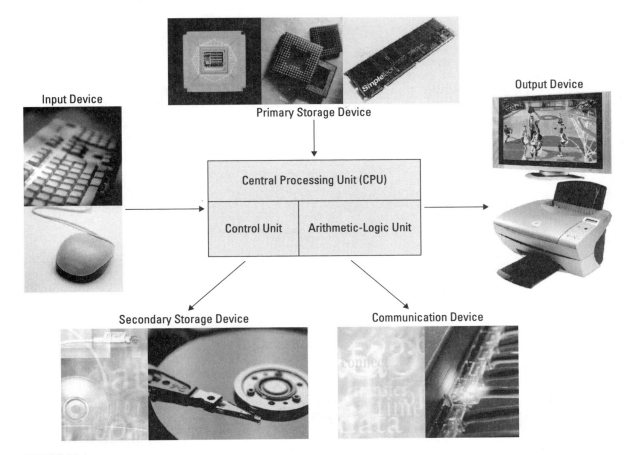

FIGURE B3.2

How the Hardware
Components Work
Together

devices what to do, based on the software instructions. The ***arithmetic-logic unit (ALU)*** performs all arithmetic operations (for example, addition and subtraction) and all logic operations (such as sorting and comparing numbers). The control unit and ALU perform different functions. The control unit obtains instructions from the software. It then interprets the instructions, decides which tasks other devices perform, and finally tells each device to perform the task. The ALU responds to the control unit and does whatever it dictates, performing either arithmetic or logic operations.

The number of CPU cycles per second determines how fast a CPU carries out the software instructions; more cycles per second means faster processing, and faster CPUs cost more than their slower counterparts. CPU speed is usually quoted in megahertz and gigahertz. ***Megahertz (MHz)*** is the number of millions of CPU cycles per second. ***Gigahertz (GHz)*** is the number of billions of CPU cycles per second. Figure B3.3 displays the factors that determine CPU speed.

Advances in CPU Design

Chip makers are pressing more functionality into CPU technology. Most CPUs are ***complex instruction set computer (CISC) chips,*** which is a type of CPU that can recognize as many as 100 or more instructions, enough to carry out most computations directly. ***Reduced instruction set computer (RISC) chips*** limit the number of instructions the CPU can execute to increase processing speed. The idea of RISC is to reduce the instruction set to the bare minimum, emphasizing the instructions used most of the time and optimizing them for the fastest possible execution. A RISC processor runs faster than a CISC processor.

CPU Speed Factors
Clock speed—the speed of the internal clock of a CPU that sets the pace at which operations proceed within the computer's internal processing circuitry. Clock speed is measured in megahertz (MHz) and gigahertz (GHz). Faster clock speeds bring noticeable gains in microprocessor-intensive tasks, such as recalculating a spreadsheet.
Word length—number of bits (0s and 1s) that can be processed by the CPU at any one time. Computers work in terms of bits and bytes using electrical pulses that have two states: on and off. A *binary digit (bit)* is the smallest unit of information that a computer can process. A bit can be either a 1 (on) or a 0 (off). A group of eight bits represents one natural language character and is called a *byte*.
Bus width—the size of the internal electrical pathway along which signals are sent from one part of the computer to another. A wider bus can move more data, hence faster processing.
Chip line width—the distance between transistors on a chip. The shorter the chip line width the faster the chip since more transistors can be placed on a chip and the data and instructions travel short distances during processing.

In the next few years, better performance, systems management capabilities, virtualization, security, and features to help track computer assets will be built directly into the CPU (see Figure B3.4). *Virtualization* is a protected memory space created by the CPU allowing the computer to create virtual machines. Each virtual machine can run its own programs isolated from other machines.

PRIMARY STORAGE

Primary storage is the computer's main memory, which consists of the random access memory (RAM), cache memory, and the read-only memory (ROM) that is directly accessible to the CPU.

Random Access Memory

Random access memory (RAM) is the computer's primary working memory, in which program instructions and data are stored so that they can be accessed directly by the CPU via the processor's high-speed external data bus.

RAM is often called read/write memory. In RAM, the CPU can write and read data. Most programs set aside a portion of RAM as a temporary workspace for data so that one can modify (rewrite) as needed until the data is ready for printing or storage on secondary storage media, such as a hard drive or memory key. RAM does not retain its contents when the power to the computer is switched off, hence individuals should save their work frequently. When the computer is

Chip Advancements
AMD: Security, virtualization, and advanced power-management technology.
IBM: Cryptography for additional security and floating point capability for faster graphics processing.
Intel: Cryptography for additional security, hardware-assisted virtualization, and Active Management Technology for asset tracking, patching, and software updates.
Sun Microsystems: Cryptography for additional security, increased speed for data transmission and receipt, and the ability to run 32 computations simultaneously.

turned off, everything in RAM is wiped clean. ***Volatility*** refers to RAM's complete loss of stored information if power is interrupted. RAM is volatile and its contents are lost when the computer's electric supply fails.

Cache Memory

Cache memory is a small unit of ultra-fast memory that is used to store recently accessed or frequently accessed data so that the CPU does not have to retrieve this data from slower memory circuits such as RAM. Cache memory that is built directly into the CPU's circuits is called primary cache. Cache memory contained on an external circuit is called secondary cache.

Read Only Memory (ROM)

Read-only memory (ROM) is the portion of a computer's primary storage that does not lose its contents when one switches off the power. ROM contains essential system programs that neither the user nor the computer can erase. Since the computer's internal memory is blank during start-up, the computer cannot perform any functions unless given start-up instructions. These instructions are stored in ROM.

Flash memory is a special type of rewriteable read-only memory (ROM) that is compact and portable. ***Memory cards*** contain high-capacity storage that holds data such as captured images, music, or text files. Memory cards are removable; when one is full the user can insert an additional card. Subsequently, the data can be downloaded from the card to a computer. The card can then be erased and used again. Memory cards are typically used in digital devices such as cameras, cellular phones, and personal digital assistants (PDA). ***Memory sticks*** provide nonvolatile memory for a range of portable devices including computers, digital cameras, MP3 players, and PDAs.

SECONDARY STORAGE

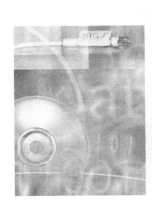

Storage is a hot area in the business arena as organizations struggle to make sense of exploding volumes of data. Storage sales grew more than 16 percent to nearly $8 billion in 2004, according to IDC market research. ***Secondary storage*** consists of equipment designed to store large volumes of data for long-term storage. Secondary storage devices are nonvolatile and do not lose their contents

when the computer is turned off. Some storage devices, such as a hard disk, offer easy update capabilities and a large storage capacity. Others, such as CD-ROMs, offer limited update capabilities but possess large storage capacities.

Storage capacity is expressed in bytes, with megabytes being the most common. A ***megabyte (MB* or *M* or *Meg)*** is roughly 1 million bytes. Therefore, a computer with 256 MB of RAM translates into the RAM being able to hold roughly 256 million characters of data and software instructions. A ***gigabyte (GB)*** is roughly 1 billion bytes. A ***terabyte (TB)*** is roughly 1 trillion bytes (refer to Figure B3.5).

Most standard desktops have a hard drive with storage capacity in excess of 80 GB. Hard drives for large organizational computer systems can hold in excess of 100 TB of information. For example, a typical double-spaced page of pure text is roughly 2,000 characters. Therefore, a 40 GB (40 gigabyte or 40 billion characters) hard drive can hold approximately 20 million pages of text.

Common storage devices include:

- Magnetic medium
- Optical medium

Term	Size
Kilobyte (KB)	1,024 Bytes
Megabyte (MB)	1,024 KB 1,048,576 Bytes
Gigabyte (GB)	1,24 MB (10^9 bytes)
Terabyte (TB)	1,024 GB (10^{12} bytes) 1 TB = Printing of 1 TB would require 50,000 trees to be made into paper and printed
Petabyte (PB)	1,024 TB (10^{15} bytes) 200 PB = All production of digital magnetic tape in 1995
Exabyte (EB)	1,024 PB (10^{18} bytes) 2 EB = total volume of information generated worldwide annually 5 EB = all words ever spoken by human beings

Magnetic Medium

Magnetic medium is a secondary storage medium that uses magnetic techniques to store and retrieve data on disks or tapes coated with magnetically sensitive materials. Like iron filings on a sheet of waxed paper, these materials are reoriented when a magnetic field passes over them. During write operations, the read/write heads emit a magnetic field that orients the magnetic materials on the disk or tape to represent encoded data. During read operations, the read/write heads sense the encoded data on the medium.

One of the first forms of magnetic medium developed was magnetic tape. ***Magnetic tape*** is an older secondary storage medium that uses a strip of thin plastic coated with a magnetically sensitive recording medium. The most popular type of magnetic medium is a hard drive. A ***hard drive*** is a secondary storage medium that uses several rigid disks coated with a magnetically sensitive material and housed together with the recording heads in a hermetically sealed mechanism. Hard drive performance is measured in terms of access time, seek time, rotational speed, and data transfer rate.

Optical Medium

Optical medium is a secondary storage medium for computers on which information is stored at extremely high density in the form of tiny pits. The presence or absence of pits is read by a tightly focused laser beam. Optical medium types include:

- **Compact disk-read-only memory (CD-ROM) drive**—an optical drive designed to read the data encoded on CD-ROMs and to transfer this data to a computer.
- **Compact disk-read-write (CD-RW) drive**—an optical drive that enables users to erase existing data and to write new data repeatedly to a CD-RW.
- **Digital video disk (DVD)**—a CD-ROM format capable of storing up to a maximum of 17 GB of data; enough for a full-length feature movie.
- **DVD-ROM drive**—a read-only drive designed to read the data encoded on a DVD and transfer the data to a computer.
- **Digital video disk-read/write (DVD-RW)**—a standard for DVD discs and player/recorder mechanisms that enables users to record in the DVD format.

CD-ROMs and DVDs offer an increasingly economical medium for storing data and programs. The overall trend in secondary storage is toward more direct-access methods, higher capacity with lower costs, and increased portability.

INPUT DEVICES

An ***input device*** is equipment used to capture information and commands. A keyboard is used to type in information, and a mouse is used to point and click on buttons and icons. Numerous input devices are available in many different environments, some of which have applications that are more suitable in a personal setting than a business setting. A keyboard, mouse, and scanner are the most common forms of input devices (see Figures B3.6 and B3.7).

New forms of input devices allow people to exercise and play video games at the same time. The Kilowatt Sport from Powergrid Fitness lets people combine strength training with their favorite video games. Players can choose any PlayStation or Xbox game that uses a joystick to run the elliptical trainer. After loading the game, participants stand on a platform while pushing and pulling a resistance rod in all directions to control what happens in the game. The varied movement targets muscle groups on the chest, arms, shoulders, abdomen, and back. The machine's display shows information such as pounds lifted and current resistance level, and players can use one-touch adjustment to vary the degree of difficulty.[3]

Another new input device is a stationary bicycle. A computer design team of graduate and undergraduate students at MIT built the Cyclescore, an integrated video game and bicycle. The MIT students tested current games on the market but found users would stop pedaling to concentrate on the game. To engage users, the team is designing games that interact with the experience of exercise itself, for example, monitoring heart rate and adjusting the difficulty of the game according to the user's bicycling capabilities. In one game, the player must pedal to make a hot-air balloon float over mountains, while collecting coins and shooting at random targets.[4]

OUTPUT DEVICES

An ***output device*** is equipment used to see, hear, or otherwise accept the results of information processing requests. Among output devices, printers and monitors are the most common; however, speakers and plotters (special printers that draw output on a page) are widely used (see Figure B3.8). In addition, output devices are responsible for converting computer-stored information into a form that can be understood.

Manual Input Devices
Joystick—widely used as an alternative to the keyboard for computer games and some professional applications, such as computer-aided design
Keyboard—provides a set of alphabetic, numeric, punctuation, symbol, and control keys
Microphone—captures sounds such as a voice for voice recognition software
Mouse—one or more control buttons housed in a palm-sized case and designed so that one can move it about on the table next to the keyboard
Pointing stick—causes the pointer to move on the screen by applying directional pressure (popular on notebooks and PDAs)
Touch screen—allows the use of a finger to point at and touch a particular function to perform
Touchpad—a form of a stationary mouse on which the movement of a finger causes the pointer on the screen to move

FIGURE B3.6

Manual Input Devices

Automated Input Devices
Bar code scanner—captures information that exists in the form of vertical bars whose width and distance apart determine a number
Digital camera—captures still images or video as a series of 1s and 0s
Magnetic ink character reader—reads magnetic ink numbers printed on checks that identify the bank, checking account, and check number
Optical-character recognition—converts text into digital format for computer input
Optical-mark recognition (OMR)—detects the presence or absence of a mark in a predetermined place (popular for multiple-choice exams).
Point-of-sale (POS)—captures information at the point of a transaction, typically in a retail environment
Radio frequency identification (RFID)—uses active or passive tags in the form of chips or smart labels that can store unique identifiers and relay this information to electronic readers

FIGURE B3.7

Automated Input Devices

Output Devices
Cathode-ray tube (CRT)—a vacuum tube that uses an electron gun (cathode) to emit a beam of electrons that illuminates phosphors on a screen as the beam sweeps across the screen repeatedly. A monitor is often called a CRT.
Liquid crystal display (LCDs)—a low-powered display technology used in laptop computers where rod-shaped crystal molecules change their orientation when an electrical current flows through them.
Laser printer—a printer that forms images using an electrostatic process, the same way a photocopier works.
Ink-jet printer—a printer that makes images by forcing ink droplets through nozzles.
Plotter—a printer that uses computer-directed pens for creating high-quality images, blueprints, schematics, etc.

FIGURE B3.8

Output Devices

A new output device based on sensor technology aims to translate American Sign Language (ASL) into speech, enabling the millions of people who use ASL to better communicate with those who do not know the rapid gesturing system. The AcceleGlove is a glove lined on the inside with sensors embedded in rings. The sensors, called accelerometers, measure acceleration and can categorize and translate finger and hand movements. Additional, interconnected attachments for the elbow and shoulder capture ASL signs that are made with full arm motion. When users wear the glove while signing ASL, algorithms in the glove's software translate the hand gestures into words. The translations can be relayed through speech synthesizers or read on a PDA-size computer screen. Inventor Jose L. Hernandez-Rebollar started with a single glove that could translate only the ASL alphabet. Now, the device employs two gloves that contain a 1,000-word vocabulary.[5]

Other new output devices are being developed every day. Needapresent.com, a British company, has developed a vibrating USB massage ball, which plugs into a computer's USB port to generate a warm massage for sore body parts during those long evenings spent coding software or writing papers. Needsapresent.com also makes a coffee cup warmer that plugs into the USB port.[6]

COMMUNICATION DEVICES

A *communication device* is equipment used to send information and receive it from one location to another. A telephone modem connects a computer to a phone line in order to access another computer. The computer works in terms of digital signals, while a standard telephone line works with analog signals. Each digital signal represents a bit (either 0 or 1). The modem must convert the digital signals of a computer into analog signals so they can be sent across the telephone line. At the other end, another modem translates the analog signals into digital signals, which can then be used by the other computer. Figure B3.9 displays the different types of modems.

Computer Categories

Supercomputers today can hit processing capabilities of well over 200 teraflops—the equivalent of everyone on earth performing 35,000 calculations per second (see Figure B3.10). For the past 20 years, federally funded supercomputing research has given birth to some of the computer industry's most significant technology breakthroughs including:

- Clustering, which allows companies to chain together thousands of PCs to build mass-market systems.
- Parallel processing, which provides the ability to run two or more tasks simultaneously and is viewed as the chip industry's future.
- Mosaic browser, which morphed into Netscape and made the Web a household name.

Federally funded supercomputers have also advanced some of the country's most dynamic industries, including advanced manufacturing, gene research in the life sciences, and real-time financial-market modeling.[7]

Carrier Technology	Description	Speed	Comments
Dial-up Access	On demand access using a modem and regular telephone line (POT).	2400 bps to 56 Kbps	■ Cheap but slow.
Cable	Special cable modem and cable line required.	512 Kbps to 20 Mbps	■ Must have existing cable access in area. ■ Bandwidth is shared.
DSL Digital Subscriber Line	This technology uses the unused digital portion of a regular copper telephone line to transmit and receive information. A special modem and adapter card are required.	128 Kbps to 8 Mbps	■ Doesn't interfere with normal telephone use. ■ Bandwidth is dedicated. ■ Must be within 5 km (3.1 miles) of telephone company switch.
Wireless (LMCS)	Access is gained by connection to a high-speed cellular like local multipoint communications system (LMCS) network via wireless transmitter/receiver.	30 Mbps or more	■ Can be used for high-speed data, broadcast TV, and wireless telephone service.
Satellite	Newer versions have two-way satellite access, removing need for phone line.	6 Mbps or more	■ Bandwidth is not shared. ■ Some connections require an existing Internet service account. ■ Setup fees can range from $500–$1000.

FIGURE B3.9

Comparing Modems

Computers come in different shapes, sizes, and colors. Some are small enough to carry around, while others are the size of a telephone booth. Size does not always correlate to power, speed, and price (see Figure B3.11).

MIT's Media Lab is developing a laptop that it will sell for $100 each to government agencies around the world for distribution to millions of underprivileged schoolchildren. Using a simplified sales model and some reengineering of the device helped MIT reach the $100 price point. Almost half the price of a current laptop comprises marketing, sales, distribution, and profit. Of the remaining costs, the display panel and backlight account for roughly half while the rest covers the operating

FIGURE B3.10

Supercomputer

Computer Category	Description	Size
Personal digital assistant (PDA)	A small hand-held computer that performs simple tasks such as taking notes, scheduling appointments, and maintaining an address book and a calendar. The PDA screen is touch-sensitive, allowing a user to write directly on the screen, capturing what is written.	Fits in a person's hand
Laptop	A fully functional computer designed to be carried around and run on battery power. Laptops come equipped with all of the technology that a personal desktop computer has, yet weigh as little as two pounds.	Similar to a textbook
Tablet	A pen-based computer that provides the screen capabilities of a PDA with the functional capabilities of a laptop or desktop computer. Similar to PDAs, tablet PCs use a writing pen or stylus to write notes on the screen and touch the screen to perform functions such as clicking on a link while visiting a Web site.	Similar to a textbook
Desktop	Available with a horizontal system box (the box is where the CPU, RAM, and storage devices are held) with a monitor on top, or a vertical system box (called a tower) usually placed on the floor within a work area.	Fits on a desk
Workstation	Similar to a desktop but has more powerful mathematical and graphics processing capabilities and can perform more complicated tasks in less time. Typically used for software development, Web development, engineering, and e-business tools.	Fits on a desk
Minicomputer (midrange computer)	Designed to meet the computing needs of several people simultaneously in a small to medium-size business environment. A common type of minicomputer is a server and is used for managing internal company networks and Web sites. Minicomputers are more powerful than desktop computers but also cost more, ranging in price from $5,000 to several hundred thousand dollars.	Ranges from fitting on a desk to the size of a filing cabinet
Mainframe computer	Designed to meet the computing needs of hundreds of people in a large business environment. Mainframe computers are a step up in size, power, capability, and cost from minicomputers. Mainframes can cost in excess of $1 million. With processing speeds greater than 1 trillion instructions per second (compared to a typical desktop that can process about 2.5 billion instructions per second), mainframes can easily handle the processing requests of hundreds of people simultaneously.	Similar to a refrigerator
Supercomputer	The fastest, most powerful, and most expensive type of computer. Organizations such as NASA that are heavily involved in research and number crunching employ supercomputers because of the speed with which they can process information. Other large, customer-oriented businesses such as General Motors and AT&T employ supercomputers just to handle customer information and transaction processing.	Similar to a car

FIGURE B3.11

Computer Categories

system. The low-cost laptop will use a display system that costs less than $25, a 500 MHz processor from AMD, a wireless LAN connection, 1 GB of storage, and the Linux operating system. The machine will automatically connect with others. China and Brazil have already ordered 3 million and 1 million laptops, respectively. MIT's goal is to produce around 150 million laptops per year.[8]

Software Basics

■ Hardware is only as good as the software that runs it. Over the years, the cost of hardware has decreased while the complexity and cost of software has increased. Some large software applications, such as customer relationship management systems, contain millions of lines of code, take years to develop, and cost millions of dollars. The two main types of software are system software and application software.

SYSTEM SOFTWARE

System software controls how the various technology tools work together along with the application software. System software includes both operating system software and utility software.

Operating System Software

Linus Torvalds, a shy Finnish programmer, may seem an unlikely choice to be one of the world's top managers. However, Linux, the software project he created while a university student, is now one of the most powerful influences on the computer world. Linux is an operating system built by volunteers and distributed for free and has become one of the primary competitors to Microsoft. Torvalds coordinates Linux development with a few dozen volunteer assistants and more than 1,000 programmers scattered around the globe. They contribute code for the kernel—or core piece—of Linux. He also sets the rules for dozens of technology companies that have lined up behind Linux, including IBM, Dell, Hewlett-Packard, and Intel.

While basic versions of Linux are available for free, Linux is having a considerable financial impact. According to market researcher IDC, the total market for Linux devices and software will increase from $11 billion in 2004 to $35.7 billion by 2008.[9]

Operating system software controls the application software and manages how the hardware devices work together. When using Excel to create and print a graph, the operating system software controls the process, ensures that a printer is attached and has paper, and sends the graph to the printer along with instructions on how to print it.

Operating system software also supports a variety of useful features, one of which is multitasking. *Multitasking* allows more than one piece of software to be used at a time. Multitasking is used when creating a graph in Excel and simultaneously printing a word processing document. With multitasking, both pieces of application software are operating at the same time. There are different types of operating system software for personal environments and for organizational environments (see Figure B3.12).

Utility Software

Utility software provides additional functionality to the operating system. Utility software includes antivirus software, screen savers, and anti-spam software. Figure B3.13 displays a few types of available utility software.

Operating System Software	
Linux	An open source operating system that provides a rich environment for high-end workstations and network servers. Open source refers to any program whose source code is made available for use or modification as users or other developers see fit.
Mac OS X	The operating system of Macintosh computers.
Microsoft Windows	Generic name for the various operating systems in the Microsoft Windows family, including Microsoft Windows CE, Microsoft Windows 98, Microsoft Windows ME, Microsoft Windows 2000, Microsoft Windows XP, Microsoft Windows NT, and Microsoft Windows Server 2003.
MS-DOS	The standard, single-user operating system of IBM and IBM-compatible computers, introduced in 1981. MS-DOS is a command-line operating system that requires the user to enter commands, arguments, and syntax.
UNIX	A 32-bit multitasking and multiuser operating system that originated at AT&T's Bell Laboratories and is now used on a wide variety of computers, from mainframes to PDAs.

APPLICATION SOFTWARE

Application software is used for specific information processing needs, including payroll, customer relationship management, project management, training, and many others. Application software is used to solve specific problems or perform specific tasks. From an organizational perspective, payroll software, collaborative software such as videoconferencing (within groupware), and inventory management software are all examples of application software (see Figure B3.14).

Types of Utility Software	
Crash-proof	Helps save information if a computer crashes.
Disk image for data recovery	Relieves the burden of reinstalling and tweaking scores of applications if a hard drive crashes or becomes irretrievably corrupted.
Disk optimization	Organizes information on a hard disk in the most efficient way.
Encrypt data	Protects confidential information from unauthorized eyes. Programs such as BestCrypt simply and effectively apply one of several powerful encryption schemes to hard drive information. Users unlock the information by entering a password in the BestCrypt control panel. The program can also secure information on rewritable optical disks or any other storage media that is assigned a drive letter.
File and data recovery	Retrieves accidental deletion of photos or documents in Windows XP by utilities such as Free Undelete, which searches designated hard drive deletion areas for recognizable data.
Text protect	In Microsoft Word, prevents users from typing over existing text after accidentally hitting the Insert key. Launch the Insert Toggle Key program, and the PC will beep whenever a user presses the Insert key.
Preventative security	Through programs such as Window Washer, erases file histories, browser cookies, cache contents, and other crumbs that applications and Windows leave on a hard drive.
Spyware	Removes any software that employs a user's Internet connection in the background without the user's knowledge or explicit permission.
Uninstaller	Can remove software that is no longer needed.

Types of Application Software	
Browser	Enables the user to navigate the World Wide Web. The two leading browsers are Netscape Navigator and Microsoft Internet Explorer.
Communication	Turns a computer into a terminal for transmitting data to and receiving data from distant computers through the telephone system.
Data management	Provides the tools for data retrieval, modification, deletion, and insertion; for example, Access, MySQL, and Oracle.
Desktop publishing	Transforms a computer into a desktop publishing workstation. Leading packages include Adobe FrameMaker, Adobe PageMaker, and QuarkXpress.
E-mail	Provides e-mail services for computer users, including receiving mail, sending mail, and storing messages. Leading e-mail software includes Microsoft Outlook, Microsoft Outlook Express, and Eudora.
Groupware	Increases the cooperation and joint productivity of small groups of co-workers.
Presentation graphics	Creates and enhances charts and graphs so that they are visually appealing and easily understood by an audience. A full-features presentation graphics package such as Lotus Freelance Graphics or Microsoft PowerPoint includes facilities for making a wide variety of charts and graphs and for adding titles, legends, and explanatory text anywhere in the chart of graph.
Programming	Possesses an artificial language consisting of a fixed vocabulary and a set of rules (called syntax) that programmers use to write computer programs. Leading programming languages include Java, C++, C#, and .NET.
Spreadsheet	Simulates an accountant's worksheet onscreen and lets users embed hidden formulas that perform calculations on the visible data. Many spreadsheet programs also include powerful graphics and presentation capabilities to create attractive products. The leading spreadsheet application is Microsoft Excel.
Word processing	Transforms a computer into a tool for creating, editing, proofreading, formatting, and printing documents. Leading word processing applications include Microsoft Word and WordPerfect.

FIGURE B3.14

Application Software

Information technology (IT) is any computer-based tool that people use to work with information and support the information and information processing needs of an organization. IT includes cell phones, PDAs, software such as spreadsheet software, and printers. There are two categories of IT: hardware and software. The six hardware components include CPU, primary storage, secondary storage, input devices, output devices, and communication devices. Computer categories include PDAs, laptops, tablets, desktops, workstations, minicomputers, mainframe computers, and supercomputers.

Software includes system software and application software. Operating system software and utility software are the two primary types of system software. There are many forms of application software from word processing to databases.

✳ KEY TERMS

Application software, 290
Arithmetic-logic unit (ALU), 280
Binary digit (bit), 281
Byte, 281
Cache memory, 282
Central processing unit (CPU)
   (or microprocessor), 279
Communication device, 286
Complex instruction set
   computer (CISC) chip, 280
Computer, 279
Control unit, 279
Flash memory, 282
Gigabyte (GB), 282

Gigahertz (GHz), 280
Hard drive, 283
Hardware, 278
Information technology (IT), 278
Input device, 284
Magnetic medium, 283
Magnetic tape, 283
Megabyte (MB, M, or Meg), 282
Megahertz (MHz), 280
Memory card, 282
Memory stick, 282
Multitasking, 289
Operating system software, 289
Output device, 284

Primary storage, 281
Random access memory
   (RAM), 281
Read-only memory (ROM), 282
Reduced instruction set
   computer (RISC) chip, 280
Secondary storage, 282
Software, 278
System software, 289
Terabyte (TB), 282
Utility software, 289
Virtualization, 281
Volatility, 282

✳ CLOSING CASE ONE

Changing Circuits at Circuit City

When Circuit City expanded the big-box warehouse format to consumer electronics retailing in the 1980s, the company was on its way to becoming the place to go for TVs and stereos. By the late 1980s, it had sidestepped its then top competitor, Silo, and it soon put the squeeze on the likes of Tweeter and RadioShack. Circuit City was doing so well in the 1990s that business consultant Jim Collins, in his best seller *Good to Great*, wrote: "From 1982 to 1999, Circuit City generated cumulative stock returns 22 times better than the market, handily beating Intel, Wal-Mart, GE, Hewlett-Packard and Coca-Cola."

Today, Circuit City is in a markedly different position. By 2001, Best Buy had raced past the Richmond, Virginia-based chain, usurping its position as the number one consumer electronics retailer. Best Buy now has 608 stores compared with Circuit City's 599 and nearly $25 billion in revenue to Circuit City's $9.7 billion. Circuit City is ranked by consultancy Retail Forward as the number three seller of consumer electronics, behind Best Buy and Wal-Mart. "Circuit City was the 800-pound gorilla," said Joseph Feldman, a research analyst with the investment bank SG Cowen & Co. However, "they woke up one morning and Best Buy had doubled its size with the same number of stores."

Catching Best Buy

Circuit City has been trying to catch up to Best Buy, or at least cement its position as a serious contender in consumer electronics retailing. Recently, its top executives announced plans to turn the company into a customer-focused business that delivers a personalized experience to all customers across all its channels (stores, Web, and call centers). Michael Jones, who took over as Circuit City's CIO in January 2004, speaks passionately about the high-profile role technology will play in delivering personalized customer experiences. However, before he can achieve his vision of store associates recognizing customers through their loyalty cards as soon as they enter the store, he has a lot of unglamorous groundwork to lay. Circuit City's strategy hinges on a robust IT infrastructure that makes information readily accessible to decision makers. Everything the company is doing to improve its business—from developing more effective promotions to deciding which products should be displayed at the ends of aisles in stores—hinges on data. "This is heavy analytical work. It's fact-based, data-driven," said Philip Schoonover, Circuit City's new president who was hired in October 2004 from Best Buy.

Circuit City is just starting to invest heavily in the technology needed to act on this strategy. It is upgrading its mostly proprietary point-of-sale (POS) system and building an enterprise data warehouse to replace siloed databases. However, some analysts say Circuit City's turnaround effort has been hampered by a stodgy, overly complacent leadership that lacks vision. Top executives saw the Best Buy locomotive coming but failed to react as it steamed past them. Indeed, some analysts say they doubt Circuit City will ever catch up.

Bottom-Up Changes

As part of its turnaround effort over the past few years, Circuit City has sold all of its noncore businesses to focus on its core: consumer electronics. It also has changed the pay structure for in-store employees, begun relocating stores (it recently closed 19), and hired new management. In addition, the company is finally starting to hone its customer-centric strategy. Circuit City is already improving the customer experience in its stores by, among other things, locating accessories and services close to big-ticket items so that customers can see more quickly what they might need to furnish their home office or outfit a home theater. For example, when a customer is looking at a high-definition television, nearby is a selection of furniture to hold the TV, the cables needed to hook it up, and DirectTV or digital cable service products. Circuit City is also making merchandising decisions based on what is important to the customer. For example, its stores are beginning to feature products deemed most important to customers on the displays at the ends of aisles. The company is trying to nail the basics of customer service by making sure that items are not out of stock.[10]

Questions

1. How would anticipating Best Buy's growth have helped Circuit City remain as an industry leader?
2. Why is keeping up with technology critical to a global company such as Circuit City?
3. Highlight some of the potential risks facing Circuit City's new business model.
4. Why is Circuit City benefiting from implementing strategic product placement techniques?

Electronic Breaking Points

What happens when someone accidentally spills a cup of hot coffee on a laptop, puts a USB memory key in a washing machine, or drops an iPod in the sand? How much abuse can electronic products take and keep on working? *PC World* tested several products to determine their breaking points.[11]

Laptop

A Gateway laptop was placed in a shoulder bag and smashed into several doors and walls. It was also dropped off a six-foot-high bookcase to simulate a drop from an airplane's overhead bin. Finally, it was knocked off a desk onto a carpeted floor without the bag. After all the abuse, the Gateway consistently rebooted and recognized the wireless network; however, the battery did become slightly dislodged and the optical drive opened.

Severe physical damage was caused when the laptop was dropped onto a hardwood floor. The laptop's screen cracked, and the black plastic molding above the keyboard cracked. Plastic splinters littered the floor, and the optical drive refused to open.

Spilling coffee in a travel-size mug onto the keyboard caused a slight sizzle, after which the Gateway's blue light winked out. The machine was quickly turned off, the battery removed, the liquid drained, the keys mopped, and the unit set aside. Unfortunately, the laptop never recovered.

Smart Phone

The PalmOne Treo 600 smart phone was stepped on, buried in the sand, bounced around in a car, and dropped off a desk onto carpeted and hardwood floors. Even though the Treo 600 was not protected by a shock-absorbent case or plastic screen cover, there were no signs of failure. Repeatedly knocking it off the desk onto a carpeted floor also left it undamaged, although the unit did turn off on several occasions.

The desk-to-hardwood-floor test produced scratches but nothing else. If dropped when in phone mode, the Treo automatically turned off. If an application was running—the calculator, for example—the device stayed on and the data remained on the screen, though a mysterious extra numeral nine appeared every time it was dropped.

MP3 Player

A 6 GB silver iPod Mini went for a bouncy car ride, was dropped on wet grass and dry pavement, was knocked off a desk onto carpeted and hardwood floors, and was finally dropped in dry sand. Bouncing inside the car caused a couple of skips. Drops on soft wet grass and carpet had no ill effect. Dropping it from the car seat to the curb and off a desk onto a hardwood floor produced a few nicks and caused songs to skip and the device to shut down repeatedly. Still, all the unit's features continued to work after the abuse, and songs played.

However, the Mini did not like the beach. Without the benefit of a protective case or plastic display covering on the unit, sand wedged under the scroll wheel, affecting all controls. Feature settings could be seen and highlighted, but the crunching sand prevented the Mini from launching them. The unit turned on but could not turn off until the iPod's automatic shutdown feature took over.

Protecting Electronic Products
Bag it. Place your products in a cushioned case or shock-absorbent travel bag. The secret is to make sure it has plenty of padding.
Get protection. Almost every technology manufacturer offers some type of warranty and equipment-replacement program. For example, Sprint provides the PCS Total Equipment Protection service, which costs $5 per month and covers loss, theft, and accidental damage to a cell phone.
Clean up spills. Try these tips to bring a laptop and data back from the dead after a spill.
1. **Disconnect the battery.** The faster the battery is disconnected the less likely components will burn out.
2. **Empty it.** Turn over the device and pour out as much liquid as possible.
3. **Open it up.** Remove the optical drive and keyboard. This can be tricky, so check the user manual for instructions. Once open, use a towel to soak up as much liquid as possible. According to Herman De Hoop, HP's technical marketing manager, you can even use a hair dryer set on cool (not hot) to dry the liquid.
4. **Leave it alone.** Let the device sit for at least 12 to 24 hours. Robert Enochs, IBM's worldwide product manager for the ThinkPad Series, warns that you should not turn the device on until all the liquid is gone and it is completely dry.
5. **Plug and pray.** Reassemble the device, and if it powers up, copy off important data, and then call the manufacturer. Even if the unit works, a professional cleaning is recommended.
6. **Enter a recovery program.** For an average price of $900, enlist the help of data recovery services like DriveSavers to rescue data from drowned hard disks.

Memory Stick

Lexar claims that its JumpDrive Sport 256 MB USB 2.0 Flash Drive is "built for the rugged life." A rubber cap protects the device, absorbing shock from any drops. For these experiments, the device was used without its cap. It was dropped, stepped on, buried in the sand, and knocked off a desk onto a hardwood floor. It also took a spin through the washing machine and dryer and was even run over by a car.

There is truth in advertising. Neither water, heat, sand, nor car could keep the memory stick from its appointed storage rounds. The car did squeeze the metal USB connector tip a tad tighter, but the device was still able to make contact with the USB port, and it worked perfectly.

Memory Card

The SanDisk SD 64 MB memory card is easy to misplace, but not easy to break. It was swatted off a desk onto a hardwood floor, dropped, stepped on, and buried in the sand. It also underwent a two-rinse cycle in the wash in a jeans pocket and then tumbled in the dryer for an hour on a high-heat setting. The SanDisk memory card aced every torture test.

For tips on how to protect electronic products, review Figure B3.15.

Questions

1. Identify the six hardware categories and place each product listed in the case in its appropriate category.
2. Describe the CPU and identify which products would use a CPU.
3. Describe the relationship between memory sticks and laptops. How can a user employ one to help protect information loss from the other?
4. Identify the different types of software each of the products listed in the case might use.

1. **Purchasing a Computer**

   Dell is considered the fastest company on earth and specializes in computer customization. Connect to Dell's Web site at www.dell.com. Go to the portion of Dell's site that allows you to customize either a laptop or a desktop computer. First, choose an already prepared system and note its price and capability in terms of CPU speed, RAM size, monitor quality, and storage capacity. Now, customize that system to increase CPU speed, add more RAM, increase monitor size and quality, and add more storage capacity. What is the difference in price between the two? Which system is more in your price range? Which system has the speed and capacity you need?

2. **Web-Enabled Cell Phones**

   When categorizing computers by size for personal needs, we focused on PDAs, laptops, and desktop computers. Other variations include Web-enabled cell phones that include instant text messaging and Web computers. For this project, you will need a group of four people, which you will then split into two groups of two. Have the first group research Web-enabled cell phones, their capabilities and costs. Have that group make a purchase recommendation based on price and capability. Have the second group do the same for Web computers. What is your vision of the future? Will we ever get rid of clunky laptops and desktops in favor of more portable and cheaper devices such as Web-enabled cell phones and Web computers? Why or why not?

3. **Small Business Computers**

   Many different types of computers are available for small businesses. Use the Internet to find three different vendors of laptops or notebooks that are good for small businesses. Find the most expensive and the least expensive that the vendor offers and create a table comparing the different computers based on the following:

   - CPU
   - Memory
   - Hard drive
   - Optical drive
   - Operating system
   - Utility software
   - Application software
   - Support plan

   Determine which computer you would recommend for a small business looking for an inexpensive laptop. Determine which computer you would recommend for a small business looking for an expensive laptop.

4. **PDA Software**

   The personal digital assistant (PDA) market is ferocious, dynamic, and uncertain. One of the uncertainties is which operating system for PDAs will become dominant. Today, Microsoft operating systems dominate the laptop and desktop market. Research the more popular PDAs available today. What are the different operating systems? What different functionality do they offer? Are they compatible with each other? Determine which one will dominate in the future.

B5
Networks and Telecommunications

1. Compare LANs, WANs, and MANs.
2. List and describe the four components that differentiate networks.
3. Compare the two types of network architectures.
4. Explain topology and the different types found in networks.
5. Describe TCP/IP along with its primary purpose.
6. Identify the different media types found in networks.

Networks and Telecommunications

Telecommunication systems enable the transmission of data over public or private networks. A ***network*** is a communications, data exchange, and resource-sharing system created by linking two or more computers and establishing standards, or protocols, so that they can work together. Telecommunication systems and networks are traditionally complicated and historically inefficient. However, businesses can benefit from today's modern network infrastructures that provide reliable global reach to employees and customers. Businesses around the world are moving to network infrastructure solutions that allow greater choice in how they go to market—solutions with global reach. Plug-In B5 takes a detailed look at key network and telecommunication technologies being integrated into businesses around the world.

Network Basics

Music is the hottest new product line at ubiquitous coffee retailer Starbucks. In Starbucks stores, customers can burn CDs while sipping coffee, thanks to the company's own online music library and increasingly sophisticated in-store network. Networks range from small two-computer networks to the biggest network of all, the Internet. A network provides two principle benefits: the ability to communicate and the ability to share. E-mail is the most popular form of network communication. Figure B5.1 highlights the three different types of networks, and Figure B5.2 graphically depicts each network type.

Network Types	
Local area network (LAN)	A computer network that uses cables or radio signals to link two or more computers within a geographically limited area, generally one building or a group of buildings. A networked office building, school, or home usually contains a single LAN. The linked computers are called workstations.
Wide area network (WAN)	A computer network that provides data communication services for business in geographically dispersed areas (such as across a country or around the world). The Internet is a WAN that spans the world.
Metropolitan area network (MAN)	A computer network that provides connectivity in a geographic area or region larger than that covered by a local area network, but smaller than the area covered by a wide area network. A college or business may have a MAN that joins the different LANs across its campus.

FIGURE B5.1

Network Types

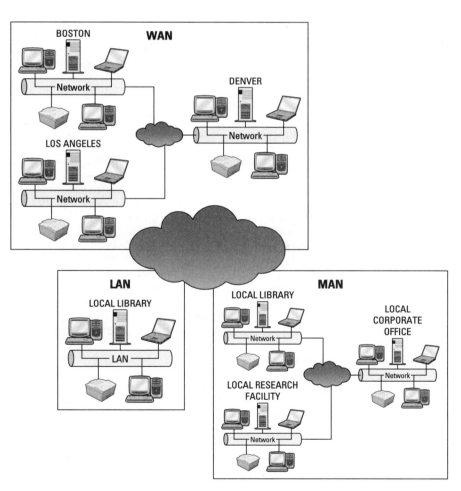

FIGURE B5.2

LAN, WAN, and MAN

Networks are differentiated by the following:

- Architecture—peer-to-peer, client/server.
- Topology—bus, star, ring, hybrid, wireless.
- Protocols—Ethernet, Transmission Control Protocol/Internet Protocol (TCP/IP).
- Media—coaxial, twisted-pair, fiber-optic.

Architecture

The two primary types of network architectures are: peer-to-peer networks and client/server networks.

PEER-TO-PEER NETWORKS

A *peer-to-peer (P2P) network* is any network without a central file server and in which all computers in the network have access to the public files located on all other workstations, as illustrated in Figure B5.3. Each networked computer can allow other computers to access its files and use connected printers while it is in use as a workstation without the aid of a server.

While Napster may be the most widely known example of a P2P implementation, it may also be one of the most narrowly focused since the Napster model takes advantage of only one of the many capabilities of P2P computing: file sharing. The technology has far broader capabilities, including the sharing of processing, memory, and storage, and the supporting of collaboration among vast numbers of distributed computers. Peer-to-peer computing enables immediate interaction among people and computer systems.

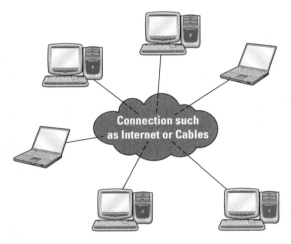

FIGURE B5.3

Peer-to-Peer (P2P) Networks

CLIENT/SERVER NETWORKS

A *client* is a computer that is designed to request information from a server. A *server* is a computer that is dedicated to providing information in response to external requests. A *client/server network* is a model for applications in which the bulk of the back-end processing, such as performing a physical search of a database, takes place on a server, while the front-end processing, which involves communicating with the users, is handled by the clients (see Figure B5.4). A *network operating system (NOS)* is the operating system that runs a network, steering information between computers and managing security and users. The client/server model has become one of the central ideas of network computing. Most business applications written today use the client/server model.

A fundamental part of client/server architecture is packet-switching. *Packet-switching* occurs when the sending computer divides a message into a number of efficiently sized units called packets, each of which contains the address of the destination computer. Each packet is sent on the network and intercepted by routers. A *router* is an intelligent connecting device that examines each packet of data it receives and then decides which way to send it onward toward its destination. The packets arrive at their intended destination, although some may have actually traveled by different physical paths, and the receiving computer assembles the packets and delivers the message to the appropriate application. The number of network routers being installed by businesses worldwide is booming (see Figure B5.5).

Eva Chen, CIO at Trend Micro, built a router that helps prevent worms and viruses from entering networks. The problem with most existing antivirus software is

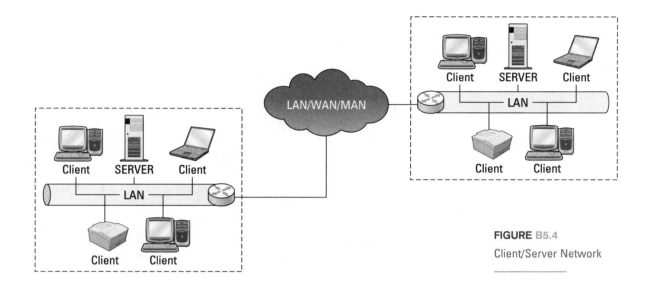

FIGURE B5.4

Client/Server Network

that it starts working after a destructive sequence of code is identified, meaning it starts doing its job only after the virus or worm has been unleashed inside the network. Chen's router, the Network VirusWall, sits on the edge of a corporate network, scanning data packets and detaining those that might contain viruses or worms. Any suspicious packets are compared with up-to-the-second information from Trend Micro's virus-tracking command center. Viruses and worms are then deleted and refused entry to the network, allowing the company to perform a preemptive strike.[1]

Topology

Networks are assembled according to certain rules. Cables, for example, have to be a certain length; each cable strand can support only a certain amount of network traffic. A **network topology** refers to the geometric arrangement of the actual physical organization of the computers (and other network devices) in a network. Topologies vary depending on cost and functionality. Figure B5.6 highlights the five common topologies used in networks, and Figure B5.7 displays each topology.

Protocols

A **protocol** is a standard that specifies the format of data as well as the rules to be followed during transmission. Simply put, for one computer (or computer program) to talk to another computer (or computer program) they must both be talking the same language, and this language is called a protocol.

A protocol is based on an agreed-upon and established standard, and this way all manufacturers of hardware and software that are using the protocol do so in a similar fashion to allow for interoperability. **Interoperability** is the capability of two or more computer systems to share data and resources, even though they are made by different manufacturers. The most popular network protocols used are Ethernet and Transmission Control Protocol/Internet Protocol (TCP/IP).

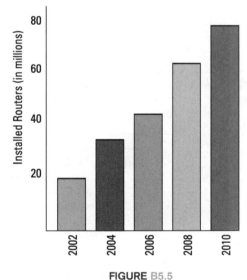

FIGURE B5.5

Worldwide Router Growth

Network Topologies	
Bus	All devices are connected to a central cable, called the bus or backbone. Bus networks are relatively inexpensive and easy to install for small networks.
Star	All devices are connected to a central device, called a hub. Star networks are relatively easy to install and manage, but bottlenecks can occur because all data must pass through the hub.
Ring	All devices are connected to one another in the shape of a closed loop, so that each device is connected directly to two other devices, one on either side of it. Ring topologies are relatively expensive and difficult to install, but they offer high bandwidth and can span large distances.
Hybrid	Groups of star-configured workstations are connected to a linear bus backbone cable, combining the characteristics of the bus and star topologies.
Wireless	Devices are connected by a receiver/transmitter to a special network interface card that transmits signals between a computer and a server, all within an acceptable transmission range.

ETHERNET

Ethernet is a physical and data layer technology for LAN networking (see Figure B5.8). Ethernet is the most widely installed LAN access method, originally developed by Xerox and then developed further by Xerox, Digital Equipment Corporation, and Intel. When it first began to be widely deployed in the 1980s, Ethernet supported a maximum theoretical data transfer rate of 10 megabits per second (Mbps). More recently, Fast Ethernet has extended traditional Ethernet technology

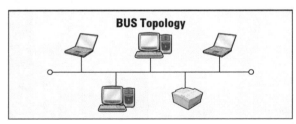

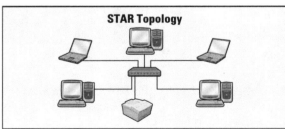

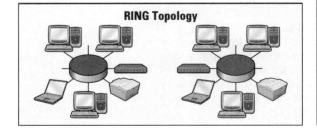

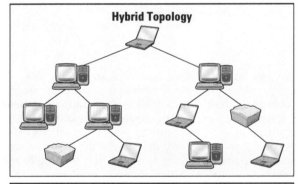

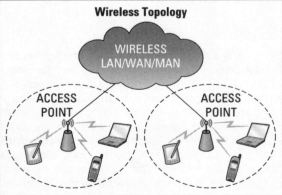

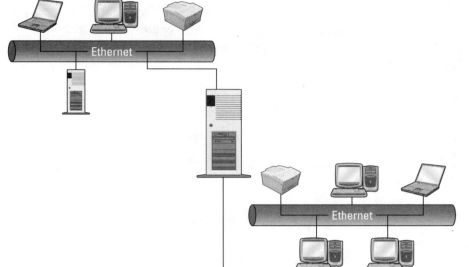

to 100 Mbps peak, and Gigabit Ethernet technology extends performance up to 1,000 Mbps.

Ethernet has survived as the major LAN technology—it is currently used for approximately 85 percent of the world's LAN-connected PCs and workstations—because its protocol has the following characteristics:

- Is easy to understand, implement, manage, and maintain.
- Allows low-cost network implementations.
- Provides extensive flexibility for network installation.
- Guarantees successful interconnection and operation of standards-compliant products, regardless of manufacturer.

TRANSMISSION CONTROL PROTOCOL/INTERNET PROTOCOL

The most common telecommunication protocol is Transmission Control Protocol/Internet Protocol (TCP/IP), which was originally developed by the Department of Defense to connect a system of computer networks that became known as the Internet. *Transmission Control Protocol/Internet Protocol (TCP/IP)* provides the technical foundation for the public Internet as well as for large numbers of private networks. The key achievement of TCP/IP is its flexibility with respect to lower-level protocols. TCP/IP uses a special transmission method that maximizes data transfer and automatically adjusts to slower devices and other delays encountered on a network. Although more than 100 protocols make up the entire TCP/IP protocol suite, the two most important of these are TCP and IP. **TCP** provides transport functions, ensuring, among other things, that the amount of data received is the same as the

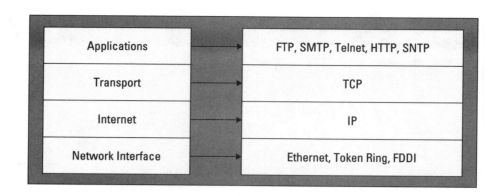

TCP/IP Applications	
File Transfer Protocol (FTP)	Allows files containing text, programs, graphics, numerical data, and so on to be downloaded off or uploaded onto a network.
Simple Mail Transfer Protocol (SMTP)	TCP/IP's own messaging system for e-mail.
Telnet Protocol	Provides terminal emulation that allows a personal computer or workstation to act as a terminal, or access device, for a server.
Hypertext Transfer Protocol (HTTP)	Allows Web browsers and servers to send and receive Web pages.
Simple Network Management Protocol (SNMP)	Allows the management of networked nodes to be managed from a single point.

amount transmitted. **IP** provides the addressing and routing mechanism that acts as a postmaster. Figure B5.9 displays TCP/IP's four-layer reference model:

- Application layer—serves as the window for users and application processes to access network services.
- Transport layer—handles end-to-end packet transportation.
- Internet layer—formats the data into packets, adds a header containing the packet sequence and the address of the receiving device, and specifies the services required from the network.
- Network interface layer—places data packets on the network for transmission.

The TCP/IP suite of applications includes five protocols—file transfer, simple mail transfer, telnet, hypertext transfer, and simple network management (see Figure B5.10).

Another communication reference model is the seven-layer Open System Interconnection (OSI) reference model. Figure B5.11 show the OSI model's seven layers.

The lower layers (1 to 3) represent local communications, while the upper layers (4 to 7) represent end-to-end communications. Each layer contributes protocol functions that are necessary to establish and maintain the error-free exchange of information between network users.

For many years, users thought the OSI model would replace TCP/IP as the preferred technique for connecting multivendor networks. But the slow pace of OSI standards as well as the expense of implementing complex OSI software and having products certified for OSI interoperability will preclude this from happening.

OSI Model
7. Application
6. Presentation
5. Session
4. Transport
3. Network
2. Data Link
1. Physical

Voice over IP (VoIP)

Originally, phone calls made over the Internet had a reputation of offering poor call quality, lame user interfaces, and low call-completion rates. With new and improved technology and IT infrastructures, Internet phone calls now offer similar quality to traditional telephone calls. Today, many consumers are making phone calls over the Internet by using voice over Internet protocol (VoIP). *Voice over IP (VoIP)* uses TCP/IP technology to transmit voice calls over long-distance telephone lines. In fact, VoIP transmits over 10 percent of all phone calls and this number is growing exponentially.

VoIP and e-mail work in similar ways. The user sends a call over the Internet in packets of audio data tagged with the same destination. VoIP reassembles the packets once they arrive at their final destination.

Numerous vendors offer VoIP services; however, the service works differently depending on the vendor's IT infrastructure. The start-up Skype pairs P2P (peer-to-peer) technology with a PC's sound card to create a voice service, which the user can use to call other Skype users. Unfortunately, the user can talk only to other Skype users. Vonage lets the user place calls to any person who has a mobile or landline (regular telephone) number. Vonage sends the call over a cable via a digital-to-analog converter. A few providers even offer an adapter for a traditional handset that plugs into a broadband modem. All of these vendors are providing VoIP, but the service and its features can vary significantly.

The telecom industry expects great benefits from combining VoIP with emerging standards that allow for easier development, interoperability among systems, and application integration. This is a big change for an industry that relies on proprietary systems to keep customers paying for upgrades and new features. The VoIP and open-standards combo should produce more choices, lower prices, and new applications.

Writing voice applications may never be as common as writing computer applications. But the spread of VoIP will make it easier to manage applications and add capabilities to the voice feature set. In a decade, the telecom network "will be like getting water out of the tap," predicts Stef van Aarle, vice president of marketing and strategy at Lucent Worldwide Services. "The only time you think of it will be when it doesn't work. And software is the glue that makes it all easy to use."

Upstarts like Vonage and Skype are bringing VoIP to the masses. But a bigger opportunity lurks in the $2 billion corporate phone market. New York-based start-up Popular Telephony is offering a new VoIP technology that dramatically cuts corporate phone costs while letting workers take their office phones anywhere. Its secret: peer-to-peer software called Peerio that is built right into handsets.

CEO Dmitry Goroshevsky founded the company three years ago to bring PC economics to the office telephone system. A traditional workplace setup requires a dedicated voice network and a private branch exchange, or PBX, to connect to the outside world and can cost up to $1 million (see Figure B5.12). Cisco has been selling an IP PBX, which uses a data network for voice calls. But Popular Telephony eliminates pricey hardware. Using an ordinary PC, network administrators assign

Telephone System	Typical Telecom System	IP-Based System	Peerio
Requirements	■ Phones ■ Private branch exchange (PBX) ■ Voice switches network ■ Dedicated voice network	■ Phones ■ IP PBX ■ Existing data network ■ Gateway	■ Phones ■ PC ■ Existing data ■ Gateway
Total Cost	$1,000,000	$500,000	$100,000

FIGURE B5.12

Typical Telephone Start-up Costs for a 1,000-Person Office

an extension to each phone. Peerio-enabled handsets, which will be sold through discount retailers and office supply stores, plug directly into a company's data network, where calls are routed through a gateway and then out. Since Peerio is based on Internet protocol, office workers can use their phones wherever there is a broadband connection. And though companies pay the usual rates to call conventional landline and mobile phone numbers, ringing up other Peerio and VoIP users will not cost a dime. A handful of licensees are manufacturing the phones.[2]

Media

Network transmission media refers to the various types of media used to carry the signal between computers. When information is sent across the network, it is converted into electrical signals. These signals are generated as electromagnetic waves (analog signaling) or as a sequence of voltage pulses (digital signaling). To be sent from one location to another, a signal must travel along a physical path. The physical path that is used to carry a signal between a signal transmitter and a signal receiver is called the transmission media. The two types of transmission media are wire (guided) and wireless (unguided).

WIRE MEDIA

Wire media are transmission material manufactured so that signals will be confined to a narrow path and will behave predictably. The three most commonly used types of guided media are (see Figure B5.13):

- Twisted-pair wiring
- Coaxial cable
- Fiber-optic cable

Twisted-Pair Wiring

Twisted-pair wiring refers to a type of cable composed of four (or more) copper wires twisted around each other within a plastic sheath. The wires are twisted to reduce outside electrical interference. Twisted-pair cables come in shielded and unshielded varieties. Shielded cables have a metal shield encasing the wires that acts as a ground for electromagnetic interference. Unshielded twisted-pair (UTP) is the most popular and is generally the best option for LAN networks. The quality of UTP may vary from telephone-grade wire to high-speed cable. The cable has four pairs of wires inside the jacket. Each pair is twisted with a different number of twists per inch

FIGURE B5.13

Twisted-Pair, Coaxial Cable, and Fiber-Optic

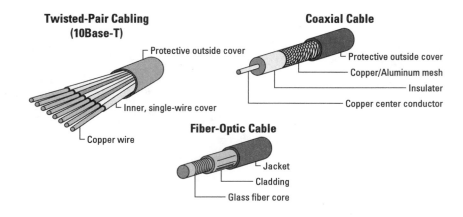

Twisted-Pair Cabling (10Base-T)
— Protective outside cover
— Inner, single-wire cover
— Copper wire

Coaxial Cable
— Protective outside cover
— Copper/Aluminum mesh
— Insulater
— Copper center conductor

Fiber-Optic Cable
— Jacket
— Cladding
— Glass fiber core

to help eliminate interference from adjacent pairs and other electrical devices. The RJ-45 connectors on twisted-pair cables resemble large telephone connectors.

Coaxial Cable

Coaxial cable is cable that can carry a wide range of frequencies with low signal loss. It consists of a metallic shield with a single wire placed along the center of a shield and isolated from the shield by an insulator. This type of cable is referred to as coaxial because it contains one copper wire (or physical data channel) that carries the signal and is surrounded by another concentric physical channel consisting of a wire mesh. The outer channel serves as a ground for electrical interference. Because of this grounding feature, several coaxial cables can be placed within a single conduit or sheath without significant loss of data integrity.

Fiber-Optic Cable

Fiber optic (or *optical fiber*) refers to the technology associated with the transmission of information as light impulses along a glass wire or fiber. The 10Base-FL and 100Base-FX optical fiber cable are the same types of cable used by most telephone companies for long-distance service. Optical fiber cable can transmit data over long distances with little loss in data integrity. In addition, because data are transferred as a pulse of light, optical fiber is not subject to interference. The light pulses travel through a glass wire or fiber encased in an insulating sheath.

Optical fiber's increased maximum effective distance comes at a price. Optical fiber is more fragile than wire, difficult to split, and labor intensive to install. For these reasons, optical fiber is used primarily to transmit data over extended distances where the hardware required to relay the data signal on less expensive media would exceed the cost of optical fiber installation. It is also used where large amounts of data need to be transmitted on a regular basis.

WIRELESS MEDIA

Wireless media are natural parts of the Earth's environment that can be used as physical paths to carry electrical signals. The atmosphere and outer space are examples of wireless media that are commonly used to carry signals. These media can carry such electromagnetic signals as microwave, infrared light waves, and radio waves.

Network signals are transmitted through all media as a type of waveform. When transmitted through wire and cable, the signal is an electrical waveform. When transmitted through fiber-optic cable, the signal is a light wave, either visible or infrared light. When transmitted through the Earth's atmosphere, the signal can take the form of waves in the radio spectrum, including microwaves, infrared, or visible light.

Recent advances in radio hardware technology have produced significant advancements in wireless networking devices: the cellular telephone, wireless modems, and wireless LANs. These devices use technology that in some cases has been around for decades but until recently was too impractical or expensive for widespread use.

E-Business Networks

To set up an e-business even a decade ago would have required an individual organization to assume the burden of developing the entire network infrastructure. Today, industry-leading companies have developed Internet-based products and services to handle many aspects of customer and supplier interactions.

"In today's retail market, you cannot be a credible national retailer without having a robust Web site," says Dennis Bowman, senior vice president and CIO of Circuit

E-Business Network Characteristics
■ Provide for the transparent exchange of information with suppliers, trading partners, and customers.
■ Reliably and securely exchange information internally and externally via the Internet or other networks.
■ Allow end-to-end integration and provide message delivery across multiple systems, in particular, databases, clients, and servers.
■ Respond to high demands with scalable processing power and networking capacity.
■ Serve as the integrator and transaction framework for both digital businesses and traditional brick-and-mortar businesses that want to leverage the Internet for any type of business.

City, who adds that customers now expect seamless retailing just as they expect stores that are clean and well stocked. For this reason, retailers are working furiously to integrate their e-business sites with their inventory and point-of-sale (POS) systems so that they can accept in-store returns of merchandise bought online and allow customers to buy on the Web and pick up in the store.

Some companies, such as Best Buy, Circuit City, Office Depot, and Sears, already have their physical and online stores integrated. These companies have been the fast movers because they already had an area in their stores for merchandise pickup (usually for big, bulky items like TVs and appliances), and because long before the Web they had systems and processes in place that facilitated the transfer of a sale from one store to another. Other retailers are partially integrated. Ann Taylor, Bed Bath & Beyond, Eddie Bauer, Linens 'n' Things, Macy's, REI, Target, The Gap, and others let customers return but not pick up online-ordered merchandise in stores. To take on the challenge of e-business integration, an organization needs a secure and reliable IT infrastructure for mission-critical systems (see Figure B5.14)

A *virtual private network (VPN)* is a way to use the public telecommunication infrastructure (e.g., Internet) to provide secure access to an organization's network (see Figure B5.15). A *valued-added network (VAN)* is a private network, provided by a third party, for exchanging information through a high capacity connection. To date, organizations engaging in e-business have relied largely on VPNs, VANs, and other dedicated links handling electronic data interchange transactions. These traditional solutions are still deployed in the market and for many companies will likely hold a

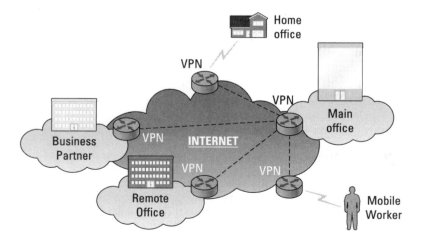

strategic role for years to come. However, conventional technologies present significant challenges:

- By handling only limited kinds of business information, these contribute little to a reporting structure intended to provide a comprehensive view of business operations.
- They offer little support for the real-time business process integration that will be essential in the digital marketplace.
- Relatively expensive and complex to implement, conventional technologies make it difficult to expand or change networks in response to market shifts.

Networks come in all sizes, from two computers connected to share a printer, to the Internet, which is the largest network of all, joining millions of computers of all types all over the world. In between are business networks, which vary in size from a dozen or fewer computers to many thousands. There are three primary types of networks: local area network (LAN), wide area network (WAN), and metropolitan area network (MAN). The following differentiate networks:

- Architecture—peer-to-peer, client/server.
- Topology—bus, star, ring, hybrid, wireless.
- Protocols—Ethernet, Transmission Control Protocol/Internet Protocol (TCP/IP).
- Media—coaxial, twisted-pair, fiber-optic.

⋆ **KEY TERMS**

Client, 316
Client/server network, 316
Coaxial cable, 323
Ethernet, 318
Fiber optic (or optical fiber), 323
Interoperability, 317
Local area network (LAN), 315
Metropolitan area network (MAN), 315
Network, 314
Network operating system (NOS), 316

Network topology, 317
Network transmission media, 322
Packet-switching, 316
Peer-to-peer (P2P) network, 316
Protocol, 317
Router, 316
Server, 316
Telecommunication system, 314
Transmission Control Protocol/Internet Protocol (TCP/IP), 319

Twisted-pair wiring, 322
Valued-added network (VAN), 324
Virtual private network (VPN), 324
Voice over Internet Protocol (VoIP), 321
Wide area network (WAN), 315
Wire media, 322
Wireless media, 323

⋆ **CLOSING CASE ONE**

Watching Where You Step—Prada

Prada estimates its sales per year at $22 million. The luxury retailer recently spent millions on IT for its futuristic "epicenter" store—but the flashy technology turned into a high-priced hassle. The company needed to generate annual sales of $75 million by 2007 to turn a profit on its new high-tech investment.

When Prada opened its $40 million Manhattan flagship, hotshot architect Rem Koolhaas promised a radically new shopping experience. And he kept the promise—though not quite according to plan. Customers were soon enduring hordes of tourists, neglected technology, and the occasional thrill of getting stuck in experimental dressing rooms. A few of the problems associated with the store:

1. **Fickle fitting rooms**—Doors that turn from clear to opaque confuse shoppers and frequently fail to open on cue.

2. **Failed RFID**—Touch screens meant to spring to life when items are placed in the RFID "closets" are often just blank.
3. **Pointless PDAs**—Salesclerks let the handheld devices gather dust and instead check the stockroom for inventory.
4. **Neglected network**—A lag between sales and inventory systems makes the wireless network nearly irrelevant.

This was not exactly the vision for the high-end boutique when it debuted in December 2001. Instead, the 22,000-square-foot SoHo shop was to be the first of four "epicenter" stores around the world that would combine cutting-edge architecture and 21st century technology to revolutionize the luxury shopping experience. Prada poured roughly 25 percent of the store's budget into IT, including a wireless network to link every item to an Oracle inventory database in real-time using radio frequency identification (RFID) tags on the clothes. The staff would roam the floor armed with PDAs to check whether items were in stock, and customers could do the same through touch screens in the dressing rooms.

But most of the flashy technology today sits idle, abandoned by employees who never quite embraced computing chic and are now too overwhelmed by large crowds to assist shoppers with handhelds. On top of that, many gadgets, such as automated dressing-room doors and touch screens, are either malfunctioning or ignored. Packed with experimental technology, the clear-glass dressing-room doors were designed to open and close automatically at the tap of a foot pedal, then turn opaque when a second pedal sent an electric current through the glass. Inside, an RFID-aware rack would recognize a customer's selections and display them on a touch screen linked to the inventory system.

In practice, the process was hardly that smooth. Many shoppers never quite understood the pedals and disrobed in full view, thinking the door had turned opaque. That is no longer a problem, since staff members usually leave the glass opaque, but often the doors get stuck. Some of the chambers are open only to VIP customers during peak traffic times.

With the smart closets and handhelds out of commission, the wireless network in the store is nearly irrelevant, despite its considerable expense. As Prada's debt reportedly climbed to around $1 billion in late 2001, the company shelved plans for the fourth epicenter store, in San Francisco. A second store opened in Tokyo to great acclaim, albeit with different architects in a different market. Though that store incorporates similar cutting-edge concepts, architect Jacques Herzog emphasized that avant-garde retail plays well only in Japan. "This building is clearly a building for Tokyo," he told *The New York Times*. "It couldn't be somewhere else."

The multimillion-dollar technology is starting to look more like technology for technology's sake than an enhancement of the shopping experience, and the store's failings have prompted Prada to reevaluate its epicenter strategy.[3]

Questions

1. Explain how Prada was anticipating using its wireless network to help its store operate more efficiently. What prevented the system from working correctly?
2. What could Prada have done to help its employees embrace the wireless network?
3. Would Prada have experienced the same issues if it had used a wire (guided) network instead of a wireless (unguided) network?
4. What security issues would Prada need to be aware of concerning its wireless network?
5. What should Prada do differently when designing its fourth store to ensure its success?

Banks Banking on Network Security

Bank of America, Commerce Bancorp, PNC Financial Services Group, and Wachovia were victims of a crime involving a person trying to obtain customer data and sell it to law firms and debt-collection agencies. New Jersey police seized 13 computers from the alleged mastermind with 670,000 account numbers and balances. There is no indication the data were used for identity theft, but it highlights how increasingly difficult it is to protect information against such schemes as the market value of personal information grows. In the past, banks were wary of the cost or customer backlash from adopting network security technologies. Today, banks are beefing up network security as more customers begin to view security as a key factor when choosing a bank.

Bank of America

Bank of America is moving toward a stronger authentication process for its 13 million online customers. Bank of America's new SiteKey service is designed to thwart scams in which customers think they are entering data on the bank's Web site, when they are actually on a thief's site built to steal data. This occurs when a worm tells a computer to reroute the bank's URL into a browser to another site that looks exactly like the bank's.

SiteKey offers two-factor authentication. When enrolling in SiteKey, a customer picks an image from a library and writes a brief phrase. Each time the customer signs on, the image and phrase are displayed, indicating that the bank recognizes the computer the customer is using and letting the customer know that he or she is at the bank's official Web site. The customer then enters a password and proceeds. When signing on from a different computer than usual, the customer must answer one of three prearranged questions.

Wells Fargo & Company

"Out-of-wallet" questions contain information that is not found on a driver's license or ATM card. Wells Fargo is implementing a security strategy that operates based on "out-of-wallet" questions as a second factor for network password enrollment and maintenance. It is also offering network security hardware such as key fobs that change passwords every 60 seconds. In the fall, it will launch a two-factor authentication pilot in which small businesses making electronic funds transfers will need a key fob to complete transactions.

E-Trade Financial Corporation

E-Trade Financial Corporation provides customers holding account balances of more than $50,000 with a free Digital Security ID for network authentication. The device displays a new six-digit code every 60 seconds, which the customer must use to log on. Accounts under $50,000 can purchase the Digital Security ID device for $25.

Barclays Bank

Barclays Bank instituted online-transfer delays of between several hours and one day. The delays, which apply the first time a transfer is attempted between two accounts, are intended to give the bank time to detect suspicious activity, such as a large number of transfers from multiple accounts into a single account. The online-transfer delay was adopted in response to a wave of phishing incidents in which thieves transferred funds from victims' bank accounts into accounts owned by "mules." Mules are people who open bank accounts based on e-mail solicitations, usually under the guise of a business proposal. From the mule accounts, the thieves withdraw cash, open credit cards, or otherwise loot the account.

Barclay's also offers account monitoring of customer's actions to compare them with historical profile data to detect unusual behavior. For instance, the service would alert the bank to contact the customer if the customer normally logs on from England and suddenly logs on from New York and performs 20 transactions.[4]

Questions

1. What reason would a bank have for not wanting to adopt an online-transfer delay policy?
2. Why is network security critical to financial institutions?
3. Explain the differences between the types of network security offered by the banks in the case. Which bank would you open an account with and why?
4. What additional types of network security, not mentioned in the case above, would you recommend a bank implement?
5. Identity three policies a bank should implement to help it improve network information security.

★ MAKING BUSINESS DECISIONS

1. Secure Access

Organizations that have traditionally maintained private, closed systems have begun to look at the potential of the Internet as a ready-made network resource. The Internet is inexpensive and globally pervasive: Every phone jack is a potential connection. However, the Internet lacks security. What obstacles must organizations overcome to allow secure network connections?

2. Rolling Out with Networks

As organizations begin to realize the benefits of adding a wireless component to their network, they must understand how to leverage this emerging technology. Wireless solutions have come to the forefront for many organizations with the rollout of more standard, cost-effective, and secure wireless protocols. With wireless networks, increased business agility may be realized by continuous data access and synchronization. However, with the increased flexibility come many challenges. Develop a report detailing the benefits an organization could obtain by implementing wireless technology. Also, include the challenges that a wireless network presents along with recommendations for any solutions.

3. Wireless Fitness

Sandifer's Fitness Club is located in beautiful South Carolina. Rosie Sandifer has owned and operated the club for twenty years. The club has 3 outdoor pools, 2 indoor pools, 10 racquetball courts, 10 tennis courts, an indoor and outdoor track, along with a 4-story exercise equipment and massage therapy building. Rosie has hired you as a summer intern specializing in information technology. The extent of Rosie's current technology includes a few PCs in the accounting department and two PCs with Internet access for the rest of the staff. Your first assignment is to create a report detailing networks and wireless technologies. The report should explain how the club could gain a business advantage by implementing a wireless network. If Rosie likes your report, she will hire you as the full-time employee in charge of information technology. Be sure to include all of the different uses for wireless devices the club could implement to improve its operations.

CHAPTER 6

Valuing Organizational Information

6.1. Describe the broad levels, formats, and granularities of information.

6.2. Differentiate between transactional and analytical information.

6.3. List, describe, and provide an example of each of the five characteristics of high quality information.

6.4. Assess the impact of low quality information on an organization and the benefits of high quality information on an organization.

Organizational Information

Google recently reported a 200 percent increase in sales of its new Enterprise Search Appliance tool released in 2002. Companies use the tool within an enterprise information portal (EIP) to search corporate information for answers to customer questions and to fulfill sales orders. Hundreds of Google's customers are already using the tool—Xerox, Hitachi Data Systems, Nextel Communications, Procter & Gamble, Discovery Communications, Cisco Systems, Boeing. The ability to search, analyze, and comprehend information is vital for any organization's success. The incredible 200 percent growth in sales of Google's new Search Appliance tool is a strong indicator that organizations are coveting technologies that help organize and provide access to information.[2]

Information is everywhere in an organization. When addressing a significant business issue, employees must be able to obtain and analyze all the relevant information so they can make the best decision possible. Organizational information comes at different levels and in different formats and "granularities." *Information granularity* refers to the extent of detail within the information (fine and detailed or coarse and abstract). Employees must be able to correlate the different levels, formats, and granularities of information when making decisions. For example, if employees are using a supply chain management system to make decisions, they might find that their suppliers send information in different formats and granularity at different levels. One supplier might send detailed information in a spreadsheet, another supplier might send summary information in a Word document, and still another might send aggregate information from a database. Employees will need to compare these different types of information for what they commonly reveal to make strategic SCM decisions. Figure 6.1 displays types of information found in organizations.

Successfully collecting, compiling, sorting, and finally analyzing information from multiple levels, in varied formats, exhibiting different granularity can provide tremendous insight into how an organization is performing. Taking a hard look at organizational information can yield exciting and unexpected results such as potential new markets, new ways of reaching customers, and even new ways of doing business.

Samsung Electronics took a detailed look at over 10,000 reports from its resellers to identify "lost deals" or orders lost to competitors. The analysis yielded

Information Types	Range	Examples
Information Levels	Individual	Individual knowledge, goals, and strategies
	Department	Departmental goals, revenues, expenses, processes, and strategies
	Enterprise	Enterprisewide revenues, expenses, processes, and strategies
Information Formats	Document	Letters, memos, faxes, e-mails, reports, marketing materials, and training materials
	Presentation	Product, strategy, process, financial, customer, and competitor presentations
	Spreadsheet	Sales, marketing, industry, financial, competitor, customer, and order spreadsheets
	Database	Customer, employee, sales, order, supplier, and manufacturer databases
Information Granularities	Detail (Fine)	Reports for each salesperson, product, and part
	Summary	Reports for all sales personnel, all products, and all parts
	Aggregate (Coarse)	Reports across departments, organizations, and companies

the enlightening result that 80 percent of lost sales occurred in a single business unit, the health care industry. Furthermore, Samsung was able to identify that 40 percent of its lost sales in the health care industry were going to one particular competitor. Before performing the analysis, Samsung was heading into its market blind. Armed with this valuable information, Samsung is changing its selling strategy in the health care industry by implementing a new strategy to work more closely with hardware vendors to win back lost sales.[3]

Not all companies are successful at managing information. Staples, the office-supplies superstore, opened its first store in 1986 with state-of-the-art technology. The company experienced rapid growth and soon found itself overwhelmed with the resulting volumes of information. The state-of-the-art technology quickly became obsolete and the company was unable to obtain any insight into its massive volumes of information. A simple query such as identifying the customers who purchased a computer, but not software or peripherals, took hours. Some of the queries required several days to complete and by the time the managers received answers to their queries it was too late.[4]

After understanding the different levels, formats, and granularities of information, it is important to look at a few additional characteristics that help determine the value of information. These characteristics include transactional, analytical, timeliness, and quality.

The Value of Transactional and Analytical Information

Transactional information encompasses all of the information contained within a single business process or unit of work, and its primary purpose is to support the performing of daily operational tasks. Examples of transactional information are withdrawing cash from an ATM, making an airline reservation, or purchasing stocks. Organizations capture and store transactional information in databases, and they use it when performing operational tasks and repetitive decisions such as analyzing daily sales reports and production schedules to determine how much inventory to carry.

Analytical information encompasses all organizational information, and its primary purpose is to support the performing of managerial analysis tasks. Analytical information includes transactional information along with other information such as market and industry information. Examples of analytical information include trends, sales, product statistics, and future growth projections. Analytical information is used when making important ad hoc decisions such as whether the organization should build a new manufacturing plant or hire additional sales personnel.

The Value of Timely Information

The need for timely information can change for each business decision. Some decisions require weekly or monthly information while other decisions require daily information. Timeliness is an aspect of information that depends on the situation. In some industries, information that is a few days or weeks old can be relevant while in other industries information that is a few minutes old can be almost worthless. Some organizations, such as 911 centers, stock traders, and banks, require consolidated, up-to-the-second information, 24 hours a day, seven days a week. Other organizations, such as insurance and construction companies, require only daily or even weekly information.

Real-time information means immediate, up-to-date information. *Real-time systems* provide real-time information in response to query requests. Many organizations use real-time systems to exploit key corporate transactional information. In a survey of 700 IT executives by Evans Data Corp., 48 percent of respondents said they were already analyzing information in or near real-time, and another 25 percent reported plans to add real-time systems.[5]

Real-time systems provide valuable information for supporting corporate strategies such as customer relationship management. Bell Mobility Inc., Canada's largest wireless carrier, staffs over 550 customer service representatives and uses E.piphany Inc.'s Real-Time tool to make the right customer offers at the right time without having to rely on guesswork. Figure 6.2 display's Bell Mobility's results from the first month after implementation of the Real-Time tool.[6]

The growing demand for real-time information stems from organizations' need to make faster and more effective decisions, keep smaller inventories, operate more efficiently, and track performance more carefully. But timeliness is relative. Organizations need fresh, timely information to make good decisions. Information also needs to be timely in the sense that it meets employees' needs—but no more. If employees can absorb information only on an hourly or daily basis, there is no need to gather real-time information in smaller increments. For example, MBIA Insurance Corp. uses overnight updates to feed its real-time systems. Employees use this information to make daily risk decisions for mortgages, insurance policies, and other services. The company found that overnight updates were sufficient, as long as

FIGURE 6.2

Results from Bell Mobility's Real-Time Tool

Bell Mobility's Real-Time Tool Results
■ 18 percent increase in sales per hour
■ 16 percent increase in total inbound marketing revenue
■ 75 percent decrease in total time to create and deploy a new marketing campaign

users could gain immediate access to the information they needed to make business decisions during the day.[7]

Most people request real-time information without understanding one of the biggest pitfalls associated with real-time information—continual change. Imagine the following scenario: Three managers meet at the end of the day to discuss a business problem. Each manager has gathered information at different times during the day to create a picture of the situation. Each manager's picture may be different because of this time discrepancy. Their views on the business problem may not match since the information they are basing their analysis on is continually changing. This approach may not speed up decision making, and may actually slow it down.

The timeliness of the information required must be evaluated for each business decision. Organizations do not want to find themselves using real-time information to make a bad decision faster.

The Value of Quality Information

Westpac Financial Services (WFS), one of the four major banks in Australia, serves millions of customers from its many core systems, each with its own database. The databases maintain information and provide users with easy access to the stored information. Unfortunately, the company failed to develop information-capturing standards, which led to inconsistent organizational information. For example, one system had a field to capture e-mail addresses while another system did not. Duplicate customer information among the different systems was another major issue, and the company continually found itself sending conflicting or competing messages to customers from different operations of the bank. A customer could also have multiple accounts within the company, one representing a life insurance policy and one representing a credit card. WFS had no way to identify that the two different customer accounts were for the same customer.

WFS had to solve its information quality problems immediately if it was to remain competitive. The company purchased NADIS (Name & Address Data Integrity Software), a software solution that filters customer information, highlighting missing, inaccurate, and redundant information. Customer service ratings are on the rise for WFS now that the company can operate its business with a single and comprehensive view of each one of its customers.[8]

Business decisions are only as good as the quality of the information used to make the decisions. Figure 6.3 reviews five characteristics common to high quality information: accuracy, completeness, consistency, uniqueness, and timeliness.

Characteristics of High Quality Information	
Accuracy	Are all the values correct? For example, is the name spelled correctly? Is the dollar amount recorded properly?
Completeness	Are any of the values missing? For example, is the address complete including street, city, state, and zip code?
Consistency	Is aggregate or summary information in agreement with detailed information? For example, do all total fields equal the true total of the individual fields?
Uniqueness	Is each transaction, entity, and event represented only once in the information? For example, are there any duplicate customers?
Timeliness	Is the information current with respect to the business requirements? For example, is information updated weekly, daily, or hourly?

FIGURE 6.3

The Five Common Characteristics of High Quality Information

Figure 6.4 highlights several issues with low quality information including:

1. The first issue is *missing* information. The customer's first name is missing. (See #1 in Figure 6.4.)

2. The second issue is *incomplete* information since the street address contains only a number and not a street name.

3. The third issue is a probable *duplication* of information since the only slight difference between the two customers is the spelling of the last name. Similar street addresses and phone numbers make this likely.

4. The fourth issue is potential *wrong* information because the customer's phone and fax numbers are the same. Some customers might have the same number for phone and fax line, but the fact that the customer also has this number in the e-mail address field is suspicious.

5. The fifth issue is definitely an example of *inaccurate* information since a phone number is located in the e-mail address field.

6. The sixth issue is *incomplete* information since there is not a valid area code for the phone and fax numbers.

Recognizing how low quality information issues occur will allow organizations to begin to correct them. The four primary sources of low quality information are:

1. Online customers intentionally enter inaccurate information to protect their privacy.

2. Information from different systems have different information entry standards and formats.

3. Call center operators enter abbreviated or erroneous information by accident or to save time.

4. Third party and external information contain inconsistencies, inaccuracies, and errors.[9]

Addressing the above sources of information inaccuracies will significantly improve the quality of organizational information and the value that can be extracted from the information.

FIGURE 6.4

Low Quality Information Example

UNDERSTANDING THE COSTS OF POOR INFORMATION

Using the wrong information can lead to making the wrong decision. Making the wrong decision can cost time, money, and even reputations. Every business decision

1. Missing information (no first name) 2. Incomplete information (no street) 5. Inaccurate information (invalid e-mail)

ID	Last Name	First Name	Street	City	State	Zip	Phone	Fax	E-mail
113	Smith		123 S. Main	Denver	CO	80210	(303) 777-1258	(303) 777-5544	ssmith@aol.com
114	Jones	Jeff	12A	Denver	CO	80224	(303) 666-6868	(303) 666-6868	(303) 666-6868
115	Roberts	Jenny	1244 Colfax	Denver	CO	85231	759-5654	853-6584	jr@msn.com
116	Robert	Jenny	1244 Colfax	Denver	CO	85231	759-5654	853-6584	jr@msn.com

3. Probable duplicate information (similar names, same address, phone number) 4. Potential wrong information (are the phone and fax numbers the same or is this an error?) 6. Incomplete information (missing area codes)

is only as good as the information used to make the decision. Bad information can cause serious business ramifications such as:

- Inability to accurately track customers, which directly affects strategic initiatives such as CRM and SCM.
- Difficulty identifying the organization's most valuable customers.
- Inability to identify selling opportunities and wasted revenue from marketing to nonexisting customers and nondeliverable mail.
- Difficulty tracking revenue because of inaccurate invoices.
- Inability to build strong relationships with customers—which increases their buyer power.

UNDERSTANDING THE BENEFITS OF GOOD INFORMATION

High quality information can significantly improve the chances of making a good decision and directly increase an organization's bottom line. Lillian Vernon Corp., a catalog company, used Web analytics to discover that men preferred to shop at Lillian Vernon's Web site instead of looking through its paper catalog. Based on this information, the company began placing male products more prominently on its Web site and soon realized a 15 percent growth in sales to men.[10]

Another company discovered that Phoenix, Arizona, is not a good place to sell golf clubs, even with its high number of golf courses. An analysis revealed that typical golfers in Phoenix are either tourists or conventioneers. These golfers usually bring their clubs with them while visiting Phoenix. The analysis further revealed that two of the best places to sell golf clubs in the United States are Rochester, New York, and Detroit, Michigan.[11]

There are numerous examples of companies that have used their high quality information to make solid strategic business decisions. High quality information does not automatically guarantee that every decision made is going to be a good one, since people ultimately make decisions. But such information ensures that the basis of the decisions is accurate. The success of the organization depends on appreciating and leveraging the true value of timely and high quality information.

OPENING CASE STUDY QUESTIONS

1. Determine if an entry in Wikipedia is an example of transactional information or analytical information.

2. Describe the impact to Wikipedia if the information contained in its database is of low quality.

3. Review the five common characteristics of high quality information and rank them in order of importance to Wikipedia.

4. Explain how Wikipedia is resolving the issue of poor information.

The Alaska Department of Fish and Game requires high quality information to manage the state's natural resources, specifically to increase fishing yields, while ensuring the future of many species. Using fish counts, the department makes daily decisions as to which districts will be open or closed to commercial fishing. If the department receives poor information from fish counts then either too many fish escape or too many are caught. Allowing too many salmon to swim upstream could deprive fishermen of their livelihoods. Allowing too many to be caught before they swim upstream to spawn could diminish fish populations—yielding devastating effects for years to come.

Because of the incredible size of Alaskan fisheries, the Commercial Fisheries Division's decisions have global impact. Its information is relied upon by individual fishermen who want to know the best places to fish, by corporations around the world that need information on which to base business strategies for seafood processing and marketing, by researchers, and by legislators. With so much at stake, the Division of Commercial Fisheries set out to improve the quality of its information by implementing a system that can gather the information from remote parts of the state and analyze it quickly to determine the daily outcomes.

Originally, the department captured information in spreadsheets that were e-mailed from station to station before being entered into the system. There was no central information set to work from, and more often than not, the information was low quality. Decisions were based on inaccurate and, because of delays in posting, untimely information.

With the implementation of an Oracle database, the department significantly improved the quality and timeliness of its information. Each time a commercial fishing boat within Alaska's jurisdiction unloads at a processing plant, the catch is weighed and details of the catch, such as species caught, weight, and quantity, are recorded on a fish ticket. This information is entered into the new system. To gather fish escapement information from remote areas, field workers positioned in towers scan rivers to visibly count fish. This information is radioed in the next morning.

Information from fish processed the previous day is keyed in by 10:00 a.m., and one hour later, the managers and fisheries across the state have all the information they require to make accurate decisions. They then announce on the radio and on their Web site, which receives more than 3,000 hits on an average day, whether or not fishermen can fish that day.

Fisheries are now managed with timely, centralized, and accurate information. Web pages summarize daily catches for certain areas, like Bristol Bay, whose annual sockeye salmon season, which lasts only a few weeks, is closely monitored by fish processors worldwide. With the enormous quantities of fish caught, salmon fisheries worldwide adjust their production levels based on the results of the annual Bristol Bay sockeye salmon season. This is just one reason why producing fast, quality information is critical to managing Alaska's natural resources.[12]

Questions

1. Describe the difference between transactional and analytical information and determine which type the Alaska Department of Fish and Game is using to make decisions.
2. Explain the importance of quality information for the Alaska Department of Fish and Game.
3. Review the five common characteristics of high quality information and rank them in order of importance for the Alaska Department of Fish and Game.
4. Do the managers at the Alaska Department of Fish and Game have all the information they require to make an accurate decision? Explain the statement "it is never possible to have all of the information required to make the best decision possible."

Storing Organizational Information—Databases

7.1. Define the fundamental concepts of the relational database model.

7.2. Evaluate the advantages of the relational database model.

7.3. Compare relational integrity constraints and business-critical integrity constraints.

7.4. Describe the role and purpose of a database management system.

7.5. List and describe the four components of a database management system.

7.6. Describe the two primary methods for integrating information across multiple databases.

Storing Organizational Information

Austrian Federal Railways maintains its entire railway system—which includes over 5,849 kilometers of track, 5,993 bridges and viaducts, 240 tunnels, and 6,768 crossings—with an Oracle database. Multiple applications run on the database including accounting, order processing, and geographic applications that pinpoint railway equipment locations. The database contains over 80 billion characters of information and supports more than 1,200 users. Many organizations use databases similar to Austrian Federal Railways' to manage large amounts of information.[13]

Relational Database Fundamentals

There are many different models for organizing information in a database, including the hierarchical database, network database, and the most prevalent—the relational database model. Broadly defined, a **database** maintains information about various types of objects (inventory), events (transactions), people (employees), and places (warehouses). In a **hierarchical database model**, information is organized into a tree-like structure that allows repeating information using parent/child relationships, in such a way that it cannot have too many relationships. Hierarchical structures were widely used in the first mainframe database management systems. However, owing to their restrictions, hierarchical structures often cannot be used to relate to structures that exist in the real world. The **network database model** is a flexible way of representing objects and their relationships. Where the hierarchical model structures data as a tree of records, with each record having one parent record and many children, the network model allows each record to have multiple parent and child records, forming a lattice structure. The **relational database model** is a type of database that stores information in the form of logically related two-dimensional tables. This text focuses on the relational database model.

Consider how the Coca-Cola Bottling Company of Egypt (TCCBCE) implemented an inventory-tracking database to improve order accuracy by 27 percent, decrease order response time by 66 percent, and increase sales by 20 percent. With over 7,400 employees, TCCBCE owns and operates 11 bottling plants and 29 sales and distribution centers, making it one of the largest companies in Egypt.

Traditionally, the company sent distribution trucks to each customer's premises to take orders and deliver stock. Many problems were associated with this process including numerous information entry errors, which caused order-fulfillment time to take an average of three days. To remedy the situation, Coca-Cola decided to create presales teams equipped with handheld devices to visit customers and take orders electronically. On returning to the office, the teams synchronized orders with the company's inventory-tracking database to ensure automated processing and rapid dispatch of accurate orders to customers.[14]

ENTITIES, ENTITY CLASSES, AND ATTRIBUTES

Figure 7.1 illustrates the primary concepts of the relational database model—entities, entity classes, attributes, keys, and relationships. An **entity** in the relational database model is a person, place, thing, transaction, or event about which information is stored. An **entity class** (often called a table) in the relational database model is a collection of similar entities. The entity classes of interests in Figure 7.1 are *CUSTOMER, ORDER, ORDER LINE, PRODUCT,* and *DISTRIBUTOR.* Notice that each entity class (the collection of similar entities) is stored in a different two-dimensional table. **Attributes,** also called fields or columns, are characteristics or properties of an entity class. In Figure 7.1 the attributes for *CUSTOMER* include *Customer ID, Customer Name, Contact Name,* and *Phone.* Attributes for *PRODUCT* include *Product ID, Product Description,* and *Price.* Each specific entity in an entity class (e.g., Dave's Sub Shop in the *CUSTOMER* table) occupies one row in its respective table. The columns in the table contain the attributes.

KEYS AND RELATIONSHIPS

To manage and organize various entity classes within the relational database model, developers must identify primary keys and foreign keys and use them to create logical relationships. A **primary key** is a field (or group of fields) that uniquely identifies a given entity in a table. In *CUSTOMER,* the *Customer ID* uniquely identifies each entity (customer) in the table and is the primary key. Primary keys are important because they provide a way of distinguishing each entity in a table.

A **foreign key** in the relational database model is a primary key of one table that appears as an attribute in another table and acts to provide a logical relationship between the two tables. Consider Hawkins Shipping, one of the distributors appearing in the *DISTRIBUTOR* table. Its primary key, *Distributor ID,* is DEN8001. Notice that *Distributor ID* also appears as an attribute in the ORDER table. This establishes the fact that Hawkins Shipping (*Distributor ID* DEN8001) was responsible for delivering orders 34561 and 34562 to the appropriate customer(s). Therefore, *Distributor ID* in the *ORDER* table creates a logical relationship (who shipped what order) between *ORDER* and *DISTRIBUTOR.*

Relational Database Advantages

From a business perspective, database information offers many advantages, including:

- Increased flexibility.
- Increased scalability and performance.
- Reduced information redundancy.
- Increased information integrity (quality).
- Increased information security.

Order Number: 34562

Coca-Cola Bottling Company of Egypt
Sample Sales Order

Customer: Dave's Sub Shop | Date: 8/6/2008

Quantity	Product	Price	Amount
100	Vanilla Coke	$0.55	$55

Distributor Fee $29.50
Order Total $67.95

CUSTOMER

Customer ID	*Customer Name*	*Contact Name*	*Phone*
23	Dave's Sub Shop	David Logan	(555)333-4545
43	Pizza Palace	Debbie Fernandez	(555)345-5432
765	T's Fun Zone	Tom Repicci	(555)565-6655

ORDER

Order ID	*Order Date*	*Customer ID*	*Distributor ID*	*Distributor Fee*	*Total Due*
34561	7/4/2008	23	DEN8001	$22.00	$145.75
34562	8/6/2008	23	DEN8001	$12.95	$67.95
34563	6/5/2008	765	NY9001	$29.50	$249.50

ORDER LINE

Order ID	*Line Item*	*Product ID*	*Quantity*
34561	1	12345AA	75
34561	2	12346BB	50
34561	3	12347CC	100
34562	1	12349EE	300
34563	1	12345AA	100
34563	2	12346BB	100
34563	3	12347CC	50
34563	4	12348DD	50
34563	5	12349EE	100

DISTRIBUTOR

Distributor ID	*Distributor Name*
DEN8001	Hawkins Shipping
CHI3001	ABC Trucking
NY9001	Van Distributors

PRODUCT

Product ID	*Product Description*	*Price*
12345AA	Coca-Cola	$0.55
12346BB	Diet Coke	$0.55
12347CC	Sprite	$0.55
12348DD	Diet Sprite	$0.55
12349EE	Vanilla Coke	$0.55

FIGURE 7.1
Potential Relational Database for Coca-Cola Bottling Company of Egypt (TCCBCE)

INCREASED FLEXIBILITY

Databases tend to mirror business structures, and a good database can handle changes quickly and easily, just as any good business needs to be able to handle changes quickly and easily. Equally important, databases provide flexibility in allowing each user to access the information in whatever way best suits his or her needs. The distinction between logical and physical views is important in understanding flexible database user views. The *physical view* of information deals with the physical storage of information on a storage device such as a hard disk. The *logical view* of information focuses on how users logically access information to meet their particular business needs. This separation of logical and physical views is what allows each user to access database information differently. That is, while a database has only one physical view, it can easily support multiple logical views. In the previous database illustration, for example, users could perform a query to determine which distributors delivered shipments to Pizza Palace last week. At the same time, another person could perform some sort of statistical analysis to determine the frequency at which Sprite and Diet Coke appear on the same order. These represent two very different logical views, but both views use the same physical view.

Consider another example—a mail-order business. One user might want a CRM report presented in alphabetical format, in which case last name should appear before first name. Another user, working with a catalog mailing system, would want customer names appearing as first name and then last name. Both are easily achievable, but different logical views of the same physical information.

INCREASED SCALABILITY AND PERFORMANCE

The official Web site of The American Family Immigration History Center, www .ellisisland.org, generated over 2.5 billion hits in its first year of operation. The site offers easy access to immigration information about people who entered America through the Port of New York and Ellis Island between 1892 and 1924. The database contains over 25 million passenger names correlated to 3.5 million images of ships' manifests.[15]

Only a database could "scale" to handle the massive volumes of information and the large numbers of users required for the successful launch of the Ellis Island Web site. *Scalability* refers to how well a system can adapt to increased demands. *Performance* measures how quickly a system performs a certain process or transaction. Some organizations must be able to support hundreds or thousands of online users including employees, partners, customers, and suppliers, who all want to access and share information. Databases today scale to exceptional levels, allowing all types of users and programs to perform information processing and information-searching tasks.

REDUCED INFORMATION REDUNDANCY

Redundancy is the duplication of information, or storing the same information in multiple places. Redundant information occurs because organizations frequently capture and store the same information in multiple locations. The primary problem with redundant information is that it is often inconsistent, which makes it difficult to determine which values are the most current or most accurate. Not having correct information is confusing and frustrating for employees and disruptive to an organization. One primary goal of a database is to eliminate information redundancy by recording each piece of information in only one place in the database. Eliminating information redundancy saves space, makes performing information updates easier, and improves information quality.

INCREASED INFORMATION INTEGRITY (QUALITY)

Information integrity is a measure of the quality of information. Within a database environment, *integrity constraints* are rules that help ensure the quality of information. Integrity constraints can be defined and built into the database design. The database (more appropriately, the database management system, which is discussed below) ensures that users can never violate these constraints. There are two types of integrity constraints: (1) relational integrity constraints and (2) business-critical integrity constraints.

Relational integrity constraints are rules that enforce basic and fundamental information-based constraints. For example, an operational integrity constraint would not allow someone to create an order for a nonexistent customer, provide a markup percentage that was negative, or order zero pounds of raw materials from a supplier. *Business-critical integrity constraints* enforce business rules vital to an organization's success and often require more insight and knowledge than relational integrity constraints. Consider a supplier of fresh produce to large grocery chains such as Kroger. The supplier might implement a business-critical integrity constraint stating that no product returns are accepted after 15 days past delivery. That would make sense because of the chance of spoilage of the produce. These types of integrity constraints tend to mirror the very rules by which an organization achieves success.

The specification and enforcement of integrity constraints produce higher quality information that will provide better support for business decisions. Organizations that establish specific procedures for developing integrity constraints typically see a decline in information error rates and an increase in the use of organizational information.

INCREASED INFORMATION SECURITY

Information is an organizational asset. Like any asset, the organization must protect its information from unauthorized users or misuse. As systems become increasingly complex and more available over the Internet, security becomes an even bigger issue. Databases offer many security features including passwords, access levels, and access controls. Passwords provide authentication of the user who is gaining access to the system. Access levels determine who has access to the different types of information, and access controls determine what type of access they have to the information. For example, customer service representatives might need read-only access to customer order information so they can answer customer order inquiries; they might not have or need the authority to change or delete order information. Managers might require access to employee files, but they should have access only to their own employees' files, not the employee files for the entire company. Various security features of databases can ensure that individuals have only certain types of access to certain types of information.

Databases can increase personal security as well as information security. Since 1995, the Chicago Police Department (CPD) has relied on a crime-fighting system called Citizen and Law Enforcement Analysis and Reporting (CLEAR). CLEAR electronically streamlines the way detectives enter and access critical information to help them solve crimes, analyze crime patterns, and ultimately promote security in a proactive manner. The CPD enters 650,000 new criminal cases and 500,000 new arrests into CLEAR each year.[16]

Database Management Systems

Ford's European plant manufactures more than 5,000 vehicles a day and sells them in over 100 countries worldwide. Every component of every model must conform to

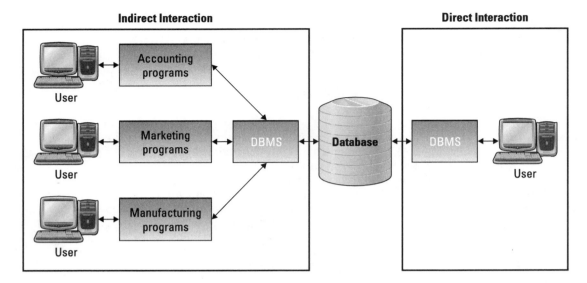

Indirect Interaction   **Direct Interaction**

Accounting programs

User

Marketing programs

DBMS

Database

DBMS

User

User

Manufacturing programs

User

FIGURE 7.2

Interacting Directly and Indirectly with a Database through a DBMS

complex European standards, including passenger safety standards and pedestrian and environmental protection standards. These standards govern each stage of Ford's manufacturing process from design to final production. The company needs to obtain many thousands of different approvals each year to comply with the standards. Over-looking just one means the company cannot sell the finished vehicle, which brings the production line to a standstill and could potentially cost Ford up to 1 million euros per day. Ford built the Homologation Timing System (HTS), based on a relational data-base, to help it track and analyze these standards. The reliability and high perform-ance of the HTS have helped Ford substantially reduce its compliance risk.[17]

A database management system is used to access information from a database. A ***database management system (DBMS)*** is software through which users and ap-plication programs interact with a database. The user sends requests to the DBMS and the DBMS performs the actual manipulation of the information in the data-base. There are two primary ways that users can interact with a DBMS: (1) directly and (2) indirectly, as displayed in Figure 7.2. In either case, users access the DBMS and the DBMS accesses the database.

A DBMS is composed of four primary components including data definition, data manipulation, application generation, and data administration (see Figure 7.3).

DATA DEFINITION COMPONENT

The ***data definition component*** of a DBMS helps create and maintain the data dic-tionary and the structure of the database. The ***data dictionary*** of a database is a file

FIGURE 7.3

Four Components of a Database Management System

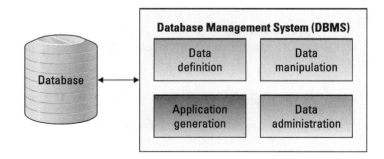

Database Management System (DBMS)

Database

| Data definition | Data manipulation |
| Application generation | Data administration |

FIGURE 7.4

Logical Field Properties in
a Database

Logical Property	Example
Field name	Name of field such as *Customer ID* or *Product ID*
Type	Alphanumeric, numeric, date, time, currency, etc.
Form	Each phone number must have the area code (XXX) XXX-XXXX
Default value	The default value for area code is (303)
Validation rule	A discount cannot exceed 100 percent
Entry rule	The field must have a valid entry—no blanks are allowed
Duplicate rule	Duplicate information is not allowed

that stores definitions of information types, identifies the primary and foreign keys, and maintains the relationships among the tables. The data dictionary essentially defines the logical properties of the information that the database contains. See Figure 7.4 for typical logical properties of information.

All the logical properties shown in Figure 7.4 are important, and they vary depending on the type of information. For example, a typical address field might have a *Type* logical property of alphanumeric, meaning that the field can accept numbers, letters, and special characters. This would be an example of a relational integrity constraint. The validation rule requiring that a discount cannot exceed 100 percent is an example of a business-critical integrity constraint.

The data dictionary is an important part of the DBMS because users can consult the dictionary to determine the different types of database information. The data dictionary also supplies users with vital information when creating reports such as column names and information formats.

DATA MANIPULATION COMPONENT

Of the four DBMS components, users probably spend the most time working with data manipulation. The ***data manipulation component*** of a DBMS allows users to create, read, update, and delete information in a database. A DBMS contains a variety of data manipulation tools including views, report generators, query-by-example tools, and structured query language.

A ***view*** allows users to see the contents of a database, make any required changes, perform simple sorting, and query the database to find the location of specific information. ***Report generators*** allow users to define formats for reports along with what information they want to see in the report (see Figure 7.5).

Most often, users will create queries to access information in a database. A query is simply a question, such as "How many customers live in California?" ***Query-by-example (QBE) tools*** allow users to graphically design the answers to specific questions. Figure 7.6 displays Microsoft's Access QBE tool with a query asking which customers have ordered which products. Using a QBE, a user can design this query by asking the DBMS to pull all of the product descriptions for each order for every customer. Figure 7.7 displays the results to this query.

Structured query language (SQL) is a standardized fourth-generation query language found in most DBMSs. SQL performs the same function as QBE, except that the user must type statements instead of pointing, clicking, and dragging in a graphical environment. The basic form of an SQL statement is SELECT . . . . . . FROM . . . . . . WHERE. Figure 7.8 displays the corresponding SQL statement required to perform the query from Figure 7.6. To write queries in SQL, users typically need some formal training and a solid technical background. Fortunately, QBE tools and their drag-and-drop design features allow nonprogrammers to quickly and easily design complex queries without knowing SQL.

FIGURE 7.5

Sample Report Using
Microsoft Access

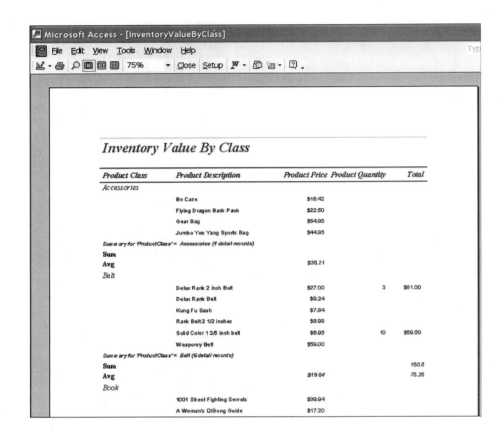

APPLICATION GENERATION AND DATA ADMINISTRATION COMPONENTS

For the most part, users will be focusing on data manipulation tools to build views, reports, and queries. IT specialists primarily use the application generation and data administration components. Even though most users will probably not be using these components, it is still important that they understand what they are and the functions they support.

The *application generation component* includes tools for creating visually appealing and easy-to-use applications. IT specialists use application generation components to build programs for users to enter and manipulate information with an interface specific to their application needs. Consider a manager involved in the management of an organization's supply chain. Using the application generation component, an IT specialist could build an SCM application software tool for the manager that would contain various menu options including add a supplier, order from a supplier, check the status of an order, and so on. This application would be easier and more intuitive for the manager to use on a consistent basis than requiring the manager to use views, report generators, and QBE tools.

The *data administration component* provides tools for managing the overall database environment by providing facilities for backup, recovery, security, and performance. Again, IT specialists directly interact with the data administration component. There are several strategic-level IT positions in most organizations— CIO (chief information officer), CTO (chief technology officer), CSO (chief security officer), and CPO (chief privacy officer). People in these positions oversee the use of the data administration component. For example, the chief privacy officer is responsible for ensuring the ethical and legal use of information. Therefore, he or she

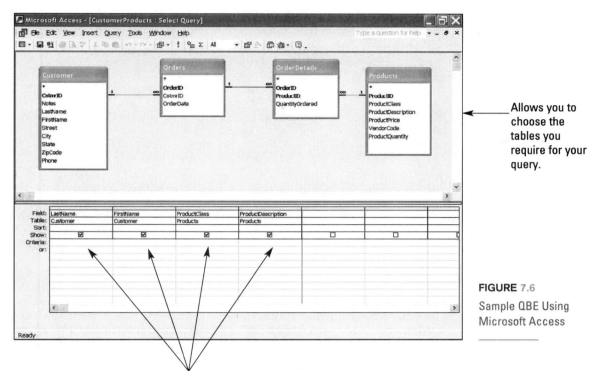

Allows you to choose the tables you require for your query.

FIGURE 7.6

Sample QBE Using Microsoft Access

This is where you define which fields you want to see for the results of your query. This query asks for the customer's last name and first name, along with the customer's corresponding product class and product description from the customer's orders.

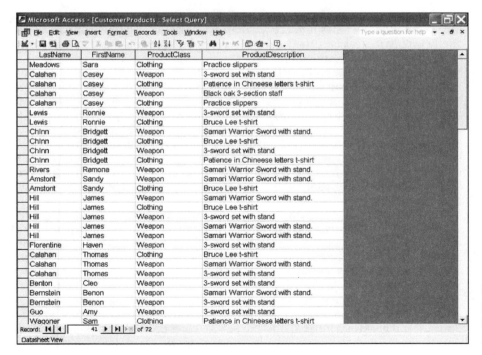

FIGURE 7.7

Results of the QBE Query in Figure 7.6

```
SELECT  Customer.LastName, Customer.FirstName,
        Products.ProductClass, Products.ProductDescription
FROM    Products
        INNER JOIN ((Customer INNER JOIN Orders ON
        (Customer.CstmrID = Orders.CstmrID) AND (Customer.CstmrID
        = Orders.CstmrID))
        INNER JOIN OrderDetails ON Orders.OrderID =
        OrderDetails.OrderID) ON Products.Product ID =
        OrderDetails.ProductID;
```

FIGURE 7.8

SQL Version of the QBE
Query in Figure 7.6

would direct the use of the security features of the data administration component, implement policies and procedures concerning who has access to different types of information, and control what functions they can perform on that information (read-only, update, delete). The chief technology officer, responsible for ensuring the efficiency of IT systems, would direct the use of the backup, recovery, and performance features of the data administration component.

The focus this far has been on a single database. However, almost all organizations maintain multiple systems—for billing, order entry, order fulfillment, etc.—and hence have multiple databases, one to support each system. The number of databases in an organization can range from just a few to several hundred. Issues of redundancy and consistency become prevalent and problematic. Having multiple databases, some containing the same information, adds another layer of complexity to managing information and ensuring its quality in an organization.

Integrating Information among Multiple Databases

Until the 1990s, each department in the UK's Ministry of Defense (MOD) and Army headquarters had its own systems, each system had its own database, and sharing information among the departments was difficult. Manually inputting the same information multiple times into the different systems was also time consuming and inefficient. In many cases, management could not even compile the information it required to answer questions and make decisions.

The Army solved the problem by integrating its systems, or building connections between its many databases. These integrations allow the Army's multiple systems to automatically communicate by passing information between the databases, eliminating the need for manual information entry into multiple systems because after entering the information once, the integrations sent the information immediately to all other databases. The integrations not only enable the different departments to share information, but have also dramatically increased the quality of the information. The Army can now generate reports detailing its state of readiness and other vital issues, nearly impossible tasks before building the integrations among the separate systems.[18]

An *integration* allows separate systems to communicate directly with each other. Similar to the UK's Army, an organization will probably maintain multiple systems, with each system having its own database. Without integrations, an organization will (1) spend considerable time entering the same information in multiple systems and (2) suffer from the low quality and inconsistency typically embedded in redundant information. While most integrations do not completely eliminate redundant information, they can ensure the consistency of it across multiple systems.

An organization can choose from two integration methods. The first is to create forward and backward integrations that link together processes (and their underlying databases) in the value chain. A *forward integration* takes information entered

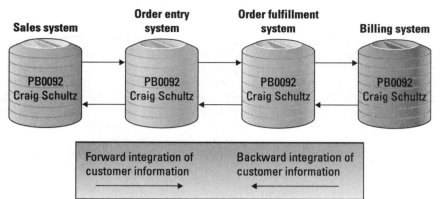

Sales system

Order entry
system

Order fulfillment
system

Billing system

PB0092
Craig Schultz

PB0092
Craig Schultz

PB0092
Craig Schultz

PB0092
Craig Schultz

Forward integration of
customer information

Backward integration of
customer information

into a given system and sends it automatically to all downstream systems and processes. A *backward integration* takes information entered into a given system and sends it automatically to all upstream systems and processes.

Figure 7.9 demonstrates how this method works across the systems or processes of sales, order entry, order fulfillment, and billing. In the order entry system, for example, an employee can update the information for a customer. That information, via the integrations, would be sent upstream to the sales system and downstream to the order fulfillment and billing systems.

Ideally, an organization wants to build both forward and backward integrations, which provide the flexibility to create, update, and delete information in any of the systems. However, integrations are expensive and difficult to build and maintain and most organizations build only forward integrations (sales through billing in Figure 7.9). Building only forward integrations implies that a change in the initial system (sales) will result in changes occurring in all the other systems. Integration of information is not possible for any changes occurring outside the initial system, which again can result in inconsistent organizational information. To address this issue, organizations can enforce business rules that all systems, other than the initial system, have read-only access to the integrated information. This will require

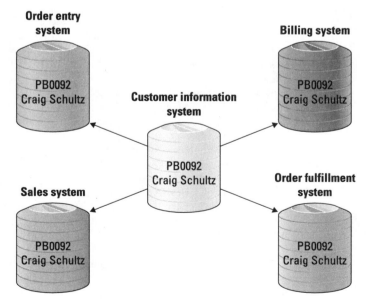

FIGURE 7.10

Integrating Customer
Information among
Databases

Order entry
system

Billing system

PB0092
Craig Schultz

PB0092
Craig Schultz

Customer information
system

PB0092
Craig Schultz

Sales system

Order fulfillment
system

PB0092
Craig Schultz

PB0092
Craig Schultz

users to change information in the initial system only, which will always trigger the integration and ensure that organizational information does not get out of sync.

The second integration method builds a central repository for a particular type of information. Figure 7.10 provides an example of customer information integrated using this method across four different systems in an organization. Users can create, update, and delete customer information only in the central customer information database. As users perform these tasks on the central customer information database, integrations automatically send the new and/or updated customer information to the other systems. The other systems limit users to read-only access of the customer information stored in them. Again, this method does not eliminate redundancy—but it does ensure consistency of the information among multiple systems.

OPENING CASE STUDY QUESTIONS

1. Identify the different types of entity classes that might be stored in Wikipedia's database.

2. Explain why database technology is so important to Wikipedia's business model.

3. Explain the difference between logical and physical views and why logical views are important to Wikipedia's customers.

Chapter Seven Case: Hotcourses Increases Revenues by 60 Percent

Hotcourses, one of the hottest new e-businesses in London, offers a comprehensive online educational marketplace. One of the biggest online databases of professional, higher, and further education courses in the United Kingdom, Hotcourses receives more than 5,000 unique visits per day on its Web site. The site attracted 7,500 course providers during its first 12 months, including every university in the United Kingdom, and is growing at a rate of 600 percent or 2,000 new courses each week.

The company was launched by the United Kingdom's leading publisher of retail guides to courses and colleges in June 2000. Hotcourses enables people to find the right course, at the right price, in the location they choose to study, and it estimated annual revenues for 2003 between $101 million and $500 million.

The company's IT goals are to provide the scalability and performance required to deploy Web applications quickly, manage content dynamically, and support tens of thousands of users concurrently. These goals are being accomplished through Hotcourses' flexible IT infrastructure, which is based upon Oracle databases. "Leveraging the Internet to put our business online and extend the service on a national basis was always part of our growth strategy," said Jeremy Hunt, joint chief executive at Hotcourses. "Providing an online portal and Web-enabled fulfillment systems would extend our reach and drive demand, both from course providers and students."

Resources available through Hotcourses are free to users, who can select and book their chosen course online. The site allows colleges to upload and amend information themselves and list their courses free of charge, but a fee is charged the facility to allow prospective students to e-mail them with further inquiries. Hotcourses also derives revenue from value-added services to course providers such as extended profiles, banners, links to Web sites, and priorities in search returns. The search engine is based on Oracle InterMedia, a core feature of Oracle database, which provides an integrated data management environment enabling users to search for, analyze, and profile information.

The business intelligence integrated with the database enables Hotcourses to assess key factors such as the number of hits and regularity of visits. "The Internet and Oracle's e-business technology have transformed our business from a London-focused directory publisher to a countrywide service, advertising and selling thousands of courses from a huge range of providers," said Hunt.

The number of courses listed on Hotcourses rose from 35,000 to over 600,000 at the end of 2003. Since then, Hotcourses has begun to extend the service by creating databases in Chinese, Japanese, and Portuguese to attract foreign students who wish to study in Britain. The company also plans to create an online, interactive directory for students and course providers, implement robust, scalable platforms to support rapid expansion, and capture key information and analyze it to provide real-time business intelligence.[19]

Questions

1. Identify the different types of entity classes and attributes potentially maintained in the Hotcourses database.
2. Describe the two different ways that employees at Hotcourses might access the information in their databases.
3. Create two questions that a manager at Hotcourses could turn into queries and run against its database to discover business intelligence.
4. List several useful reports management would like to see based on data in the database.
5. Would different entity types be required for different countries?

<< TECHNOLOGY PLUG-IN POINTERS

Review **Technology Plug-In T5 "Designing Database Applications"** for an overview of the steps to follow while designing a small database application, including defining entity classes, identifying primary and foreign keys, and completing the first three steps of normalization (up through and including eliminating many-to-many relationships).

Review **Technology Plug-In T6 "Basic Skills and Tools Using Access"** for a comprehensive tutorial on how to create tables and define relationships.

CHAPTER 8

Accessing Organizational Information—Data Warehouse

LEARNING OUTCOMES

8.1. Describe the roles and purposes of data warehouses and data marts in an organization.

8.2. Compare the multidimensional nature of data warehouses (and data marts) with the two-dimensional nature of databases.

8.3. Identify the importance of ensuring the cleanliness of information throughout an organization.

8.4. Explain the relationship between business intelligence and a data warehouse.

Accessing Organizational Information

Applebee's Neighborhood Grill & Bar posts annual sales in excess of $3.2 billion and is actively using information from its data warehouse to increase sales and cut costs. The company gathers daily information for the previous day's sales into its data warehouse from 1,500 restaurants located in 49 states and seven countries. Understanding regional preferences, such as patrons in Texas preferring steaks more than patrons in New England, allows the company to meet its corporate strategy of being a neighborhood grill appealing to local tastes. The company has found tremendous value in its data warehouse by being able to make business decisions about customers' regional needs. The company also uses data warehouse information to perform the following:

- Base its labor budgets on actual number of guests served per hour.
- Develop promotional sale item analysis to help avoid losses from overstocking or understocking inventory.
- Determine theoretical and actual costs of food and the use of ingredients.[20]

History of Data Warehousing

In the 1990s as organizations began to need more timely information about their business, they found that traditional operational information systems were too cumbersome to provide relevant data efficiently and quickly. Operational systems typically include accounting, order entry, customer service, and sales and are not appropriate for business analysis for the following reasons:

- Information from other operational applications is not included.
- Operational systems are not integrated, or not available in one place.
- Operational information is mainly current—does not include the history that is required to make good decisions.
- Operational information frequently has quality issues (errors)— the information needs to be cleansed.

- Without information history, it is difficult to tell how and why things change over time.
- Operational systems are not designed for analysis and decision support.

During the latter half of the 20th century, the numbers and types of databases increased. Many large businesses found themselves with information scattered across multiple platforms and variations of technology, making it almost impossible for any one individual to use information from multiple sources. Completing reporting requests across operational systems could take days or weeks using antiquated reporting tools that were designed more or less to execute the business rather than run the business. From this idea, the data warehouse was born as a place where relevant information could be held for completing strategic reports for management. The key here is the word *strategic* as most executives were less concerned with the day-to-day operations than they were with a more overall look at the model and business functions.

A key idea within data warehousing is to take data from multiple platforms/technologies (as varied as spreadsheets, databases, and word files) and place them in a common location that uses a common querying tool. In this way operational databases could be held on whatever system was most efficient for the operational business, while the reporting/strategic information could be held in a common location using a common language. Data warehouses take this a step further by giving the information itself commonality by defining what each term means and keeping it standard. An example of this would be gender, which can be referred to in many ways (Male, Female, M/F, 1/0), but should be standardized on a data warehouse with one common way of referring to each sex (M/F).

This design makes decision support more readily available without affecting day-to-day operations. One aspect of a data warehouse that should be stressed is that it is *not* a location for *all* a business's information, but rather a location for information that is interesting, or information that will assist decision makers in making strategic decisions relative to the organization's overall mission.

Data warehousing is about extending the transformation of data into information. Data warehouses offer strategic level, external, integrated, and historical information so businesses can make projections, identify trends, and decide key business issues. The data warehouse collects and stores integrated sets of historical information from multiple operational systems and feeds them to one or more data marts. It may also provide end-user access to support enterprisewide views of information.

Data Warehouse Fundamentals

A *data warehouse* is a logical collection of information—gathered from many different operational databases—that supports business analysis activities and decision-making tasks. The primary purpose of a data warehouse is to aggregate information throughout an organization into a single repository in such a way that employees can make decisions and undertake business analysis activities. Therefore, while databases store the details of all transactions (for instance, the sale of a product) and events (hiring a new employee), data warehouses store that same information but in an aggregated form more suited to supporting decision-making tasks. Aggregation, in this instance, can include totals, counts, averages, and the like. Because of this sort of aggregation, data warehouses support only analytical processing.

The data warehouse modeled in Figure 8.1 compiles information from internal databases or transactional/operational databases and external databases through *extraction, transformation, and loading (ETL),* which is a process that extracts information from internal and external databases, transforms the information using a common set of enterprise definitions, and loads the information into a data warehouse. The data warehouse then sends subsets of the information to data marts. A *data mart* contains a subset of data warehouse information. To distinguish between

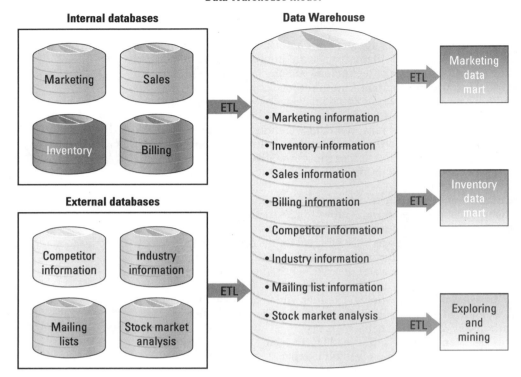

Data Warehouse Model

Internal databases

Marketing Sales

Inventory Billing

External databases

Competitor information Industry information

Mailing lists Stock market analysis

ETL

Data Warehouse

- Marketing information
- Inventory information
- Sales information
- Billing information
- Competitor information
- Industry information
- Mailing list information
- Stock market analysis

ETL → Marketing data mart

ETL → Inventory data mart

ETL → Exploring and mining

FIGURE 8.1

Model of a Typical Data Warehouse

data warehouses and data marts, think of data warehouses as having a more organizational focus and data marts as having focused information subsets particular to the needs of a given business unit such as finance or production and operations.

Lands' End created an organizationwide data warehouse so all its employees could access organizational information. Lands' End soon found out that there could be "too much of a good thing" because many of its employees would not use the data warehouse because it was simply too big, too complicated, and had too much irrelevant information. Lands' End knew there was valuable information in its data warehouse, and it had to find a way for its employees to easily access the information. Data marts were the perfect solution to the company's information overload problem. Once the employees began using the data marts, they were ecstatic at the wealth of information. Data marts were a huge success for Lands' End.[21]

MULTIDIMENSIONAL ANALYSIS AND DATA MINING

A relational database contains information in a series of two-dimensional tables. In a data warehouse and data mart, information is multidimensional, meaning it contains layers of columns and rows. For this reason, most data warehouses and data marts are *multidimensional databases*. A *dimension* is a particular attribute of information. Each layer in a data warehouse or data mart represents information according to an additional dimension. A **cube** is the common term for the representation of multidimensional information. Figure 8.2 displays a cube (cube *a*) that represents store information (the layers), product information (the rows), and promotion information (the columns).

Once a cube of information is created, users can begin to slice and dice the cube to drill down into the information. The second cube (cube *b*) in Figure 8.2 displays a slice representing promotion II information for all products, at all stores. The third

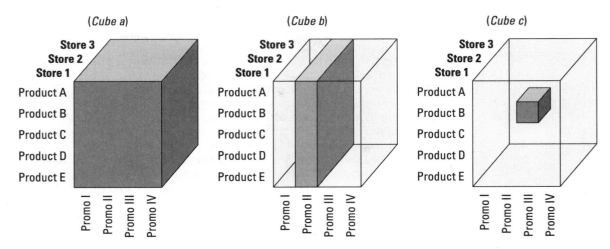

FIGURE 8.2

A Cube of Information for Performing a Multidimensional Analysis on Three Different Stores, for Five Different Products, and Four Different Promotions

cube (cube *c*) in Figure 8.2 displays only information for promotion III, product B, at store 2. By using multidimensional analysis, users can analyze information in a number of different ways and with any number of different dimensions. For example, users might want to add dimensions of information to a current analysis including product category, region, and even forecasted versus actual weather. The true value of a data warehouse is its ability to provide multidimensional analysis that allows users to gain insights into their information.

Data warehouses and data marts are ideal for off-loading some of the querying against a database. For example, querying a database to obtain an average of sales for product B at store 2 while promotion III is under way might create a considerable processing burden for a database, essentially slowing down the time it takes another person to enter a new sale into the same database. If an organization performs numerous queries against a database (or multiple databases), aggregating that information into a data warehouse could be beneficial.

Data mining is the process of analyzing data to extract information not offered by the raw data alone. For example, Ruf Strategic Solutions helps organizations employ statistical approaches within a large data warehouse to identify customer segments that display common traits. Marketers can then target these segments with specially designed products and promotions.[22]

Data mining can also begin at a summary information level (coarse granularity) and progress through increasing levels of detail (drilling down), or the reverse (drilling up). To perform data mining, users need data-mining tools. ***Data-mining tools*** use a variety of techniques to find patterns and relationships in large volumes of information and infer rules from them that predict future behavior and guide decision making. Data-mining tools for data warehouses and data marts include query tools, reporting tools, multidimensional analysis tools, statistical tools, and intelligent agents.

Sega of America, one of the largest publishers of video games, uses a data warehouse and statistical tools to distribute its annual advertising budget of more than $50 million. With its data warehouse, product line specialists and marketing strategists "drill" into trends of each retail store chain. Their goal is to find buying trends that help them determine which advertising strategies are working best and how to reallocate advertising resources by media, territory, and time.[23]

INFORMATION CLEANSING OR SCRUBBING

It should come as no surprise that maintaining quality information in a data warehouse or data mart is extremely important. The Data Warehousing Institute estimates that low quality information costs U.S. businesses $600 billion annually. That number may seem high, but it is not. If an organization is using a data warehouse or data mart to allocate dollars across advertising strategies (such as in the case of Sega of America), low quality information will definitely have a negative impact on its ability to make the right decision.[24]

To increase the quality of organizational information and thus the effectiveness of decision making, businesses must formulate a strategy to keep information clean. This is the concept of information cleansing or scrubbing. ***Information cleansing or scrubbing*** is a process that weeds out and fixes or discards inconsistent, incorrect, or incomplete information.

Specialized software tools exist that use sophisticated algorithms to parse, standardize, correct, match, and consolidate data warehouse information. This is vitally important because data warehouses often contain information from several different databases, some of which can be external to the organization. In a data warehouse, information cleansing occurs first during the ETL process and second on the information once it is in the data warehouse. Companies can choose information cleansing software from several different vendors including Oracle, SAS, Ascential Software, and Group 1 Software. Ideally, scrubbed information is error free and consistent.

Dr Pepper/Seven Up, Inc., was able to integrate its myriad databases in a data warehouse (and subsequently data marts) in less than two months, giving the company access to consolidated, clean information. Approximately 600 people in the company regularly use the data marts to analyze and track beverage sales across multiple dimensions, including various distribution routes such as bottle/can sales, fountain food-service sales, premier distributor sales, and chain and national accounts. The company is now performing in-depth analysis of up-to-date sales information that is clean and error free.[25]

Looking at customer information highlights why information cleansing is necessary. Customer information exists in several operational systems. In each system all details of this customer information could change from the customer ID to contact information (see Figure 8.3). Determining which contact information is accurate and correct for this customer depends on the business process that is being executed.

Figure 8.4 displays a customer name entered differently in multiple operational systems. Information cleansing allows an organization to fix these types of inconsistencies and cleans the information in the data warehouse. Figure 8.5 displays the typical events that occur during information cleansing.

Achieving perfect information is almost impossible. The more complete and accurate an organization wants its information to be, the more it costs (see Figure 8.6). The trade-off for perfect information lies in accuracy versus completeness. Accurate information means it is correct, while complete information means there are no

FIGURE 8.3

Contact Information in Operational Systems

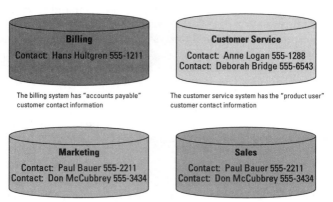

Billing
Contact: Hans Hultgren 555-1211

The billing system has "accounts payable" customer contact information

Customer Service
Contact: Anne Logan 555-1288
Contact: Deborah Bridge 555-6543

The customer service system has the "product user" customer contact information

Marketing
Contact: Paul Bauer 555-2211
Contact: Don McCubbrey 555-3434

Sales
Contact: Paul Bauer 555-2211
Contact: Don McCubbrey 555-3434

The marketing and sales system has "decision maker" customer contact information.

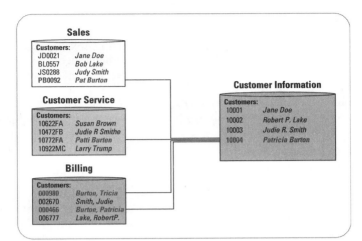

FIGURE 8.4

Standardizing Customer
Name from Operational
Systems

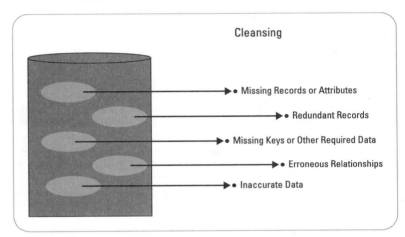

FIGURE 8.5

Information Cleansing
Activities

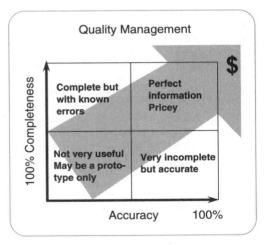

FIGURE 8.6

Accurate and Complete
Information

blanks. A birth date of 2/31/10 is an example of complete but inaccurate information (February 31 does not exist). An address containing Denver, Colorado, without a ZIP code is an example of incomplete information that is accurate. For their information, most organizations determine a percentage high enough to make good decisions at a reasonable cost, such as 85 percent accurate and 65 percent complete.

Business Intelligence

Business intelligence (BI) is information that people use to support their decision-making efforts. An early reference to business intelligence occurs in Sun Tzu's book titled *The Art of War*. Sun Tzu claims that to succeed in war, one should have full knowledge of one's own strengths and weaknesses and full knowledge of the enemy's strengths and weaknesses. Lack of either one might result in defeat. A certain school of thought draws parallels between the challenges in business and those of war, specifically:

- Collecting information.
- Discerning patterns and meaning in the information.
- Responding to the resultant information.

Before the start of the information age in the late 20th century, businesses sometimes collected information from nonautomated sources. Businesses then lacked the computing resources to properly analyze the information and often made commercial decisions based primarily on intuition.

As businesses started automating more and more systems, more and more information became available. However, collection remained a challenge due to a lack of infrastructure for information exchange or to incompatibilities between systems. Reports sometimes took months to generate. Such reports allowed informed long-term strategic decision making. However, short-term tactical decision making continued to rely on intuition.

In modern businesses, increasing standards, automation, and technologies have led to vast amounts of available information. Data warehouse technologies have set up repositories to store this information. Improved ETL have increased the speedy collecting of information. Business intelligence has now become the art of sifting through large amounts of data, extracting information, and turning that information into actionable knowledge.

ENABLING BUSINESS INTELLIGENCE

Competitive organizations accumulate business intelligence to gain sustainable competitive advantage, and they may regard such intelligence as a valuable core competence in some instances. The principal BI enablers are technology, people, and corporate culture.

Technology

Even the smallest company with BI software can do sophisticated analyses today that were unavailable to the largest organizations a generation ago. The largest companies today can create enterprisewide BI systems that compute and monitor metrics on virtually every variable important for managing the company. How is this possible? The answer is technology—the most significant enabler of business intelligence.

People

Understanding the role of people in BI allows organizations to systematically create insight and turn these insights into actions. Organizations can improve their decision making by having the right people making the decisions. This usually means a manager who is in the field and close to the customer rather than an analyst rich in data but poor in experience. In recent years "business intelligence for the masses" has been an important trend, and many organizations have made great strides in providing sophisticated yet simple analytical tools and information to a much larger user population than previously possible.

Culture

A key responsibility of executives is to shape and manage corporate culture. The extent to which the BI attitude flourishes in an organization depends in large part on the organization's culture. Perhaps the most important step an organization can take to encourage BI is to measure the performance of the organization against a set of key indicators. The actions of publishing what the organization thinks are the most important indicators, measuring these indicators, and analyzing the results to guide improvement display a strong commitment to BI throughout the organization.

OPENING CASE STUDY QUESTIONS

1. Determine how Wikipedia could use a data warehouse to improve its business operations.

2. Explain why Wikipedia must cleanse or scrub the information in its data warehouse.

3. Explain how a company could use information from Wikipedia to gain business intelligence.

Chapter Eight Case: Mining the Data Warehouse

According to a Merrill Lynch survey in 2006, business intelligence software and data-mining tools were at the top of CIOs' technology spending list. Following are a few examples of how companies are using data warehousing and data-mining tools to gain valuable business intelligence.

Ben & Jerry's

These days, when we all scream for ice cream, Ben & Jerry's cuts through the din by using integrated query, reporting, and online analytical processing technology from BI software vendor Business Objects. Through an Oracle database and with BI from Business Objects, Ben & Jerry's tracks the ingredients and life of each pint. If a consumer calls in with a complaint, the consumer affairs staff matches the pint with which supplier's milk, eggs, cherries, or whatever did not meet the organization's near-obsession with quality.

The BI tools let Ben & Jerry's officials access, analyze, and act on customer information collected by the sales, finance, purchasing, and quality-assurance departments. The company can determine what milk customers prefer in the making of the ice cream. The technology helped Ben & Jerry's track more than 12,500 consumer contacts in 2005. The information ranged from comments about the ingredients used in ice cream to queries about social causes supported by the company.

California Pizza Kitchen

California Pizza Kitchen (CPK) is a leading casual dining chain in the premium pizza segment with a recognized consumer brand and an established, loyal customer base. Founded in 1985, there are currently more than 130 full-service restaurants in over 26 states, the District of Columbia, and five foreign countries.

Before implementing its BI tool, Cognos, CPK used spreadsheets to plan and track its financial statements and line items. The finance team had difficulty managing the volumes of data, complex calculations, and constant changes to the spreadsheets. It took several weeks of two people working full time to obtain one version of the financial statements and future forecast. In addition, the team was limited by the software's inability to link cells and calculations across multiple spreadsheets, so updating other areas of corporate records became a time-consuming task. With Cognos, quarterly forecasting cycles have been reduced from eight days to two days. The finance team can now spend more time reviewing the results rather than collecting and entering the data.

Noodles & Company

Noodles & Company has more than 70 restaurants throughout Colorado, Illinois, Maryland, Michigan, Minnesota, Texas, Utah, Virginia, and Wisconsin. The company recently purchased Cognos BI tools to help implement reporting standards and communicate real-time operational information to field management throughout the United States.

Before implementing the first phase of the Cognos solution, IT and finance professionals spent days compiling report requests from numerous departments including sales and marketing, human resources, and real estate. Since completing phase one, operational Cognos reports are being accessed on a daily basis through the Noodles & Company Web site. This provides users with a single, 360-degree view of the business and consistent reporting throughout the enterprise.

Noodles & Company users benefit from the flexible query and reporting capabilities, allowing them to see patterns in the data to leverage new business opportunities. Cognos tools can pull information directly from a broad array of relational, operational, and other systems.[26]

Questions

1. Explain how Ben & Jerry's is using business intelligence tools to remain successful and competitive in a saturated market.
2. Identify why information cleansing is critical to California Pizza Kitchen's business intelligence tool's success.
3. Illustrate why 100 percent accurate and complete information is impossible for Noodles & Company to obtain.
4. Describe how each of the companies above is using BI to gain a competitive advantage.

TECHNOLOGY PLUG-IN POINTERS >>

Review **Technology Plug-In T3 "Problem Solving Using Excel"** for a comprehensive tutorial on how to create and sort a list in a workbook, use filters, organize and analyze entries by using subtotals, and create summary information by using pivot tables and pivot charts.

Review **Technology Plug-In T7 "Problem Solving Using Access"** for a comprehensive tutorial on using the query-by-example tool to select data from a table or tables, as well as to sort and filter data.

CHAPTER 17

Building Software to Support an Agile Organization

17.1. Identify the business benefits associated with successful software development.

17.2. Describe the seven phases of the systems development life cycle.

17.3. Summarize the different software development methodologies.

17.4. Explain project management and its three interdependent variables.

Systems Development

Nike's SCM system failure, which spun out of control to the tune of $400 million, is legendary. Nike blamed the system failure on its SCM vendor i2 Technologies. Nike stated that i2 Technologies' demand and supply planning module created serious inventory problems. The i2 deployment, part of a multimillion-dollar e-business upgrade, caused Nike CEO Philip Knight to famously say, "This is what we get for our $400 million?" The SCM vendor saw its stock plummet with the Nike disaster, along with its reputation. I2's chief marketing officer, Katrina Roche, asserted that Nike failed to use the vendor's implementation methodology and templates, which contributed to the problem.[2]

Organizations must learn how to build and implement disruptive technologies, such as software for wireless devices, to remain competitive. Software that is built correctly can support agile organizations and can transform as the organization and its business transforms. Software that effectively meets employee needs will help an organization become more productive and enhance decision making. Software that does not meet employee needs may have a damaging effect on productivity and can even cause a business to fail. Employee involvement along with the right implementation methodology when developing software is critical to the success of an organization.

Software development problems often lead to high-profile disasters. Hershey Food's glitch in its ERP implementation made the front page of *The Wall Street Journal* and cost the company millions. Hershey said computer problems with its SAP software system created a backlog of orders, causing slower deliveries, and resulting in lower earnings. Statistics released in 2006 by the National Research Council show that U.S. companies spent $250 billion in 2005 to repair damage caused by software defects.[3]

If software does not work, the organization will not work. Traditional business risk models typically ignored software development, largely because most organizations considered the impact from software and software development on the business to be minor. In the digital age, however, software success, or failure, can lead directly to business success, or failure. Almost every large organization in the world relies on software, either to drive its business operations or to make its products work. As organizations' reliance on software grows, so do the business-related consequences of software successes and failures including:

- **Increase or decrease revenues**—Organizations have the ability to directly increase profits by implementing successful IT systems. Organizations can also lose millions when software fails or key information is stolen or compromised.

  Nike's poorly designed supply chain management software delayed orders, increased excess inventories, and caused third-quarter earnings to fall 24 percent below expectations.

- **Repair or damage to brand reputation**—Technologies such as CRM can directly enhance a company's brand reputation. Software can also severely damage a company's reputation if it fails to work as advertised or has security vulnerabilities that affect its customers' trust.

  H&R Block customers were furious when the company accidentally placed its customers' passwords and Social Security numbers on its Web site.

- **Prevent or incur liabilities**—Technology such as CAT scans, MRIs, and mammograms can save lives. Faulty technology used in airplanes, automobiles, pacemakers, or nuclear reactors can cause massive damage, injury, or death.

  The parent company of bankrupt pharmaceutical distributor FoxMeyer sued SAP for $500 million over ERP software failure that allegedly crippled its operations.

- **Increase or decrease productivity**—CRM and SCM software can directly increase a company's productivity. Large losses in productivity can also occur when software malfunctions or crashes.

  The Standish Group estimates that defective software code accounted for 45 percent of computer-system downtime and cost U.S. companies $100 billion in lost productivity in 2003 alone.[4]

The lucrative advantages of successful software implementations provide significant incentives to manage software development risks. But according to the Standish Group's Chaos report, more than half the software development projects undertaken in the United States come in late or over budget and the majority of successful projects maintain fewer features and functions than originally specified. Organizations also cancel around 33 percent of these projects during development. Understanding the basics of software development, or the systems development life cycle, will help organizations avoid potential software development pitfalls and ensure that software development efforts are successful.[5]

Developing Software—The Systems Development Life Cycle (SDLC)

Information systems are the support infrastructure that helps an organization change quickly when adapting to shifting business environments and markets. Many factors must come together to develop successful software. This chapter focuses on the *systems development life cycle (SDLC),* also known as the "software life cycle" or the "application life cycle," which is the overall process for developing information systems from planning and analysis through implementation and maintenance (see Figure 17.1).

1. **Planning**—The *planning phase* involves establishing a high-level plan of the intended project and determining project goals. Planning is the first and most critical phase of any systems development effort an organization undertakes, regardless of whether the effort is to develop a system that allows customers to order products over the Internet, determine the best logistical structure for warehouses around the world, or form a strategic information alliance with another organization. Organizations must carefully plan the activities (and determine why they are necessary) to be successful.

FIGURE 17.1

The Systems Development
Life Cycle

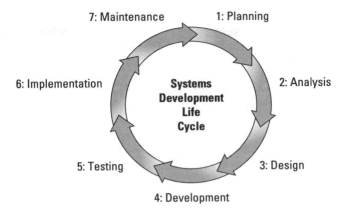

2. **Analysis**—The *analysis phase* involves analyzing end-user business requirements and refining project goals into defined functions and operations of the intended system. *Business requirements* are the detailed set of business requests that the system must meet in order to be successful. The analysis phase is obviously critical. A good start is essential, and the organization must spend as much time, energy, and resources as necessary to perform a detailed, accurate analysis.

3. **Design**—The *design phase* involves describing the desired features and operations of the system including screen layouts, business rules, process diagrams, pseudo code, and other documentation.

4. **Development**—The *development phase* involves taking all of the detailed design documents from the design phase and transforming them into the actual system. In this phase the project transitions from preliminary designs to the actual physical implementation.

5. **Testing**—The *testing phase* involves bringing all the project pieces together into a special testing environment to test for errors, bugs, and interoperability and verify that the system meets all of the business requirements defined in the analysis phase.

   According to a report issued in June 2003 by the National Institute of Standards and Technology (NIST), defective software costs the U.S. economy an estimated $59.5 billion each year. Of that total, software users incur 64 percent of the costs and software developers 36 percent. NIST suggests that improvements in testing could reduce this cost significantly—by about a third, or $22.5 billion—but that testing improvements would not eliminate most software errors.[6]

6. **Implementation**—The *implementation phase* involves placing the system into production so users can begin to perform actual business operations with the system.

7. **Maintenance**—Maintaining the system is the final sequential phase of any systems development effort. The *maintenance phase* involves performing changes, corrections, additions, and upgrades to ensure the system continues to meet the business goals. This phase continues for the life of the system because the system must change as the business evolves and its needs change, demanding constant monitoring, supporting the new system with frequent minor changes (for example, new reports or information capturing), and reviewing the system to be sure it is moving the organization toward its strategic goals.

Software Development Methodologies

Today, systems are so large and complex that teams of architects, analysts, developers, testers, and users must work together to create the millions of lines of custom-written code that drive enterprises. For this reason, developers have created a

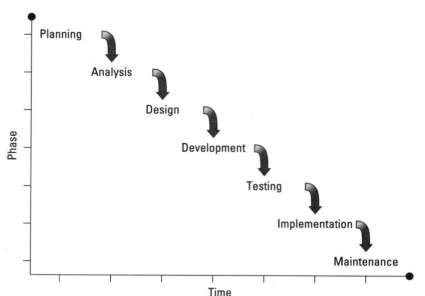

FIGURE 17.2

The Traditional Waterfall
Methodology

number of different system development life cycle methodologies including *water-fall; rapid application development (RAD); extreme programming;* and *agile.* The old-est of these, and the best known, is the waterfall methodology: a sequence of phases in which the output of each phase becomes the input for the next (see Figure 17.2).

WATERFALL METHODOLOGY

The traditional **waterfall methodology** is a sequential, activity-based process in which each phase in the SDLC is performed sequentially from planning through implemen-tation and maintenance. The waterfall methodology is one of the oldest software de-velopment methods and has been around for more than 30 years. The success rate for software development projects that follow this approach is only about 1 in 10. One pri-mary reason for such a low success rate is that the waterfall methodology does not suf-ficiently consider the level of uncertainty in new projects and the creativity required to complete software development projects in several aspects:

- **The business problem:** Any flaws in accurately defining and articulating the business problem in terms of what the business users actually require flow on-ward to the next phase.
- **The plan:** Managing costs, resources, and time constraints is difficult in the wa-terfall sequence. What happens to the schedule if a programmer quits? How will a schedule delay in a specific phase impact the total cost of the project? Unex-pected contingencies may sabotage the plan.
- **The solution:** The waterfall methodology is problematic in that it assumes users can specify all business requirements in advance. Defining the appropriate IT in-frastructure that is flexible, scalable, and reliable is a challenge. The final IT infra-structure solution must meet not only current but also future needs in terms of time, cost, feasibility, and flexibility. Vision is inevitably limited at the head of the waterfall.

Unfortunately, business requirements change as the business changes, which calls for considerable feedback and iterative consultation for all business require-ments. Essentially, software is "soft" and it must be easily changed and manipulated to meet the changing dynamics of an organization. As people's understanding of the business problems evolve, so must the software. For this reason, it is counter-productive to define all requirements precisely upfront since, by the time the software goes into production, which can be several months or even years after completing the initial analysis phase, chances are the business problems have changed as well as the business.

RAPID APPLICATION DEVELOPMENT METHODOLOGY (RAD)

In response to the faster pace of business, rapid application development has become a popular route for accelerating systems development. *Rapid application development (RAD) (*also called *rapid prototyping) methodology* emphasizes extensive user involvement in the rapid and evolutionary construction of working prototypes of a system to accelerate the systems development process. The fundamentals of RAD include:

- Focus initially on creating a prototype that looks and acts like the desired system.
- Actively involve system users in the analysis, design, and development phases.
- Accelerate collecting the business requirements through an interactive and iterative construction approach.

A *prototype* is a smaller-scale representation or working model of the users' requirements or a proposed design for an information system. The prototype is an essential part of the analysis phase when using the RAD methodology.

PHH Vehicle Management Services, a Baltimore fleet-management company with over 750,000 vehicles, wanted to build an enterprise application that opened the entire vehicle information database to customers over the Internet. To build the application quickly, the company abandoned the traditional waterfall approach. Instead, a team of 30 developers began prototyping the Internet application, and the company's customers evaluated each prototype for immediate feedback. The development team released new prototypes that incorporated the customers' feedback every six weeks. The PHH Interactive Vehicle application went into production seven months after the initial work began. Over 20,000 customers, using a common browser, can now access the PHH Interactive site at any time from anywhere in the world to review their accounts, analyze billing information, and order vehicles.[7]

EXTREME PROGRAMMING METHODOLOGY

Extreme programming (XP) methodology breaks a project into tiny phases, and developers cannot continue on to the next phase until the first phase is complete. The primary difference between the waterfall and XP methodologies is that XP divides its phases into iterations with user feedback. The waterfall approach develops the entire system, whereas XP develops the system in iterations (see Figure 17.3). XP is a lot like a jigsaw puzzle; there are many small pieces. Individually the pieces make no sense, but when they are combined (again and again) an organization can gain visibility into the entire new system.

Microsoft Corporation developed Internet Explorer and Netscape Communications Corporation developed Communicator using extreme programming. Both companies did a nightly compilation (called a build) of the entire project, bringing together all the current components. They established release dates and expended considerable effort to involve customers in each release. The extreme programming approach allowed both Microsoft and Netscape to manage millions of lines of code as specifications changed and evolved over time. Most important, both companies frequently held user design reviews and strategy sessions to solicit and incorporate user feedback.[8]

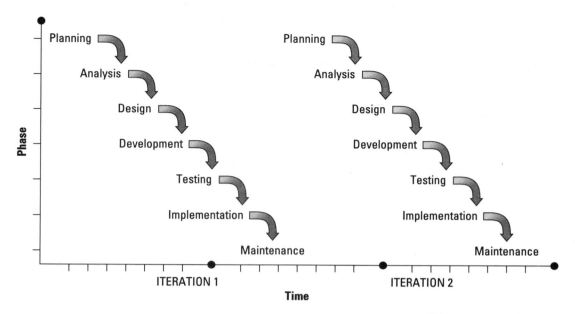

FIGURE 17.3

The Iterative Approach

XP is a significant departure from traditional software development methodologies, and many organizations in different industries have developed successful software using it. One reason for XP's success is its stress on customer satisfaction. XP empowers developers to respond to changing customer and business requirements, even late in the systems development life cycle, and XP emphasizes teamwork. Managers, customers, and developers are all part of a team dedicated to delivering quality software. XP implements a simple, yet effective way to enable groupware-style development. The XP methodology promotes quickly being able to respond to changing requirements and technology.

AGILE METHODOLOGY

The *agile methodology,* a form of XP, aims for customer satisfaction through early and continuous delivery of useful software components. Agile is similar to XP but with less focus on team coding and more on limiting project scope. An agile project sets a minimum number of requirements and turns them into a deliverable product. Agile means what it sounds like: fast and efficient; small and nimble; lower cost; fewer features; shorter projects.

The Agile Alliance is a group of software developers whose mission is to improve software development processes and whose manifesto includes the following tenets:

- Early and continuous delivery of valuable software will satisfy the customer.
- Changing requirements, even late in development, are welcome.
- Businesspeople and developers must work together daily throughout the project.
- Projects should be built around motivated individuals. Give them the environment and support they need, and trust them to get the job done.
- The best architectures, requirements, and designs emerge from self-organizing teams.
- At regular intervals, the team should reflect on how to become more effective, then tune and adjust its behavior accordingly.[9]

Developing Successful Software

The Gartner Group estimates that 65 percent of agile projects are successful. This success rate is extraordinary compared to the 10 percent success rate of waterfall projects. The following are the primary principles an organization should follow for successful agile software development.[10]

SLASH THE BUDGET

Small budgets force developers and users to focus on the essentials. Small budgets also make it easier to kill a failing project. For example, imagine that a project that has already cost $20 million is going down the tubes. With that much invested, it is tempting to invest another $5 million to rescue it rather than take a huge loss. All too often, the system fails and the company ends up with an even bigger loss.

Jim Johnson, chairman of The Standish Group, says he forced the CIO of one Fortune 500 company to set a $100,000 ceiling on all software development projects. There were no exceptions to this business rule without approval from the CIO and CEO. Johnson claims the company's project success rate went from 0 percent to 50 percent.[11]

IF IT DOESN'T WORK, KILL IT

Bring all key stakeholders together at the beginning of a project and as it progresses bring them together again to evaluate the software. Is it doing what the business wants and, more important, requires? Eliminate any software that is not meeting business expectations. This is called triage, and it's "the perfect place to kill a software project," said Pat Morgan, senior program manager at Compaq's Enterprise Storage Group. He holds monthly triage sessions and says they can be brutal. "At one [meeting], engineering talked about a cool process they were working on to transfer information between GUIs. No one in the room needed it. We killed it right there. In our environment, you can burn a couple of million dollars in a month only to realize what you're doing isn't useful."[12]

KEEP REQUIREMENTS TO A MINIMUM

Start each project with what the software must absolutely do. Do not start with a list of everything the software should do. Every software project traditionally starts with a requirements document that will often have hundreds or thousands of business requirements. The Standish Group estimates that only 7 percent of the business requirements are needed for any given application. Keeping requirements to a minimum also means that scope creep and feature creep must be closely monitored. *Scope creep* occurs when the scope of the project increases. *Feature creep* occurs when developers add extra features that were not part of the initial requirements. Both scope creep and feature creep are major reasons software development fails.[13]

TEST AND DELIVER FREQUENTLY

As often as once a week, and not less than once a month, complete a part of the project or a piece of software. The part must be working and it must be bug-free. Then have the customers test and approve it. This is the agile methodology's most radical departure from traditional development. In some traditional software projects, the customers did not see any working parts or pieces for years.

ASSIGN NON-IT EXECUTIVES TO SOFTWARE PROJECTS

Non-IT executives should coordinate with the technical project manager, test iterations to make sure they are meeting user needs, and act as liaisons between executives and IT. Having the business side involved full-time will bring project ownership and a desire to succeed to all parties involved. SpreeRide, a Salt Lake City market research outfit, used the agile methodology to set up its company's Web site. The project required several business executives designated full-time. The company believes this is one of the primary reasons that the project was successfully deployed in less than three months.[14]

Project Managing the Systems Development Effort

No one would think of building an office complex by turning loose 100 different construction teams to build 100 different rooms, with no single blueprint or agreed-upon vision of the completed structure. Yet this is precisely the situation in which many large organizations find themselves when managing systems development projects. Organizations routinely overschedule their resources (human and otherwise), develop redundant projects, and damage profitability by investing in nonstrategic efforts that do not contribute to the organization's bottom line. Project management offers a strategic framework for coordinating the numerous activities associated with organizational projects.

According to the Project Management Institute, ***project management*** is the application of knowledge, skills, tools, and techniques to project activities in order to meet or exceed stakeholder needs and expectations from a project. ***Project management software*** specifically supports the long-term and day-to-day management and execution of the steps in a project (such as building a new warehouse or designing and implementing a new IT system).

Project management is essential to the success of almost every aspect of IT. Without it, projects tend to be delayed, over budget, and often never reach completion. Horizon Blue Cross Blue Shield of New Jersey, a $6-billion-plus health insurance provider, allocated several hundred million dollars to IT over a five-year period to tackle tasks such as consolidating five enterprise software platforms, managing compliance with regulatory offices, and simplifying new product development. These IT initiatives involve hundreds of skilled people working on hundreds of concurrently developing projects. Horizon's executives needed to gain visibility into all projects, subsets of projects, and existing and planned projects collectively. The company considered a rigorous and formalized project management strategy fundamental to the project's success.

Horizon decided to implement IT project management software from Business Engine Inc. to manage its projects. The software collects information through standardized templates created for Microsoft Project, which are stored in an enterprise database and then fed into Business Engine's analytical tool, called Ben. Each user can then view and manipulate spreadsheets and graphs, share documents, track revisions, and run what-if scenarios in their personalized digital dashboard view. With the help from Business Engine, Horizon is managing IT projects and assets as if they were investments, tracking their performance against business goals, assessing their individual return and value to the company, and helping sort out which projects require greater attention and resources and which require reduced attention and resources. Horizon found itself ahead of schedule on over 70 percent of its IT projects.[15]

Figure 17.4 displays the relationships between the three primary variables in any project—(1) time, (2) cost, and (3) scope. These three variables are interdependent.

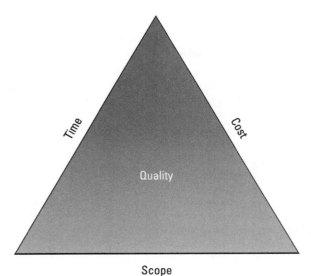

FIGURE 17.4

Project Management
Interdependent Variables

For example, decreasing a project's time frame means either increasing the cost of the project or decreasing the scope of the project to meet the new deadline. Increasing a project's scope means either increasing the project's time frame or increasing the project's cost—or both—to meet the increased scope changes. Project management is the science of making intelligent trade-offs between time, cost, and scope. All three of the factors combined determine a project's quality.

Benjamin Franklin's timeless advice—by failing to prepare, you prepare to fail—especially applies to many of today's software development projects. A recent survey concluded that the failure rate of IT projects is much higher in organizations that do not exercise disciplined project management. Figure 17.5 displays the top six reasons why IT projects fail, according to *Information Week*'s research survey of 150 IT managers.[16]

A successful project is typically on time, within budget, meets the business's requirements, and fulfills the customer's needs. The Hackett Group, an Atlanta-based consultancy, analyzed its client database (which includes 2,000 companies, including 81 Fortune 100 companies) and discovered:

- Three in 10 major IT projects fail.
- 21 percent of the companies state that they cannot adjust rapidly to market changes.
- One in four validate a business case for IT projects after completion.[17]

Nicolas Dubuc, collaborative project manager at Rhodia Inc., a $6 billion worldwide manufacturer of specialty chemicals, uses Microsoft's software to develop project management templates and methodologies for its 18 divisions. "We're designing a platform for rapid application development that will enhance opportunities for innovation," Duboc said.

Today, the leaders in the project management software market include Microsoft, Primavera, Oracle, and SAP. Microsoft Project is the core project management tool for many organizations and dominates with more than 8 million users and over 80 percent of the market share. Figure 17.6 displays the expected growth for project management software over the next few years. If an organization wants to deliver successful, quality software on time and under budget, it must take advantage of project management software.

FIGURE 17.5

Why IT Projects Fall
Behind Schedule or Fail

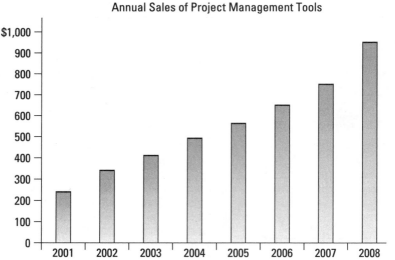

Annual Sales of Project Management Tools

FIGURE 17.6

Expected Growth for
Project Management
Software

(in $millions)

1. How are hospitals using new software to improve their operations?

2. List and describe the seven phases in the systems development life cycle and determine which phase is most important to a hospital when developing new systems.

3. Review the primary principles of successful software development and list them in order of importance for Hackensack University Medical Center's business strategy.

4. Why is building agile software important to Hackensack University Medical Center?

5. Assess the impact to a hospital if it decided to use the waterfall methodology to build its customers' information systems.

Chapter Seventeen Case: Transforming the Entertainment Industry—Netflix

The online DVD rental pioneer Netflix is transforming the movie business with its unique business model and streamlined shipping strategy. Netflix is quickly becoming one of Hollywood's most promising new business partners and is experiencing staggering growth with over 1 million subscribers, accounting for 3 to 5 percent of all U.S. home video rentals.

Typically, traditional video rental stores focus on major films and ignore older movies and smaller titles with niche audiences. Netflix is turning that idea upside down by offering a serious market for every movie, not just blockbusters. How? Netflix attributes its success to its proprietary software, called the Netflix Recommendation System, which constantly suggests movies a customer might like, based on how the customer rates any of the 15,000 titles in the company's catalog. Beyond recommendations, Netflix has figured out how to get DVDs from one subscriber to the next with unbelievable efficiency.

Netflix operates by allowing its 3.5 million subscribers to rent unlimited videos for $9.99 a month, as long as they have no more than three DVDs rented at a time. Currently there are more than 5 million discs in the hands of its customers at any given time, with an average of 500,000 DVDs shipped out of the company's 36 leased distribution centers daily. To handle the rental logistics for its 10 million DVD library the company created a proprietary supply chain management system.

As with any change or market advance, when new competition invades, existing competitors will not stand still. Walmart.com recently launched its own version of the Netflix model; it has already built six distribution centers, and is charging less per month for the same services offered by Netflix. Blockbuster purchased a similar service called FilmCaddy and is deciding how it will promote the service nationally. Other companies threatening to steal Netflix's market share are satellite and cable companies that now offer on-demand movies. To remain disruptive, Netflix will need to analyze its competition and strategize new ways to continue to increase subscriptions and revenues.

Netflix's Value Proposition

A crucial competitive weapon for maintaining its market share (estimated at two-thirds of online rentals) is new, homegrown software that improves upon the Oracle database the company uses to automate the DVD distribution process. The software consults the database to match a customer request with the movies in inventory. Based on algorithms devised to maximize delivery time by mail, the application decides which distribution center will fulfill each movie. The program then generates a "pull list" for workers at each center to fulfill the orders and ship them to customers.

Blockbuster, with 1 million online subscribers and 5,700 retail stores, is attacking with similar technology to orchestrate DVD delivery by mail from the chain's stores. Central to the Blockbuster strategy is the integration of 28 systems into one that feeds data about online orders to retail locations quickly.[18]

Questions

1. Assess the business-related consequences of a failure in Netflix's proprietary supply chain management system.

2. List and describe the seven phases in the systems development life cycle and determine which phase you think is most important to Netflix when it is developing software.

3. Determine the primary differences between the waterfall development methodology and the agile development methodology. Which methodology would you recommend Netflix use and why?

4. Why would prototyping be a good idea for Netflix if it decides to build a CRM system?

5. Given $10,000, would you recommend purchasing Netflix or Blockbuster stock?

<< BUSINESS PLUG-IN POINTERS

Review **Business Plug-In B14 "Systems Development"** for in-depth coverage of the SDLC and its associated activities including performing feasibility studies, gathering business requirements, analyzing a buy versus build decision, designing and building systems, writing and performing testing, supporting users, etc.

Review **Business Plug-In B15 "Project Management"** for an overview of the fundamentals of project management including prioritizing projects and developing project plans, along with a detailed look at risk management and change management.

B14

Systems Development

1. Summarize the activities associated with the planning phase in the SDLC.
2. Summarize the activities associated with the analysis phase in the SDLC.
3. Summarize the activities associated with the design phase in the SDLC.
4. Summarize the activities associated with the development phase in the SDLC.
5. Summarize the activities associated with the testing phase in the SDLC.
6. Summarize the activities associated with the implementation phase in the SDLC.
7. Summarize the activities associated with the maintenance phase in the SDLC.

Introduction

Today, systems are so large and complex that teams of architects, analysts, developers, testers, and users must work together to create the millions of lines of custom-written code that drive enterprises. For this reason, developers have created a number of different system development methodologies including waterfall, prototyping, rapid application development (RAD), extreme programming, agile, and others. All these methodologies are based on the *systems development life cycle (SDLC),* which is the overall process for developing information systems from planning and analysis through implementation and maintenance (see Figure B14.1).

The systems development life cycle is the foundation for all systems development methodologies, and there are literally hundreds of different activities associated with each phase in the SDLC. Typical activities include determining budgets, gathering system requirements, and writing detailed user documentation. The activities performed during each systems development project will vary. This plug-in takes a detailed look at a few of the more common activities performed during the systems development life cycle, along with common issues facing software development projects (see Figure B14.2).

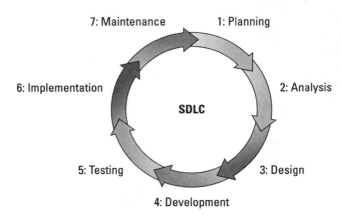

SDLC Phase	Activities
1. Planning	■ Identify and select the system for development ■ Assess project feasibility ■ Develop the project plan
2. Analysis	■ Gather business requirements ■ Create process diagrams ■ Perform a buy versus build analysis
3. Design	■ Design the IT infrastructure ■ Design system models
4. Development	■ Develop the IT infrastructure ■ Develop the database and programs
5. Testing	■ Write the test conditions ■ Perform the system testing
6. Implementation	■ Determine implementation method ■ Provide training for the system users ■ Write detailed user documentation
7. Maintenance	■ Build a help desk to support the system users ■ Perform system maintenance ■ Provide an environment to support system changes

FIGURE B14.2

Common Activities
Performed During
Systems Development

Systems Development Life Cycle

PHASE 1: PLANNING

The *planning phase* involves establishing a high-level plan of the intended project and determining project goals. The three primary activities involved in the planning phase are:

1. Identify and select the system for development.
2. Assess project feasibility.
3. Develop the project plan.

Evaluation Criteria	Description
Value chain analysis	The value chain determines the extent to which the new system will add value to the organization. Systems with greater value are given priority over systems with less value.
Strategic alignment	Projects that are in line with the organization's strategic goals and objectives are given priority over projects not in line with the organization's strategic goals and objectives.
Cost-benefit analysis	A cost/benefit analysis determines which projects offer the organization the greatest benefits with the least amount of cost.
Resource availability	Determine the amount and type of resources required to complete the project and determine if the organization has these resources available.
Project size, duration, and difficulty	Determine the number of individuals, amount of time, and technical difficulty of the project.

Identify and Select the System for Development

Systems are successful only when they solve the right problem or take advantage of the right opportunity. Systems development focuses on either solving a problem or taking advantage of an opportunity. Determining which systems are required to support the strategic goals of an organization is one of the primary activities performed during the planning phase. Typically, employees generate proposals to build new information systems when they are having a difficult time performing their jobs. Unfortunately, most organizations have limited resources and cannot afford to develop all proposed information systems. Therefore, they look to critical success factors to help determine which systems to build.

A *critical success factor (CSF)* is a factor that is critical to an organization's success. To determine which system to develop, an organization tracks all the proposed systems and prioritizes them by business impact or critical success factors. This allows the business to prioritize which problems require immediate attention and which problems can wait. Figure B14.3 displays possible evaluation criteria for determining which projects to develop.

Assess Project Feasibility

A *feasibility study* determines if the proposed solution is feasible and achievable from a financial, technical, and organizational standpoint. Typically, an organization will define several alternative solutions that it can pursue to solve a given problem. A feasibility study is used to determine if the proposed solution is achievable, given the organization's resources and constraints in regard to technology, economics, organizational factors, and legal and ethical considerations. Figure B14.4 displays the many different types of feasibility studies an organization can perform.

Develop the Project Plan

Developing a project plan is one of the final activities performed during the planning phase and it is one of the hardest and most important activities. The project plan is the guiding force behind on-time delivery of a complete and successful system. It logs and tracks every single activity performed during the project. If an activity is missed, or takes longer than expected to complete, the project plan must be updated to reflect these changes. Updating of the project plan must be performed in every subsequent phase during the systems development effort.

Types of Feasibility Studies	
Economic feasibility study (often called a **cost-benefit analysis**)	Identifies the financial benefits and costs associated with the systems development project.
Legal and contractual feasibility study	Examines all potential legal and contractual ramifications of the proposed system.
Operational feasibility study	Examines the likelihood that the project will attain its desired objectives.
Schedule feasibility study	Assesses the likelihood that all potential time frames and completion dates will be met.
Technical feasibility study	Determines the organization's ability to build and integrate the proposed system.

FIGURE B14.4

Types of Feasibility Studies

PHASE 2: ANALYSIS

The *analysis phase* involves analyzing end-user business requirements and refining project goals into defined functions and operations of the intended system. The three primary activities involved in the analysis phase are:

1. Gather business requirements.
2. Create process diagrams.
3. Perform a buy versus build analysis.

Gather Business Requirements

Business requirements are the detailed set of business requests that the system must meet to be successful. At this point, there is little or no concern with any implementation or reference to technical details. For example, the types of technology used to build the system, such as an Oracle database or the Java programming language, are not yet defined. The only focus is on gathering the true business requirements for the system. A sample business requirement might state, "The system must track all customer sales by product, region, and sales representative." This requirement states what the system must do from the business perspective, giving no details or information on how the system is going to meet this requirement.

Gathering business requirements is basically conducting an investigation in which users identify all the organization's business needs and take measurements of these needs. Figure B14.5 displays a number of ways to gather business requirements.

The *requirements definition document* contains the final set of business requirements, prioritized in order of business importance. The system users review the requirements definition document and determine if they will sign off on the business requirements. *Sign-off* is the system users' actual signatures indicating they approve all of the business requirements. One of the first major milestones on the project plan is usually the users' sign-off on business requirements.

A large data storage company implemented a project called Python whose purpose was to control all the company's information systems. Seven years later, tens of millions of dollars and 35 programmers later Python was canceled. At the end of the project, Python had over 1,800 business requirements of which 900 came from engineering and were written in order to make the other 900 customer requirements work. By the time the project was canceled, it was unclear what the primary goals,

Methods for Gathering Business Requirements
Perform a *joint application development (JAD)* session where employees meet, sometimes for several days, to define or review the business requirements for the system.
Interview individuals to determine current operations and current issues.
Compile questionnaires to survey employees to discover issues.
Make observations to determine how current operations are performed.
Review business documents to discover reports, policies, and how information is used throughout the organization.

objectives, and needs of the project were. Management should have realized Python's issues when the project's requirements phase dragged on, bulged, and took years to complete. The sheer number of requirements should have raised a red flag.[1]

Create Process Diagrams

Once a business analyst takes a detailed look at how an organization performs its work and its processes, the analyst can recommend ways to improve these processes to make them more efficient and effective. *Process modeling* involves graphically representing the processes that capture, manipulate, store, and distribute information between a system and its environment. One of the most common diagrams used in process modeling is the data flow diagram. A *data flow diagram (DFD)* illustrates the movement of information between external entities and the processes and data stores within the system (see Figure B14.6). Process models and data flow diagrams establish the specifications of the system. *Computer-aided software engineering (CASE)* tools

FIGURE B14.6

Sample Data Flow
Diagram

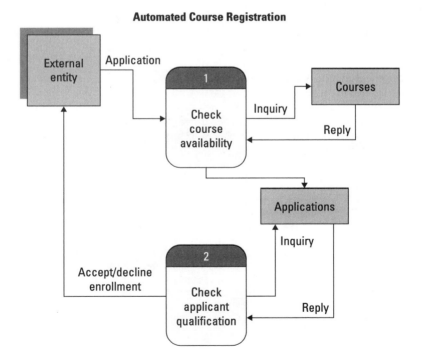

Automated Course Registration

are software suites that automate systems analysis, design, and development. Process models and data flow diagrams can provide the basis for the automatic generation of the system if they are developed using a CASE tool.

Perform a Buy versus Build Analysis

An organization faces two primary choices when deciding to develop an information system: (1) it can *buy* the information system from a vendor or (2) it can *build* the system itself. ***Commercial off-the-shelf (COTS)*** software is a software package or solution that is purchased to support one or more business functions and information systems. Most customer relationship management, supply chain management, and enterprise resource planning solutions are COTS. Typically, a cost-benefit analysis forms the basis of the buy versus build decision. Organizations must consider the questions displayed in Figure B14.7 during the buy versus build decision.

Three key factors an organization should also consider when contemplating the buy versus build decision are: (1) time to market, (2) corporate resources, and (3) core competencies. Weighing the complex relationship between each of these three variables will help an organization make the right choice (see Figure B14.8).

When making the all-important buy versus build decision consider when the product must be available, how many resources are available, and how the organization's core competencies affect the product. If these questions can be definitely answered either yes or no, then the answer to the buy versus build question is easy. However, most organizations cannot answer these questions with a solid yes or no. Most organizations need to make a trade-off between the lower cost of buying a system and the need for a system that meets all of their requirements. Finding a system to buy that meets all an organization's unique business requirements is next to impossible.

Buy versus Build Decision Questions
Do any currently available products fit the organization's needs?
Are unavailable features important enough to warrant the expense of in-house development?
Can the organization customize or modify an existing COTS to fit its needs?
Is there a justification to purchase or develop based on the cost of acquisition?

FIGURE B14.7

Buy versus Build Decision Questions

Three Key Factors in Buy versus Build Decisions	
1. Time to market	If time to market is a priority, then purchasing a good base technology and potentially building on to it will likely yield results faster than starting from scratch.
2. Availability of corporate resources	The buy versus build decision is a bit more complex to make when considering the availability of corporate resources. Typically, the costs to an organization to buy systems such as SCM, CRM, and ERP are extremely high. These costs can be so high—in the multiple millions of dollars—that acquiring these technologies might make the entire concept economically unfeasible. Building these systems, however, can also be extremely expensive, take indefinite amounts of time, and constrain resources.
3. Corporate core competencies	The more an organization wants to build a technical core competency, the less likely it will want to buy.

FIGURE B14.8

Key Factors in Buy versus Build Decisions

PHASE 3: DESIGN

The **design phase** involves describing the desired features and operations of the system including screen layouts, business rules, process diagrams, pseudo code, and other documentation. The two primary activities involved in the design phase are:

1. Design the IT infrastructure.
2. Design system models.

Design the IT Infrastructure

The system must be supported by a solid IT infrastructure or chances are the system will crash, malfunction, or not perform as expected. The IT infrastructure must meet the organization's needs in terms of time, cost, technical feasibility, and flexibility. Most systems run on a computer network with each employee having a client and the application running on a server. During this phase, the IT specialists recommend what types of clients and servers to buy including memory and storage requirements, along with software recommendations. An organization typically explores several different IT infrastructures that must meet current as well as future system needs. For example, databases must be large enough to hold the current volume of customers plus all new customers that the organization expects to gain over the next several years (see Figure B14.9).

Design System Models

Modeling is the activity of drawing a graphical representation of a design. An organization should model everything it builds including reports, programs, and

FIGURE B14.9

Sample IT Infrastructure

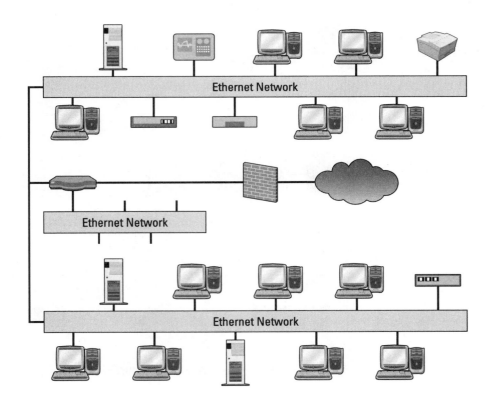

databases. Many different types of modeling activities are performed during the design phase, including:

- The ***graphical user interface (GUI)*** is the interface to an information system. ***GUI screen design*** is the ability to model the information system screens for an entire system using icons, buttons, menus, and submenus.

- ***Data models*** represent a formal way to express data relationships to a database management system (DBMS).

- ***Entity relationship diagram (ERD)*** is a technique for documenting the relationships between entities in a database environment (see Figure B14.10).

FIGURE B14.10

Sample Entity
Relationship Diagram

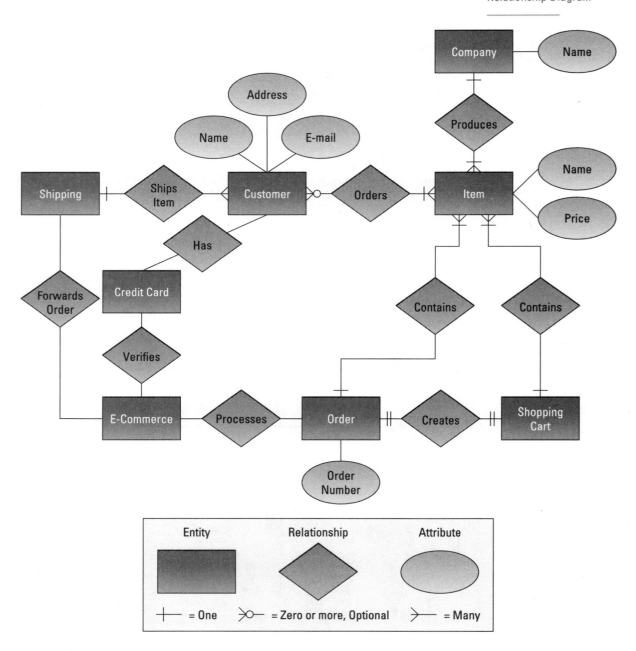

PHASE 4: DEVELOPMENT

The ***development phase*** involves taking all of the detailed design documents from the design phase and transforming them into the actual system. The two primary activities involved in the development phase are:

1. Develop the IT infrastructure.
2. Develop the database and programs.

Develop the IT Infrastructure

The platform upon which the system will operate must be built before building the actual system. In the design phase, an organization creates a blueprint of the proposed IT infrastructure displaying the design of the software, hardware, and telecommunication equipment. In the development phase, the organization purchases and implements the required equipment to support the IT infrastructure.

Most new systems require new hardware and software. It may be as simple as adding memory to a client or as complex as setting up a wide area network across several states.

Develop the Database and Programs

Once the IT infrastructure is built, the organization can begin to create the database and write the programs required for the system. IT specialists perform these functions and it may take months or even years to design and create all the needed elements to complete the system.

PHASE 5: TESTING

According to a report issued in June 2003 by the National Institute of Standards and Technology (NIST), defective software costs the U.S. economy an estimated $59.5 billion each year. Of that total, software users incurred 64 percent of the costs and software developers 36 percent. NIST suggests that improvements in testing could reduce this cost by about a third, or $22.5 billion, but that unfortunately testing improvements would not eliminate all software errors.[2]

The ***testing phase*** involves bringing all the project pieces together into a special testing environment to test for errors, bugs, and interoperability, in order to verify that the system meets all the business requirements defined in the analysis phase. The two primary activities involved in the testing phase are:

1. Write the test conditions.
2. Perform the system testing.

Write the Test Conditions

Testing is critical. An organization must have excellent test conditions to perform an exhaustive test. ***Test conditions*** are the detailed steps the system must perform along with the expected results of each step. Figure B14.11 displays several test conditions for testing user log-on functionality in a system. The tester will execute each test condition and compare the expected results with the actual results in order to verify that the system functions correctly. Notice in Figure B14.11 how each test condition is extremely detailed and states the expected results that should occur when executing each test condition. Each time the actual result is different from the expected result, a "bug" is generated and the system goes back to development for a bug fix.

Test condition 6 in Figure B14.11 displays a different actual result than the expected result because the system failed to allow the user to log on. After this test condition fails, it is obvious that the system is not functioning correctly and it must be sent back to development for a bug fix.

Test Condition Number	Date Tested	Tested	Test Condition	Expected Result	Actual Result	Pass/ Fail
1	1/1/09	Emily Hickman	Click on System Start Button	Main Menu appears	Same as expected result	Pass
2	1/1/09	Emily Hickman	Click on Log-on Button in Main Menu	Log-on Screen appears asking for User name and Password	Same as expected result	Pass
3	1/1/09	Emily Hickman	Type Emily Hickman in the User Name Field	Emily Hickman appears in the User Name Field	Same as expected result	Pass
4	1/1/09	Emily Hickman	Type Zahara123 in the password field	XXXXXXXXX appears in the password field	Same as expected result	Pass
5	1/1/09	Emily Hickman	Click on O.K. button	User log-on request is sent to database and user name and password are verified	Same as expected result	Pass
6	1/1/09	Emily Hickman	Click on Start	User name and password are accepted and the system main menu appears	Screen appeared stating log on failed and user name and password were incorrect	Fail

FIGURE B14.11

Sample Test Conditions

A typical system development effort has hundreds or thousands of test conditions. Every single test condition must be executed to verify that the system performs as expected. Writing all the test conditions and performing the actual testing of the software takes a tremendous amount of time and energy. Testing is critical to the successful development of any system.

Perform the System Testing

System developers must perform many different types of testing to ensure that the system works as expected. Figure B14.12 displays a few of the more common types of tests performed during this phase.

PHASE 6: IMPLEMENTATION

The *implementation phase* involves placing the system into production so users can begin to perform actual business operations with the system. The three primary activities involved in the implementation phase are:

1. Write detailed user documentation.
2. Determine implementation method.
3. Provide training for the system users.

Write Detailed User Documentation

Systems users require *user documentation* that highlights how to use the system. This is the type of documentation that is typically provided along with the new system. Systems users find it extremely frustrating to have a new system without documentation.

Types of Tests Performed During the Testing Phase	
Application (or system) testing	Verifies that all units of code work together and the total system satisfies all of its functional and operational requirements.
Backup and recovery testing	Tests the ability of an application to be restarted after failure.
Documentation testing	Verifies that the instruction guides are helpful and accurate.
Integration testing	Exposes faults in the integration of software components or software units.
Regression testing	Determines if a functional improvement or repair to the system has affected the other functional aspects of the software.
Unit testing	Tests each unit of code as soon as the unit is complete to expose faults in the unit regardless of its interaction with other units.
User acceptance testing (UAT)	Determines whether a system satisfies its acceptance criteria, enabling the customer to decide whether or not to accept a system.

Determine Implementation Method

An organization must choose the right implementation method to ensure a successful system implementation. Figure B14.13 highlights the four primary implementation methods an organization can choose from.

Provide Training for the System Users

An organization must provide training for the system users. The two most popular types of training are online training and workshop training. **Online training** runs over the Internet or off a CD-ROM. System users perform the training at any time, on their own computers, at their own pace. This type of training is convenient for system users because they can set their own schedule for the training. **Workshop training** is set in a classroom-type environment and led by an instructor. Workshop training is recommended for difficult systems where the system users require one-on-one time with an individual instructor.

Primary Implementation Methods	
1. Parallel implementation	Using both the old and new systems until it is evident that the new system performs correctly.
2. Phased implementation	Implementing the new system in phases (e.g., accounts receivables then accounts payable) until it is evident that the new system performs correctly and then implementing the remaining phases of the new system.
3. Pilot implementation	Having only a small group of people use the new system until it is evident that the new system performs correctly and then adding the remaining people to the new system.
4. Plunge implementation	Discarding the old system completely and immediately using the new system.

PHASE 7: MAINTENANCE

The *maintenance phase* involves performing changes, corrections, additions, and upgrades to ensure the system continues to meet the business goals. Once a system is in place, it must change as the organization changes. The three primary activities involved in the maintenance phase are:

1. Build a help desk to support the system users.
2. Perform system maintenance.
3. Provide an environment to support system changes.

Build a Help Desk to Support the System Users

A *help desk* is a group of people who respond to internal system user questions. Typically, internal system users have a phone number for the help desk they call whenever they have issues or questions about the system. Staffing a help desk that answers internal user questions is an excellent way to provide comprehensive support for new systems.

Perform System Maintenance

Maintenance is fixing or enhancing an information system. Many different types of maintenance must be performed on the system to ensure it continues to operate as expected. These include:

- **Adaptive maintenance**—making changes to increase system functionality to meet new business requirements.
- **Corrective maintenance**—making changes to repair system defects.
- **Perfective maintenance**—making changes to enhance the system and improve such things as processing performance and usability.
- **Preventive maintenance**—making changes to reduce the chance of future system failures.

Provide an Environment to Support System Changes

As changes arise in the business environment, an organization must react to those changes by assessing the impact on the system. It might well be that the system needs to adjust to meet the ever-changing needs of the business environment. If so, an organization must modify its systems to support the business environment.

A *change management system* includes a collection of procedures to document a change request and define the steps necessary to consider the change based on the expected impact of the change. Most change management systems require that a change request form be initiated by one or more project stakeholders (users, customers, analysts, developers). Ideally, these change requests are reviewed by a *change control board (CCB)* responsible for approving or rejecting all change requests. The CCB's composition typically includes a representative for each business area that has a stake in the project. The CCB's decision to accept or reject each change is based on an impact analysis of the change. For example, if one department wants to implement a change to the software that will increase both deployment time and cost, then the other business owners need to agree that the change is valid and that it warrants the extended time frame and increased budget.

Software Problems Are Business Problems

Only 28 percent of projects are developed within budget and delivered on time and as promised, says the Standish Group, a Massachusetts-based consultancy, in a recent report. The primary reasons for project failure are:

- Unclear or missing business requirements.
- Skipping SDLC phases.

- Failure to manage project scope.
- Failure to manage project plan.
- Changing technology.[3]

UNCLEAR OR MISSING BUSINESS REQUIREMENTS

The most common reason systems fail is because the business requirements are either missing or incorrectly gathered during the analysis phase. The business requirements drive the entire system. If they are not accurate or complete, the system will not be successful.

It is important to discuss the relationship between the SDLC and the cost for the organization to fix errors. An error found during the analysis and design phase is relatively inexpensive to fix. All that is typically required is a change to a Word document. However, exactly the same error found during the testing or implementation phase is going to cost the organization an enormous amount to fix because it has to change the actual system. Figure B14.14 displays how the cost to fix an error grows exponentially the later the error is found in the SDLC.

SKIPPING SDLC PHASES

The first thing individuals tend to do when a project falls behind schedule is to start skipping phases in the SDLC. For example, if a project is three weeks behind in the development phase, the project manager might decide to cut testing down from six weeks to three weeks. Obviously, it is impossible to perform all the testing in half the time. Failing to test the system will lead to unfound errors, and chances are high that the system will fail. It is critical that an organization perform all phases in the SDLC during every project. Skipping any of the phases is sure to lead to system failure.

FAILURE TO MANAGE PROJECT SCOPE

As the project progresses, the project manager must track the status of each activity and adjust the project plan if an activity is added or taking longer than expected. **Scope creep** occurs when the scope of the project increases. **Feature creep** occurs when developers add extra features that were not part of the initial requirements. Scope creep and feature creep are difficult to manage and can easily cause a project to fall behind schedule.

FIGURE B14.14

The Cost of Finding Errors

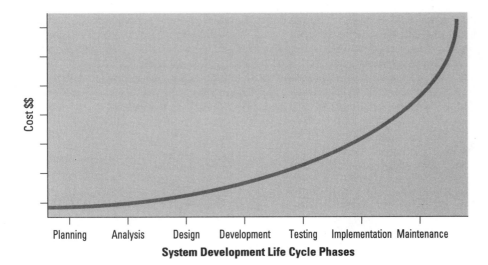

System Development Life Cycle Phases

FAILURE TO MANAGE PROJECT PLAN

Managing the project plan is one of the biggest challenges during systems development. The project plan is the road map the organization follows during the development of the system. Developing the initial project plan is the easiest part of the project manager's job. Managing and revising the project plan is the hard part. The project plan is a living document since it changes almost daily on any project. Failing to monitor, revise, and update the project plan can lead to project failure.

CHANGING TECHNOLOGY

Many real-world projects have hundreds of business requirements, take years to complete, and cost millions of dollars. Gordon Moore, co-founder of Intel Corporation, observed in 1965 that chip density doubles every 18 months. This observation, known as Moore's law, simply means that memory sizes, processor power, and so on, all follow the same pattern and roughly double in capacity every 18 months. As Moore's law states, technology changes at an incredibly fast pace; therefore it is possible to have to revise an entire project plan in the middle of a project as a result of a change in technology. Technology changes so fast that it is almost impossible to deliver an information system without feeling the pain of changing technology.

T he systems development life cycle (SDLC) is the foundation for all systems development methodologies. Understanding the phases and activities involved in the systems development life cycle is critical when developing information systems regardless of which methodology is being used. The SDLC contains the following phases:

1. The *planning phase* involves establishing a high-level plan of the intended project and determining project goals.

2. The *analysis phase* involves analyzing end-user business requirements and refining project goals into defined functions and operations of the intended system.

3. The *design phase* involves describing the desired features and operations of the system including screen layouts, business rules, process diagrams, pseudo code, and other documentation.

4. The *development phase* involves taking all the detailed design documents from the design phase and transforming them into the actual system.

5. The *testing phase* involves bringing all the project pieces together into a special testing environment to test for errors, bugs, and interoperability, in order to verify that the system meets all the business requirements defined in the analysis phase.

6. The *implementation phase* involves placing the system into production so users can begin to perform actual business operations with the system.

7. The *maintenance phase* involves performing changes, corrections, additions, and upgrades to ensure the system continues to meet the business goals.

★ KEY TERMS

Analysis phase, 463
Business requirement, 463
Change control board
   (CCB), 471
Change management
   system, 471
Commercial off-the-shelf
   (COTS), 465
Computer-aided software
   engineering (CASE), 464
Critical success factor
   (CSF), 462
Data flow diagram (DFD), 464
Data model, 467
Design phase, 466

Development phase, 468
Entity relationship diagram
   (ERD), 467
Feasibility study, 462
Feature creep, 472
Graphical user interface
   (GUI), 467
GUI screen design, 467
Help desk, 471
Implementation phase, 469
Joint application development
   (JAD), 464
Maintenance, 471
Maintenance phase, 471
Modeling, 466

Online training, 470
Planning phase, 461
Process modeling, 464
Requirements definition
   document, 463
Scope creep, 472
Sign-off, 463
Systems development life cycle
   (SDLC), 460
Test condition, 468
Testing phase, 468
User documentation, 469
Workshop training, 470

Disaster at Denver International Airport

One good way to learn how to develop successful systems is to review past failures. One of the most infamous system failures is Denver International Airport's (DIA) baggage system. When the automated baggage system design for DIA was introduced, it was hailed as the savior of modern airport design. The design relied on a network of 300 computers to route bags and 4,000 telecars to carry luggage across 21 miles of track. Laser scanners were to read bar-coded luggage tags, while advanced scanners tracked the movement of toboggan-like baggage carts.

When DIA finally opened its doors for reporters to witness its revolutionary baggage handling system the scene was rather unpleasant. Bags were chewed up, lost, and misrouted in what has since became a legendary systems nightmare.

One of the biggest mistakes made in the baggage handling system fiasco was that not enough time was allowed to properly develop the system. In the beginning of the project, DIA assumed it was the responsibility of individual airlines to find their own way of moving the baggage from the plane to the baggage claim area. The automated baggage system was not involved in the initial planning of the DIA project. By the time the developers of DIA decided to create an integrated baggage system, the time frame for designing and implementing such a complex and huge system was not possible.

Another common mistake that occurred during the project was that the airlines kept changing their business requirements. This caused numerous issues including the implementation of power supplies that were not properly updated for the revised system design, which caused overloaded motors and mechanical failures. Besides the power supplies design problem, the optical sensors did not read the bar codes correctly, causing issues with baggage routing.

Finally, BAE, the company that designed and implemented the automated baggage system for DIA, had never created a baggage system of this size before. BAE had created a similar system in an airport in Munich, Germany, where the scope was much smaller. Essentially, the baggage system had an inadequate IT infrastructure since it was designed for a much smaller system.

DIA simply could not open without a functional baggage system so the city had no choice but to delay the opening date for over 16 months, costing taxpayers roughly $1 million per day, which totaled around $500 million.[4]

Questions

1. One of the problems with DIA's baggage system was inadequate testing. Describe the different types of tests DIA could have used to help ensure its baggage system's success.
2. Evaluate the different implementation approaches. Which one would have most significantly increased the chances of the project's success?
3. Explain the cost of finding errors. How could more time spent in the analysis and design phase have saved Colorado taxpayers hundreds of millions of dollars?
4. Why could BAE not take an existing IT infrastructure and simply increase its scale and expect it to work?

Reducing Ambiguity in Business Requirements

The number one reason projects fail is bad business requirements. Business requirements are considered "bad" because of ambiguity or insufficient involvement of end users during analysis and design.

A requirement is unambiguous if it has the same interpretation for all parties. Different interpretations by different participants will usually result in unmet expectations. Here is an example of an ambiguous requirement and an example of an unambiguous requirement:

- **Ambiguous requirement:** The financial report must show profits in local and U.S. currencies.
- **Unambiguous requirement:** The financial report must show profits in local and U.S. currencies using the exchange rate printed in *The Wall Street Journal* for the last business day of the period being reported.

Ambiguity is impossible to prevent completely because it is introduced into requirements in natural ways. For example:

- Requirements can contain technical implications that are obvious to the IT developers but not to the customers.
- Requirements can contain business implications that are obvious to the customer but not to the IT developers.
- Requirements may contain everyday words whose meanings are "obvious" to everyone, yet different for everyone.
- Requirements are reflections of detailed explanations that may have included multiple events, multiple perspectives, verbal rephrasing, emotion, iterative refinement, selective emphasis, and body language—none of which are captured in the written statements.

Tips for Reviewing Business Requirements

When reviewing business requirements always look for the following words to help dramatically reduce ambiguity:

- **"And and Or"** have well-defined meanings and ought to be completely unambiguous, yet they are often understood only informally and interpreted inconsistently. For example, consider the statement "The alarm must ring if button T is pressed and if button F is pressed." This statement may be intended to mean that to ring the alarm, both buttons must be pressed or it may be intended to mean that either one can be pressed. A statement like this should never appear in a requirement because the potential for misinterpretation is too great. A preferable approach is to be very explicit, for example, "The alarm must ring if both buttons T and F are pressed simultaneously. The alarm should not ring in any other circumstance."
- **"Always"** might really mean "most of the time," in which case it should be made more explicit. For example, the statement "We always run reports A and B together" could be challenged with "In other words, there is never any circumstance where you would run A without B and B without A?" If you build a system with an "always" requirement, then you are actually building the system to never run report A without report B. If a user suddenly wants report B without report A, you will need to make significant system changes.
- **"Never"** might mean "rarely," in which case it should be made more explicit. For example, the statement "We never run reports A and B in the same month" could be challenged with, "So that means that if I see that A has been run, I can be absolutely certain that no one will want to run B." Again, if you build a system that supports a "never" requirement then the system users can never perform that requirement. For example, the system would never allow a user to run reports A and B in the same month, no matter what the circumstances.
- **Boundary conditions** are statements about the line between true and false and do and do not. These statements may or may not be meant to include end points. For example, "We want to use method X when there are up to 10 pages, but method Y otherwise." If you were building this system, would you include page 10 in method X or in method Y? The answer to this question will vary causing an ambiguous business requirement.[5]

Questions

1. Why are ambiguous business requirements the leading cause of system development failures?
2. Why do the words *and* and *or* tend to lead to ambiguous requirements?

3. Research the Web and determine other reasons for "bad" business requirements.

4. What is wrong with the following business requirement: "The system must support employee birthdays since every employee always has a birthday every year."

1. **Understanding Project Failure**

   You are the director of project management for Stello, a global manufacturer of high-end writing instruments. The company sells to primarily high-end customers, and the average price for one of its fine writing instruments is about $350. You are currently implementing a new customer relationship management system and you want to do everything you can to ensure a successful systems development effort. Create a document summarizing the five primary reasons why this project could fail, along with your strategy to eliminate the possibility of system development failure on your project.

2. **Missing Phases in the Systems Development Life Cycle**

   Hello Inc. is a large concierge service for executives operating in Chicago, San Francisco, and New York. The company performs all kinds of services from dog walking to airport transportation. Your manager, Dan Martello, wants to skip the testing phase during the company's financial ERP implementation. Dan feels that since the system came from a vendor it should work correctly. To meet the project's looming deadline he wants to skip the testing phase. Draft a memo explaining to Dan the importance of following the SDLC and the ramifications to the business if the financial system is not tested.

3. **Saving Failing Systems**

   Crik Candle Company manufactures low-end candles for restaurants. The company generates over $40 million in annual revenues and has over 300 employees. You are in the middle of a large multimillion-dollar supply chain management implementation. Your project manager has just come to you with the information that the project might fail for the following reasons:

   - Several business requirements were incorrect and the scope has to be doubled.
   - Three developers recently quit.
   - The deadline has been moved up a month.

   Develop a list of options that your company can follow to ensure the project remains on schedule and within budget.

4. **Refusing to Sign-Off**

   You are the primary client on a large extranet development project. After carefully reviewing the requirements definition document, you are positive that there are missing, ambiguous, inaccurate, and unclear requirements. The project manager is pressuring you for your sign-off since he has already received sign-off from five of your co-workers. If you fail to sign off on the requirements, you are going to put the entire project at risk since the time frame is nonnegotiable. What would you do? Why?

5. **Feasibility Studies**

   John Lancert is the new managing operations director for a large construction company, LMC. John is currently looking for an associate who can help him prioritize the 60 proposed company projects. You are interested in working with John and have decided to apply for the job. John has asked you to compile a report detailing why project prioritization is critical for LMC, along with the different types of feasibility studies you would recommend that LMC use when determining which projects to pursue.

B15

Project Management

1. Describe the three primary activities performed by a project manager.
2. Explain change management and how an organization can prepare for change.
3. Explain risk management and how an organization can mitigate risk.
4. Summarize the strategies a project manager can use to ensure a successful project.

Introduction

The core units introduced project management. A **project** is a temporary endeavor undertaken to create a unique product or service. According to the Project Management Institute, **project management** is the application of knowledge, skills, tools, and techniques to project activities in order to meet or exceed stakeholder needs and expectations from a project. This plug-in takes a detailed look at the fundamentals of project management, along with change management and risk management.

Project Management Fundamentals

Project deliverables are any measurable, tangible, verifiable outcome, result, or item that is produced to complete a project or part of a project. Examples of project deliverables include design documents, testing scripts, and requirements documents. **Project milestones** represent key dates when a certain group of activities must be performed. For example, completing the planning phase might be a project milestone. If a project milestone is missed, then chances are the project is experiencing problems. A **project manager** is an individual who is an expert in project planning and management, defines and develops the project plan, and tracks the plan to ensure all key project milestones are completed on time. The art and science of project management must coordinate numerous activities as displayed in Figure B15.1. Project managers perform numerous activities, and three of these primary activities are:

1. Choosing strategic projects.
2. Setting the project scope.
3. Managing resources and maintaining the project plan.

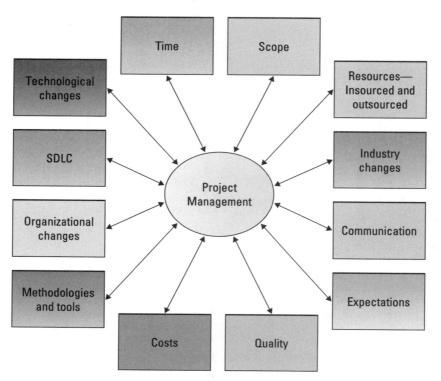

CHOOSING STRATEGIC PROJECTS

Calpine Corp., a large energy producer, uses project management software to look at its IT investments from a business perspective. The company classifies projects in one of three ways: (1) run the business, (2) grow the business, and (3) transform the business. Calpine splits its $100 million in assets accordingly: 60 percent for running the business, 20 percent for growing the business, and 20 percent for transforming the business. Calpine evaluates each of its 30 to 35 active projects for perceived business value against project costs. For the company to pursue a project it must pass a return on investment (ROI) hurdle. A business project must minimally provide two times ROI, and a transformation project must provide five times ROI.[1]

One of the most difficult decisions organizations make is determining the projects in which to invest time, energy, and resources. An organization must identify what it wants to do and how it is going to do it. The "what" part of this question focuses on issues such as justification for the project, definition of the project, and expected results of the project. The "how" part of the question deals with issues such as project approach, project schedule, and analysis of project risks. Determining which projects to focus corporate efforts on is as necessary to projects as each project is to an organization. The three common techniques an organization can use to select projects include:

1. Focus on organizational goals.
2. Categorize projects.
3. Perform a financial analysis (see Figure B15.2).

Before its merger with Hewlett-Packard, Compaq decided to analyze and prioritize its system development projects. Knowing that the CIO wanted to be able to view every project, project management leaders quickly identified and removed nonstrategic projects. At the end of the review process, the company canceled 39 projects, saving the organization $15 million. Most Fortune 100 companies are

Techniques for Choosing Strategic Projects

1. **Focus on organizational goals**—Managers are finding tremendous value in choosing projects that align with the organization's goals. Projects that address organizational goals tend to have a higher success rate since they are important to the entire organization.

2. **Categorize projects**—There are various categories that an organization can group projects into to determine a project's priority. One type of categorization includes problem, opportunity, and directives. Problems are undesirable situations that prevent an organization from achieving its goals. Opportunities are chances to improve the organization. Directives are new requirements imposed by management, government, or some other external influence. It is often easier to obtain approval for projects that address problems or directives because the organization must respond to these categories to avoid financial losses.

3. **Perform a financial analysis**—A number of different financial analysis techniques can be performed to help determine a project's priority. A few of these include net present value, return on investment, and payback analysis. These financial analysis techniques help determine the organization's financial expectations for the project.

receiving bottom-line benefits similar to Compaq's from implementing a project management solution.[2]

Organizations also need to choose and prioritize projects in such a way that they can make responsible decisions as to which projects to eliminate. Jim Johnson, chairman of the Standish Group, has identified project management as the process that can make the difference in project success. According to Johnson, "Companies need a process for taking a regular look at their projects and deciding, again and again, if the investment is going to pay off. As it stands now, for most companies, projects can take on a life of their own."[3]

An organization must build in continuous self-assessment, which allows earlier termination decisions on failing projects, with the associated cost savings. This frees capital and personnel for dedication to projects that are worth pursuing. The elimination of a project should be viewed as successful resource management, not as an admission of failure.

SETTING THE PROJECT SCOPE

Once an organization defines the projects it wants to pursue, it must set the project scope. *Project scope* defines the work that must be completed to deliver a product with the specified features and functions. The project scope statement is important because it specifies clear project boundaries. The project scope typically includes the following:

- *Project product*—a description of the characteristics the product or service has undertaken.
- *Project objectives*—quantifiable criteria that must be met for the project to be considered a success.
- *Project deliverables*—any measurable, tangible, verifiable outcome, result, or item that is produced to complete a project or part of a project.
- *Project exclusions*—products, services, or processes that are not specifically a part of the project.

The project objectives are one of the most important areas to define because they are essentially the major elements of the project. When an organization achieves the project objectives, it has accomplished the major goals of the project and the project scope is satisfied. Project objectives must include metrics so that the project's success can be measured. The metrics can include cost, schedule, and quality metrics along with a number of other metrics. Figure B15.3 displays the SMART criteria—useful reminders on how to ensure that the project has created understandable and measurable objectives.

MANAGING RESOURCES AND MAINTAINING THE PROJECT PLAN

Managing people is one of the hardest and most critical efforts a project manager undertakes. How to resolve conflicts within the team and how to balance the needs of the project with the personal/professional needs of the team are a few of the challenges facing project managers. More and more project managers are the main (and sometimes sole) interface with the client during the project. As such, communication, negotiation, marketing, and salesmanship are just as important to the project manager as financial and analytical acumen. There are many times when the people management side of project management made the difference in pulling off a successful project.

A **project plan** is a formal, approved document that manages and controls project execution. A well-defined project plan is characterized by the following:

- Easy to understand.
- Easy to read.
- Communicated to all key participants (key stakeholders).
- Appropriate to the project's size, complexity, and criticality.
- Prepared by the team, rather than by the individual project manager.

The most important part of the plan is communication. The project manager must communicate the plan to every member of the project team and to any key stakeholders and executives. The project plan must also include any project assumptions and be detailed enough to guide the execution of the project. A key to achieving project success is earning consensus and buy-in from all key stakeholders. By including key stakeholders in project plan development, the project manager allows them to have ownership of the plan. This often translates to greater commitment, which in turn results in enhanced motivation and productivity.

The two primary diagrams most frequently used in project planning are PERT and Gantt charts. A **PERT (Program Evaluation and Review Technique) chart** is a graphical network model that depicts a project's tasks and the relationships between those tasks. A **dependency** is a logical relationship that exists between the project tasks, or between a project task and a milestone. PERT charts define dependency between project tasks before those tasks are scheduled (see Figure B15.4). The boxes in Figure B15.4 represent project tasks, and the project manager can adjust the contents of the boxes to display various project attributes such as schedule and actual start and finish times. The arrows indicate that one task is dependent on the start or completion of another task. The **critical path** is a path from the start to the finish that passes through all the tasks that are critical to completing the project in the shortest amount of time. PERT charts frequently display a project's critical path.

A **Gantt chart** is a simple bar chart that depicts project tasks against a calendar. In a Gantt chart, tasks are listed vertically and the project's time frame is listed horizontally. A Gantt chart works well for representing the project schedule. It also shows actual progress of tasks against the planned duration. Figure B15.5 displays a software development project using a Gantt chart.

Change Management and Risk Management

Business leaders face a rapidly moving and unforgiving global marketplace that will force them to use every possible tool to sustain competitiveness. A good project manager understands not only the fundamentals of project management, but also how to effectively deal with change management and risk management.

- Specific
- Measurable
- Agreed upon
- Realistic
- Time framed

FIGURE B15.3

SMART Criteria for Successful Objective Creation

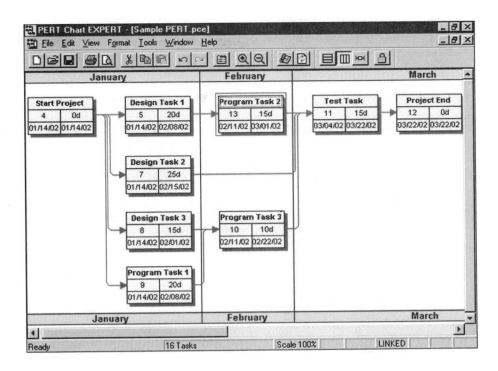

CHANGE MANAGEMENT

What works at Snap-on, a maker of tools and equipment for specialists such as car mechanics, is the organization's ability to manage change. The company recently increased profits by 12 percent while sales were down 6.7 percent. Dennis Leitner, vice president of IT, runs the IT group on a day-to-day basis and leads the

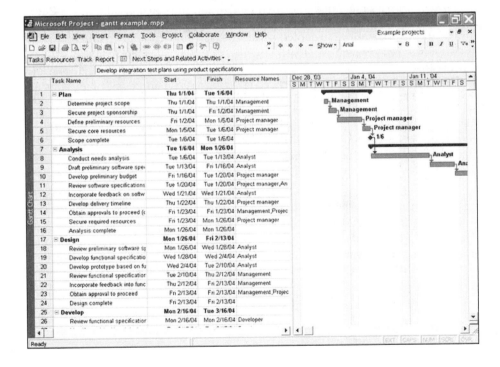

Common Reasons Change Occurs
1. An omission in defining initial scope
2. A misunderstanding of the initial scope
3. An external event such as government regulations that create new requirements
4. Organizational changes, such as mergers, acquisitions, and partnerships, that create new business problems and opportunities
5. Availability of better technology
6. Shifts in planned technology that force unexpected and significant changes to the business organization, culture, and/or processes
7. The users or management simply wanting the system to do more than they originally requested or agreed to
8. Management reducing the funding for the project or imposing an earlier deadline

FIGURE B15.6

Common Reasons
Change Occurs

implementation of all major software development initiatives. Each software development initiative is managed by both the business and IT. In fact, business resources are on the IT group's payroll and they spend as much as 80 percent of their time learning what a business unit is doing and how IT can help make it happen. Leitner's role focuses primarily on strategic planning, change management, and setting up metrics to track performance.[4]

Dynamic organizational change is inevitable and an organization must effectively manage change as it evolves. With the numerous challenges and complexities that organizations face in today's rapidly changing environment, effective change management thus becomes a critical core competency. *Change management* is a set of techniques that aid in evolution, composition, and policy management of the design and implementation of a system. Figure B15.6 displays a few of the more common reasons change occurs.

A *change management system* includes a collection of procedures to document a change request and define the steps necessary to consider the change based on the expected impact of the change. Most change management systems require that a change request form be initiated by one or more project stakeholders (systems owners, users, customers, analysts, developers). Ideally, these change requests are considered by a *change control board (CCB)* that is responsible for approving or rejecting all change requests. The CCB's composition typically includes a representative from each business area that has a stake in the project. The CCB's decision to accept or reject each change is based on an impact analysis of the change. For example, if one department wants to implement a change to the software that will increase both deployment time and cost, then the other business owners need to agree that the change is valid and that it warrants the extended time frame and increased budget.

PREPARING FOR CHANGE

Change is an opportunity, not a threat. Realizing that change is the norm rather than the exception will help an organization stay ahead. Becoming a change leader and accepting the inevitability of change can help ensure that an organization can survive and even thrive in times of change. Change leaders make change effective both inside and outside their organization by following three important guidelines:

1. Institute change management policies.
2. Anticipate change.
3. Seek change (see Figure B15.7).

Three Important Guidelines for Effectively Dealing with Change Management
1. **Institute change management polices**—Create clearly defined policies and procedures that must be followed each time a request for change is received.
2. **Anticipate change**—View change as an opportunity and embrace it.
3. **Seek change**—Every 6 to 12 months look for changes that may be windows of opportunity. Review successes and failures to determine if there are any opportunities for innovation.

General Electric has successfully tackled change management through an innovative program trademarked "Work Out." Work Out is shorthand for the idea of taking excess work out of the system. The purpose is to eliminate bureaucracy and free people's time for more productive activities. The positive time-saving and productivity-enhancing results of the Work Out change management program include:

- **Reports:** Teams calculated the time it took to prepare routine reports and compared it with the value generated from the reports. It quickly became apparent that much more effort went into preparing the reports than their comparative value to the recipients warranted. Valuable time was freed when those reports were eliminated or scaled back.
- **Approvals:** The approval process was questioned and adjusted accordingly. One instance discovered that a simple purchase order request required 12 approval signatures.
- **Meetings:** Teams evaluated the need for meetings and changed the way they were conducted to take advantage of technologies like teleconferencing.[5]

Change, whether it comes in the form of a crisis, a market shift, or a technological development, is challenging for all organizations. Successful organizations and successful people learn to anticipate and react appropriately to change.

RISK MANAGEMENT

Altria Group, Inc., the tobacco and food-products conglomerate, has a well-defined process for choosing projects based on project risk. The company gathers project information such as cash flow, return on investment, interfaces, and regulatory-compliance issues and creates a risk-based score of each project. The company then plots them on a grid with risk on the horizontal axis and value on the vertical axis. Managers then choose projects based on an optimal balance of risk and return.[6]

Project risk is an uncertain event or condition that, if it occurs, has a positive or negative effect on a project objective(s). *Risk management* is the process of proactive and ongoing identification, analysis, and response to risk factors. The best place to address project risk is during the project plan creation. Elements of risk management are outlined in Figure B15.8.

Elements of Risk Management
Risk identification—Determining which risks might affect the project and documenting their characteristics
Qualitative risk analysis—Performing a qualitative analysis of risks and conditions to prioritize their effects on project objectives
Quantitative risk analysis—Measuring the probability and consequences of risks as well as estimating their implications for the project objectives
Risk response planning—Developing procedures and techniques to enhance opportunities and reduce threats to the project's objectives

Common Project Risk Factors
Changing business circumstances that undermine expected benefits
Reluctance to report negative information or to "blow the whistle" on a project
Significant change management issues including resistance to change
The rush to get a project done quickly, often compromising the end result and desired outcome
Executives who are strongly wedded to a project and unwilling to admit that it may have been a mistake
A common tendency in IT projects to overengineer technology solutions, stemming from a belief in the superiority of technical solutions over simpler, people-based solutions
Building the project plan in conjunction with the budget or to validate some basic assumptions about the project's fiscal requirements and business base payback calculations

FIGURE B15.9

Common Project Risk Factors

Risks vary throughout a project and in general are more significant at the later phases of a project. Risk factors that may not be immediately obvious and are often the root causes of IT project success or failure are displayed in Figure B15.9.

MITIGATING RISK

An organization must devise strategies to reduce or mitigate risk. A wide range of strategies can be applied, with each risk category necessitating different mitigation strategies. When considering risk mitigation, the importance of choice, opportunities, and inexactitude should be kept clearly in mind. Organizations should take several actions at the enterprise level to improve risk management capabilities; these are displayed in Figure B15.10.

Audit and tax firm KPMG LLP and software maker SeeCommerce unveiled a service, called SeeRisk, to help companies assess supply chain management risk. SeeRisk helps a company establish common metrics and measure performance against them by identifying operational problems and risks. The SeeRisk system is integrated with operational and transactional systems along with external vendor systems. The goal of the system is to improve revenue as well as reduce costs by increasing visibility of inventory, and by knowing what is on the shelf and what is downstream in production. SeeRisk can calculate the implications that defective components would have on revenue, operating costs, what it would cost to start production over, and ultimately the effect on corporate profitability.[7]

Actions to Improve Risk Management Capabilities
Promote project leadership skills—Hire individuals with strong project management and project leadership skills as well as business management skills. These individuals can be extremely helpful in advisory and steering committee roles as well as coaching roles.
Learn from previous experience—Over many years of collective experiences, organizations have encountered hundreds of large IT projects. Document and revisit development methodologies, software tools, and software development best practices in order to share this vital information across the organization.
Share knowledge—Working in team or group environments tends to yield the most successful projects since individuals can share their unique learning experiences.
Create a project management culture—Orient people from day one on the importance of project management, change management, and risk management. Be sure to measure and reward project management skills and promote individuals based on successful projects.

FIGURE B15.10

Actions to Improve Risk Management Capabilities

Successful Project Management Strategies

Recreational Equipment, Inc. (REI) needs to consistently develop quality products and decrease the time to deliver them to market. To do that, REI needs to efficiently manage product development processes, projects, and information. The REI Gear and Apparel division takes an integrated project management approach to designing, managing, and tracking its product development projects, while collaborating and managing its workflow. REI's strategy entails combining Microsoft .NET technology, the Microsoft Office Enterprise Project Management (EPM) Solution, and software based on Microsoft Office Visio 2003 to create an integrated business solution it can use to model as-is business processes, experiment with what-if scenarios, and then convert the optimized processes into detailed project plans.

Project managers can further develop these plans, assign resources division-wide, manage projects online, and collaborate globally. REI predicts this integrated solution will help it improve its efficiency, consistency, and scalability so it can deliver its products to market more quickly.[8] Figure B15.11 displays the top five successful project management strategies outlined in *CIO* magazine.

FIGURE B15.11

Top Five Successful Project Management Strategies

Top Five Successful Project Management Strategies

1. **Define project success criteria.** At the beginning of the project, make sure the stakeholders share a common understanding of how they will determine whether the project is successful. Too often, meeting a predetermined schedule is the only apparent success factor, but there are certainly others. Some examples are increasing market share, reaching a specified sales volume or revenue, achieving specific customer satisfaction measures, retiring a high-maintenance legacy system, and achieving a particular transaction processing volume and correctness.

2. **Develop a solid project plan.** The hard part of developing a plan is the thinking, negotiating, balancing, and communication project managers will have to do to develop a solid and realistic plan. The time they spend analyzing what it will take to solve the business problem will reduce the number of changes later in the project.

3. **Divide and conquer.** Break all large tasks into multiple small tasks to provide more accurate estimates, reveal hidden work activities, and allow for more accurate, fine-grained status tracking.

4. **Plan for change.** Things never go precisely as planned on a project; therefore, the budget and schedule should include some contingency buffers at the end of major phases to accommodate change.

5. **Manage project risk.** Failure to identify and control risks will allow the risks to control the project. Be sure to spend significant time during project planning to brainstorm possible risk factors, evaluate their potential threat, and determine the best way to mitigate or prevent them.

L arge IT projects require significant investment of time and resources. Successful software development projects have proven challenging and often elusive, wasting many resources and jeopardizing the goodwill of stakeholders, including customers and employees. Bringing strong, effective project, change, and risk management disciplines to large IT projects is essential to successful organizations. The days when a project manager could just concentrate on bringing a project in on time, on budget, and with agreed-upon deliverables are fading.

KEY TERMS

CLOSING CASE ONE

Staying on Track—Toronto Transit

Schedules are at the heart of Toronto Transit Commission's (TTC) celebrated transit system, which services over 1 million customers daily. More than 50 large engineering and construction projects are under way to expand, upgrade, and maintain Toronto's transit systems and structures. One such project is the Sheppard project, which consists of constructing the new six-kilometer line north of the city. Sheppard is estimated to take more than five years to complete, with a total cost of $875 million.

TTC's challenge is to keep its 50 individual projects, most of which fall within the $2 million to $100 million price range and span an average of five years, on schedule and under budget. Staying on top of so many multifaceted, multiyear, and often interdependent projects adds additional complexity for the company. TTC uses Primavera Project Planner (P3) to create a single master schedule for all of its engineering and construction projects.

TTC's 50 individual projects average 100 to 150 activities each, with some projects encompassing as many as 500 to 600 activities. "Seeing the big picture is important, not only for the 300 people who work in the Engineering and Construction branch of the TTC, but for the entire 9,000-person organization," said Vince Carroll, head scheduler for the Engineering and Construction branch. "Engineering managers need to see how other projects may impact their own. Materials and procurement managers need to track project progress. Senior managers need to be able to communicate with city government to secure funding. Marketing and public relations people need the latest information to set public expectations. And most important of all," said Carroll, "the operations group needs to stay informed of what is happening so that they can adjust the schedules that run the trains."

Carroll and his team of 25 people create, update, and publish a master schedule that summarizes the individual status of each project, shows the logical links between projects, and provides an integrated overview of all projects. The master schedule helps the team effectively and regularly communicate the status of all projects currently under way throughout the Toronto Transit system.

The master schedule organizes projects according to their location in the capital budget. For example, projects can be organized according to those that have been allotted funding for expansion, state of good repair, legislative reasons, or environmental reasons. Each project is organized by its logical flow—from planning, analysis, design, through the maintenance phase. The final report shows positive and negative balances for each project and a single overview of the status of all the engineering and construction projects. Carroll and his team use PERT charts to create time-scaled logic diagrams and then convert this information to bar charts for presentation purposes in the master schedule. TTC is currently linking its master schedule directly to its payroll system, enabling it to track the number of hours actually worked versus hours planned.[9]

Questions

1. Describe Gantt charts and explain how TTC could use one to communicate project status.
2. Describe PERT charts and explain how TTC could use one to communicate project status.
3. How could TTC use its master schedule to gain efficiencies in its supply chain?
4. How could TTC use its master schedule to identify change management and risk management issues?

 CLOSING CASE TWO

Change at Toyota

At Toyota Motor Sales USA's headquarters in Torrance, California, a circular patch of manicured earth separates the IS building and corporate headquarters. A brook winds its way through lush flowers and pine trees, and a terraced path connects the two buildings. For many years, this was about the only thing the two groups shared with each other.

For the business executives at Toyota Motor Sales (TMS) peering across the courtyard at the Data building, the deep black windows were a symbol of IS's opacity. These executives felt that IS was unresponsive, and they had little clue where the money was going. "One of the complaints was that we spent a lot of money on IT projects, and the business was frequently disappointed with the results," recalled Bob Daly, group vice president of Toyota Customer Services. Daly says badly handled projects, such as a delayed PeopleSoft ERP implementation and a protracted parts inventory initiative, led to finger-pointing between the two factions.

Meanwhile, behind the darkened windows of the Data building, CIO Barbra Cooper's IS staff was buried under the weight of six enterprisewide projects. Called the Big Six, they included a new extranet for Toyota dealers and the PeopleSoft ERP rollout, as well as four new systems for order management, parts forecasting, advanced warranty and financial document management. Feeling besieged, the IS group made the mistake of not explaining to the business side all the things it was doing and how much it all cost. It was a classic case of mismanaged expectations and fractured alignment.

By late 2002, Cooper realized that if she wanted to win back the respect of the business managers—and remain in her post—she would have to make some radical changes. A conversation with Toyota Motor Sales CEO, in which he questioned the sharp incline of IS's spending curve, stopped her in her tracks. In her 30 years in IT, Cooper had developed something of a reputation for coming in to clean up other CIO's messes. Now, she had to take a long look in the mirror and fix herself.

Cooper's Path to Success

Cooper could no longer ignore the rumblings from across the courtyard that had worked their way into the rank-and-file business staff. To them, IS had become an unresponsive, bureaucratic machine.

Cooper started soliciting informal feedback from a wide range of businesspeople. What she discovered was an accumulation of "very painful projects for both IT and the business," she said. "Clearly there was not enough communication and education on our part."

In late 2002, Cooper hired an outside consultancy to interview TMS's top 20 executives. She wanted their honest opinions of how IS was doing. The results did not provide all the answers to the ailments, but she certainly saw the trouble spots. "Parts of the survey results were stinging," Cooper said. "But you can't be a CIO and not face that."

Cooper spent many introspective weeks in 2003 formulating her vision for a new IT department. What she developed was a strategy for a decentralized and transparent IS organization that focused all of its energy on the major business segments. In the summer of 2003, she presented her vision to her senior IS staffers. Some of the managers were excited by the prospect of change; others were less so.

The first thing Cooper did was set up the Toyota Value Action Program, a team of eight staffers responsible for translating her vision into actionable items for the department and her direct reports. Using the survey results and Cooper's direction, the team winnowed the list to 18 initiatives, including increasing employee training and development, gaining cost savings, making process improvements, ridding IS inefficiencies, and implementing a metrics program. Each initiative got a project owner and a team. Cooper insisted that each initiative have a mechanism to check its success. The most significant initiative called for improved alignment with the business side. At the heart of this new effort would be a revamped Office of the CIO structure—with new roles, reporting lines, and responsibilities.

As part of the rehaul, Cooper took top-flight personnel out of the Data building and embedded them as divisional information officers, or DIOs, in all of the business units. These DIOs are accountable for IT strategy, development, and services, and they sit on the management committees headed by top business executives. The DIOs' goal is to forge relationships with tier-one executives and executives at the vice president level.

The DIOs were not alone. Business operation managers and relationship managers from IS sat along side the business folks. "I still believe in managing IT centrally, but it was incumbent on us to physically distribute IT into the businesses," Cooper said. "They could provide more local attention while keeping the enterprise vision alive."

Cooper upended the structure of Toyota's IS department in six months in a bid to weave IT functions more closely into the daily business operations. The process was painful: She changed IS employees' jobs, exposed all of IS's shortcomings, and forced her staff into the business offices. However, just over a year into the new plan, IS and the business are now standing shoulder-to-shoulder when planning and implementing IT projects. And Cooper is still CIO of Toyota Motor Sales.

A Little Kicking and Screaming

Change can be scary for anyone, especially during an upheaval of an entire 400-person IS department. Cooper changed the jobs of 50 percent of her staffers within six months, yet no one left or was let go. Some took on new responsibilities; others took on expanded or new roles. Cooper said some mid- and upper-level staffers were initially uncomfortable with their new roles, but she spent a lot of time fostering a new attitude about the change. "I dragged them into the conversations kicking and screaming," Cooper said. "But I said to them, `Unless you think of what it means to change on this level, you will never make it happen.'" The key, Cooper said, is that all IS staffers were brought into the development of the new organization early.[10]

Questions

1. What would be the impact on Toyota's business if it failed to implement a project management solution and managed its projects using a myriad of spreadsheets and Word documents?
2. Why would Toyota find it important to focus on implementing good project management techniques?
3. Why are project management, change management, and risk management critical to a global company such as Toyota?
4. Describe the ramifications to Toyota's business if it failed to anticipate change.

✳ MAKING BUSINESS DECISIONS

1. Explaining Project Management

Prime Time Inc. is a large consulting company that specializes in outsourcing people with project management capabilities and skills. You are in the middle of an interview for a job with Prime Time. The manager performing the interview asks you to explain why managing a project plan is critical to a project's success. The manager also wants you to explain scope creep and feature creep and your tactics for managing them on a project. Finally, the manager wants you to elaborate on your strategies for delivering successful projects and reducing risks.

2. Applying Project Management Techniques

You have been hired by a medium-sized airline company, Sun Best. Sun Best currently flies over 300 routes in the East. The company is experiencing tremendous issues coordinating its 3,500 pilots, 7,000 flight attendants, and 2,000 daily flights. Determine how Sun Best could use a Gantt chart to help it coordinate its pilots, flight attendants, and daily flights. Using Excel, create a sample Gantt chart highlighting the different types of activities and resources Sun Best could track with the tool.

3. Prioritizing Projects

Nick Zele is the new managing operations director for a large construction company, CMA. Nick is looking for a project manager who can help him manage the 60 ongoing company projects. You are interested in working with Nick and have decided to apply for the job. Nick has asked you to compile a report detailing why project prioritization is critical for CMA, along with the different types of prioritization techniques you would recommend CMA use when determining which projects to pursue.

4. Managing Expectations

Trader is the name for a large human resource project that is currently being deployed at your organization. Your boss, Pam Myers, has asked you to compile an expectations management matrix for the project. The first thing you need to determine are management's expectations. Compile a list of questions you would ask to help determine management's expectations for the Trader project.

5. Mitigating Risk

Alicia Fernandez owns and operates a chain of nine seafood restaurants in the Boston area. Alicia is currently considering purchasing one of her competitors, which would give her an additional six restaurants. Alicia's primary concerns with the purchase are the constantly changing seafood prices and high staff turnover rate in the restaurant industry. Explain to Alicia what risk management is and how she can use it to mitigate the risks for the potential purchase of her competitor.

Information Security

1. Describe the relationship between information security policies and an information security plan.
2. Summarize the five steps to creating an information security plan.
3. Provide an example of each of the three primary security areas: (1) authentication and authorization, (2) prevention and resistance, and (3) detection and response.
4. Describe the relationships and differences between hackers and viruses.

Introduction

The core units introduced **information security,** which is a broad term encompassing the protection of information from accidental or intentional misuse by persons inside or outside an organization. With current advances in technologies and business strategies such as CRM, organizations are able to determine valuable information such as who are the top 20 percent of the customers that produce 80 percent of all revenues. Most organizations view this type of information as valuable intellectual capital, and they are implementing security measures to prevent the information from walking out the door or falling into the wrong hands. This plug-in discusses how an organization can implement information security lines of defense through people first and through technology second.

The First Line of Defense—People

Adding to the complexity of information security is the fact that organizations must enable employees, customers, and partners to access information electronically to be successful in this electronic world. Doing business electronically automatically creates tremendous information security risks for organizations. Surprisingly, the biggest issue surrounding information security is not a technical issue, but a people issue.

The CSI/FBI Computer Crime and Security Survey reported that 38 percent of respondents indicated security incidents originated within the enterprise. **Insiders** are legitimate users who purposely or accidentally misuse their access to the environment and cause some kind of business-affecting incident. Most information security breaches result from people misusing an organization's information either advertently or inadvertently. For example, many individuals freely give up their passwords or write them on sticky notes next to their computers, leaving the door wide open to intruders.[1]

The director of information security at a large health care company discovered how easy it was to create an information security breach when she hired outside auditors to test her company's security awareness. In one instance, auditors found that staff members testing a new system had accidentally exposed the network to outside hackers. In another, auditors were able to obtain the passwords of 16 employees when the auditors posed as support staff; hackers frequently use such "social engineering" to obtain passwords. ***Social engineering*** is using one's social skills to trick people into revealing access credentials or other information valuable to the attacker. Dumpster diving, or looking through people's trash, is another way social engineering hackers obtain information.[2]

Information security policies identify the rules required to maintain information security. An ***information security plan*** details how an organization will implement the information security policies. Figure B6.1 is an example of the University of Denver's Information Security Plan.

FIGURE B6.1

Sample Information Security Plan

Interim Information Security Plan

This Information Security Plan ("Plan") describes the University of Denver's safeguards to protect information and data in compliance ("Protected Information") with the Financial Services Modernization Act of 1999, also known as the Gramm Leach Bliley Act, 15 U.S.C. Section 6801. These safeguards are provided to:

■ Ensure the security and confidentiality of Protected Information;
■ Protect against anticipated threats or hazards to the security or integrity of such information; and
■ Protect against unauthorized access to or use of Protected Information that could result in substantial harm or inconvenience to any customer.

This Information Security Plan also provides for mechanisms to:

■ Identify and assess the risks that may threaten Protected Information maintained by the University of Denver;
■ Develop written policies and procedures to manage and control these risks;
■ Implement and review the plan; and
■ Adjust the plan to reflect changes in technology, the sensitivity of covered data and information and internal or external threats to information security.

Identification and Assessment of Risks to Customer Information

The University of Denver recognizes that it has both internal and external risks. These risks include, but are not limited to:

■ Unauthorized access of Protected Information by someone other than the owner of the covered data and information
■ Compromised system security as a result of system access by an unauthorized person
■ Interception of data during transmission
■ Loss of data integrity
■ Physical loss of data in a disaster
■ Errors introduced into the system
■ Corruption of data or systems
■ Unauthorized access of covered data and information by employees
■ Unauthorized requests for covered data and information
■ Unauthorized access through hardcopy files or reports
■ Unauthorized transfer of covered data and information through third parties

The University of Denver recognizes that this may not be a complete list of the risks associated with the protection of Protected Information. Since technology growth is not static, new risks are created regularly. Accordingly, the Information Technology Department and the Office of Student Affairs will actively participate with and seek advice from an advisory committee made up of university representatives for identification of new risks. The University of Denver believes current safeguards used by the Information Technology Department are reasonable and, in light of current risk assessments are sufficient to provide security and confidentiality to Protected Information maintained by the University.

(Continued)

Information Security Plan Coordinators

The University CIO and the Vice President for Student Affairs, in consultation with an advisory committee, have been appointed as the coordinators of this Plan. They are responsible for assessing the risks associated with unauthorized transfers of covered data and information and implementing procedures to minimize those risks to the University of Denver.

Design and Implementation of Safeguards Program

Employee Management and Training

During employee orientation, each new employee in departments that handle Protected Information will receive proper training on the importance of confidentiality of Protected Information.

Physical Security

The University of Denver has addressed the physical security of Protected Information by limiting access to only those employees who have a business reason to know such information.

Information Systems

The University of Denver has policies governing the use of electronic resources and firewall and wireless policies. The University of Denver will take reasonable and appropriate steps consistent with current technological developments to make sure that all Protected Information is secure and to safeguard the integrity of records in storage and transmission. The University of Denver will develop a plan to ensure that all electronic Protected Information is encrypted in transit.

Selection of Appropriate Service Providers

Due to the specialized expertise needed to design, implement, and service new technologies, vendors may be needed to provide resources that the University of Denver determines not to provide on its own. In the process of choosing a service provider that will maintain or regularly access Protected Information, the evaluation process shall include the ability of the service provider to safeguard Protected Information. Contracts with service providers may include the following provisions:

■ A stipulation that the Protected Information will be held in strict confidence and accessed only for the explicit business purpose of the contract;
■ An assurance from the contract partner that the partner will protect the Protected Information it receives.

Continuing Evaluation and Adjustment

This Information Security Plan will be subject to periodic review and adjustment, especially when due to the constantly changing technology and evolving risks. The Coordinators, in consultation with the Office of General Counsel, will review the standards set forth in this policy and recommend updates and revisions as necessary. It may be necessary to adjust the plan to reflect changes in technology, the sensitivity of student/customer data and internal or external threats to information security.

FIGURE B6.1

(Continued)

The first line of defense an organization should follow is to create an information security plan detailing the various information security policies. A detailed information security plan can alleviate people-based information security issues. Figure B6.2 displays the five steps for creating an information security plan. Figure B6.3 provides the top 10 questions from Ernst & Young that managers should ask to ensure their information is secure.

The Second Line of Defense—Technology

Arkansas State University (ASU) recently completed a major network upgrade that brought gigabit-speed network capacity to every dorm room and office on its campus. The university was concerned that the new network would be a tempting playground for hackers. To reduce its fear the university decided to install intrusion detection software (IDS) from Cisco Systems to stay on top of security and potential network abuses. Whenever the IDS spots a potential security threat, such as a virus or a hacker, it alerts the central management system. The system automatically pages the IT staff, who deal with the attack by shutting off access to the system, identifying the hacker's location, and calling campus security.[3]

Once an organization has protected its intellectual capital by arming its people with a detailed information security plan, it can begin to focus its efforts on deploying the right types of information security technologies such as the IDS installed at Arkansas State.

Five Steps for Creating an Information Security Plan	
1. **Develop the information security policies**	Identify who is responsible and accountable for designing and implementing the organization's information security policies. Simple, yet highly effective types of information security policies include requiring users to log off of their systems before leaving for lunches or meetings, never sharing passwords with anyone, and changing personal passwords every 60 days. The chief security officer (CSO) will typically be responsible for designing these information security policies.
2. **Communicate the information security policies**	Train all employees on the policies and establish clear expectations for following the policies. For example, let all employees know that they will receive a formal reprimand for leaving a computer unsecured.
3. **Identify critical information assets and risks**	Require the use of user IDs, passwords, and antivirus software on all systems. Ensure any systems that contain links to external networks have the appropriate technical protections such as firewalls or intrusion detection software. A **firewall** is hardware and/or software that guards a private network by analyzing the information leaving and entering the network. **Intrusion detection software (IDS)** searches out patterns in information and network traffic to indicate attacks and quickly responds to prevent any harm.
4. **Test and reevaluate risks**	Continually perform security reviews, audits, background checks, and security assessments.
5. **Obtain stakeholder support**	Gain the approval and support of the information security polices from the board of directors and all stakeholders.

FIGURE B6.2

Creating an Information Security Plan

International Data Corp. estimated that worldwide spending on IT security software, hardware, and services would top $35 billion in 2004. Organizations can deploy numerous technologies to prevent information security breaches. When determining which types of technologies to invest in, it helps to understand the three primary information security areas:

1. Authentication and authorization.
2. Prevention and resistance.
3. Detection and response.[4]

Top 10 Questions Managers Should Ask Regarding Information Security
1. Does the board of directors recognize information security is a board-level issue that cannot be left to the IT department alone?
2. Is there clear accountability for information security in the organization?
3. Do the board members articulate an agreed-upon set of threats and critical assets? How often do they review and update these?
4. How much is spent on information security and what is it being spent on?
5. What is the impact on the organization of a serious security incident?
6. Does the organization view information security as an enabler? (For example, by implementing effective security, could the organization increase business over the Internet?)
7. What is the risk to the business of getting a reputation for low information security?
8. What steps have been taken to ensure that third parties will not compromise the security of the organization?
9. How does the organization obtain independent assurance that information security is managed effectively?
10. How does the organization measure the effectiveness of its information security activities?

FIGURE B6.3

Top 10 Questions Managers Should Ask Regarding Information Security

AUTHENTICATION AND AUTHORIZATION

Authentication is a method for confirming users' identities. Once a system determines the authentication of a user, it can then determine the access privileges (or authorization) for that user. *Authorization* is the process of giving someone permission to do or have something. In multiple-user computer systems, user access or authorization determines such things as file access, hours of access, and amount of allocated storage space. Authentication and authorization techniques are broken down into three categories, and the most secure type involves a combination of all three:

1. Something the user knows such as a user ID and password.
2. Something the user has such as a smart card or token.
3. Something that is part of the user such as a fingerprint or voice signature.

Something the User Knows such as a User ID and Password

The first type of authentication, using something the user knows, is the most common way to identify individual users and typically consists of a unique user ID and password. However, this is actually one of the most *ineffective* ways for determining authentication because passwords are not secure. All it typically takes to crack a password is enough time. More than 50 percent of help-desk calls are password related, which can cost an organization significant money, and passwords are vulnerable to being coaxed out of somebody by a social engineer.

Identity theft is the forging of someone's identity for the purpose of fraud. The fraud is often financial fraud, to apply for and use credit cards in the victim's name or to apply for a loan. Figure B6.4 displays several examples of identity theft.

Phishing is a common way to steal identities online. *Phishing* is a technique to gain personal information for the purpose of identity theft, usually by means of fraudulent e-mail. One way to accomplish phishing is to send out e-mail messages that look as though they came from legitimate businesses such as AOL, MSN, or Amazon. The messages appear to be genuine with official-looking formats and logos. These e-mails typically ask for verification of important information like passwords and account numbers. The reason given is often that this personal information is required for accounting or auditing purposes. Since the

FIGURE B6.4

Examples of Identity Theft

Identity Theft Examples
An 82-year-old woman in Fort Worth, Texas, discovered that her identity had been stolen when the woman using her name was involved in a four-car collision. For 18 months, she kept getting notices of lawsuits and overdue medical bills that were really meant for someone else. It took seven years for her to get her financial good name restored after the identity thief charged over $100,000 on her 12 fraudulently acquired credit cards.
A 42-year-old retired Army captain in Rocky Hill, Connecticut, found that an identity thief had spent $260,000 buying goods and services that included two trucks, a Harley-Davidson motorcycle, and a time-share vacation home in South Carolina. The victim discovered his problem only when his retirement pay was garnished to pay the outstanding bills.
In New York, members of a pickpocket ring forged the driver's licenses of their victims within hours of snatching the women's purses. Stealing a purse typically results in around $200, if not less. But stealing the person's identity can net on average between $4,000 and $10,000.
A crime gang took out $8 million worth of second mortgages on victims' homes. It turned out the source of all the instances of identity theft came from a car dealership.
The largest identity-theft scam to date in U.S. history was broken up by police in 2002 when they discovered that three men had downloaded credit reports using stolen passwords and sold them to criminals on the street for $60 each. Many millions of dollars were stolen from people in all 50 states.

e-mails look authentic, up to one in five recipients respond with the information, and subsequently becomes a victim of identity theft and other fraud. Figure B6.5 displays the amount of money lost to identity thefts based on stolen passwords, among other things.[5]

Something the User Has such as a Smart Card or Token

The second type of authentication, using something that the user has, offers a much more effective way to identify individuals than a user ID and password. Tokens and smart cards are two of the primary forms of this type of authentication. *Tokens* are small electronic devices that change user passwords automatically. The user enters his/her user ID and token displayed password to gain access to the network. A *smart card* is a device that is around the same size as a credit card, containing embedded technologies that can store information and small amounts of software to perform some limited processing. Smart cards can act as identification instruments, a form of digital cash, or a data storage device with the ability to store an entire medical record.

Something That Is Part of the User such as a Fingerprint or Voice Signature

The third kind of authentication, using something that is part of the user, is by far the best and most effective way to manage authentication. *Biometrics* (narrowly defined) is the identification of a user based on a physical characteristic, such as a fingerprint, iris, face, voice, or handwriting. Unfortunately, biometric authentication can be costly and intrusive. For example, iris scans are expensive and considered intrusive by most people. Fingerprint authentication is less intrusive and inexpensive but is also not 100 percent accurate.

PREVENTION AND RESISTANCE

Prevention and resistance technologies stop intruders from accessing intellectual capital. A division of Sony Inc., Sony Pictures Entertainment (SPE), defends itself from attacks by using an intrusion detection system to detect new attacks as they occur. SPE develops and distributes a wide variety of products including movies, television, videos, and DVDs. A compromise to SPE security could result in costing the company valuable intellectual capital as well as millions of dollars and months of time. The company needed an advanced threat management solution that would take fewer resources to maintain and require limited resources to track and respond to suspicious network activity. The company installed an advanced intrusion detection system allowing it to monitor all of its network activity including any potential security breaches.[6]

The cost of downtime or network operation failures can be devastating to any business. For example, eBay experienced a 22-hour outage in June 2000 that caused the company's market cap to plunge an incredible $5.7 billion. Downtime costs for businesses can vary from $100 to $1 million per hour. An organization must prepare for and anticipate these types of outages resulting most commonly from hackers and viruses. Technologies available to help prevent and build resistance to attacks include **1.** content filtering, **2.** encryption, and **3.** firewalls.[7]

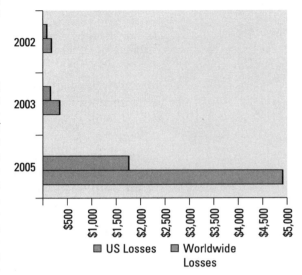

Identity thefts are expected to increase anywhere from 900% to 2,250% over the next two years; dollar figures are billions.

FIGURE B6.5

Identity Theft Losses by 2005 (billions of dollars)

2003 $20.5

2007 $198

FIGURE B6.6

Corporate Losses Caused by Spam Worldwide (2003 and 2007 in billions)

Content Filtering

Content filtering occurs when organizations use software that filters content to prevent the transmission of unauthorized information. Organizations can use content filtering technologies to filter e-mail and prevent e-mails containing sensitive information from transmitting, whether the transmission was malicious or accidental. It can also filter e-mails and prevent any suspicious files from transmitting such as potential virus-infected files. E-mail content filtering can also filter for *spam,* a form of unsolicited e-mail. Estimates predict that organizational losses from spam will be about $198 billion by 2007 (see Figure B6.6).[8]

Encryption

Encryption scrambles information into an alternative form that requires a key or password to decrypt the information. If there is an information security breach and the information was encrypted, the person stealing the information will be unable to read it. Encryption can switch the order of characters, replace characters with other characters, insert or remove characters, or use a mathematical formula to convert the information into some sort of code. Companies that transmit sensitive customer information over the Internet, such as credit card numbers, frequently use encryption.

Some encryption technologies use multiple keys like public key encryption. *Public key encryption (PKE)* is an encryption system that uses two keys: a public key that everyone can have and a private key for only the recipient (see Figure B6.7). When implementing security using multiple keys, the organization provides the public key to all of its customers (end consumers and other businesses). The customers use the public key to encrypt their information and send it along the Internet. When it arrives at its destination, the organization would use the private key to unscramble the encrypted information.

Firewalls

One of the most common defenses for preventing a security breach is a firewall. A *firewall* is hardware and/or software that guards a private network by analyzing the information leaving and entering the network. Firewalls examine each message that wants entrance to the network. Unless the message has the correct markings, the firewall prevents it from entering the network. Firewalls can even detect computers communicating with the Internet without approval. As Figure B6.8 illustrates, organizations typically place a firewall between a server and the Internet.

FIGURE B6.7

Public Key Encryption (PKE) System

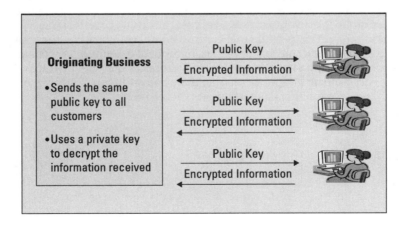

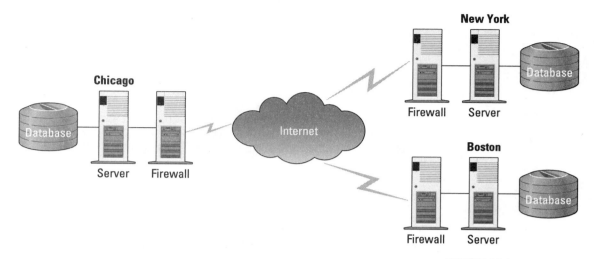

FIGURE B6.8

Sample Firewall Architecture Connecting Systems Located in Chicago, New York, and Boston

DETECTION AND RESPONSE

The final area where organizations can allocate resources is in detection and response technologies. If prevention and resistance strategies fail and there is a security breach, an organization can use detection and response technologies to mitigate the damage. The most common type of defense within detection and response technologies is antivirus software.

A single worm can cause massive damage. In August 2003, the "Blaster worm" infected over 50,000 computers worldwide and was one of the worst outbreaks of the year. Jeffrey Lee Parson, 18, was arrested by U.S. cyber investigators for unleashing the damaging worm on the Internet. The worm replicated itself repeatedly, eating up computer capacity, but did not damage information or programs. The worm generated so much traffic that it brought entire networks down.

The FBI used the latest technologies and code analysis to find the source of the worm. Prosecutors said Microsoft suffered financial losses that significantly exceeded $5,000, the statutory threshold in most hacker cases. Parson, charged with intentionally causing or attempting to cause damage to a computer, was sentenced to 18 months in prison, three years of supervised release, and 100 hours of community service. "What you've done is a terrible thing. Aside from injuring people and their computers, you shook the foundation of technology," U.S. District Judge Marsha Pechman told Parsons.

"With this arrest, we want to deliver a message to cyber-hackers here and around the world," said U.S. Attorney John McKay in Seattle. "Let there be no mistake about it, cyber-hacking is a crime. We will investigate, arrest, and prosecute cyber-hackers."[9]

Typically, people equate viruses (the malicious software) with hackers (the people). While not all types of hackers create viruses, many do. Figure B6.9 provides an overview of the most common types of hackers and viruses.

Some of the most damaging forms of security threats to e-business sites include malicious code, hoaxes, spoofing, and sniffers (see Figure B6.10).

Hackers—people very knowledgeable about computers who use their knowledge to invade other people's computers.

- *White-hat hackers*—work at the request of the system owners to find system vulnerabilities and plug the holes.

- *Black-hat hackers*—break into other people's computer systems and may just look around or may steal and destroy information.

- *Hactivists*—have philosophical and political reasons for breaking into systems and will often deface the Web site as a protest.

- *Script kiddies* or *script bunnies*—find hacking code on the Internet and click-and-point their way into systems to cause damage or spread viruses.

- *Cracker*—a hacker with criminal intent.

- *Cyberterrorists*—seek to cause harm to people or to destroy critical systems or information and use the Internet as a weapon of mass destruction.

Viruses—software written with malicious intent to cause annoyance or damage.

- *Worm*—a type of virus that spreads itself, not only from file to file, but also from computer to computer. The primary difference between a virus and a worm is that a virus must attach to something, such as an executable file, in order to spread. Worms do not need to attach to anything to spread and can tunnel themselves into computers.

- *Denial-of-service attack (DoS)*—floods a Web site with so many requests for service that it slows down or crashes the site.

- *Distributed denial-of-service attack (DDoS)*—attacks from multiple computers that flood a Web site with so many requests for service that it slows down or crashes. A common type is the Ping of Death, in which thousands of computers try to access a Web site at the same time, overloading it and shutting it down.

- *Trojan-horse virus*—hides inside other software, usually as an attachment or a downloadable file.

- *Backdoor programs*—viruses that open a way into the network for future attacks.

- *Polymorphic viruses and worms*—change their form as they propagate.

Security Threats to E-Business
Elevation of privilege is a process by which a user misleads a system into granting unauthorized rights, usually for the purpose of compromising or destroying the system. For example, an attacker might log on to a network by using a guest account, and then exploit a weakness in the software that lets the attacker change the guest privileges to administrative privileges.
Hoaxes attack computer systems by transmitting a virus hoax, with a real virus attached. By masking the attack in a seemingly legitimate message, unsuspecting users more readily distribute the message and send the attack on to their co-workers and friends, infecting many users along the way.
Malicious code includes a variety of threats such as viruses, worms, and Trojan horses.
Spoofing is the forging of the return address on an e-mail so that the e-mail message appears to come from someone other than the actual sender. This is not a virus but rather a way by which virus authors conceal their identities as they send out viruses.
Spyware is software that comes hidden in free downloadable software and tracks online movements, mines the information stored on a computer, or uses a computer's CPU and storage for some task the user knows nothing about. According to the National Cyber Security Alliance, 91 percent of the study had spyware on their computers that can cause extremely slow performance, excessive pop-up ads, or hijacked home pages.
A **sniffer** is a program or device that can monitor data traveling over a network. Sniffers can show all the data being transmitted over a network, including passwords and sensitive information. Sniffers tend to be a favorite weapon in the hacker's arsenal.
Packet tampering consists of altering the contents of packets as they travel over the Internet or altering data on computer disks after penetrating a network. For example, an attacker might place a tap on a network line to intercept packets as they leave the computer. The attacker could eavesdrop or alter the information as it leaves the network.

Implementing information security lines of defense through people first and through technology second is the best way for an organization to protect its vital intellectual capital. The first line of defense is securing intellectual capital by creating an information security plan detailing the various information security policies. The second line of defense is investing in technology to help secure information through authentication and authorization, prevention and resistance, and detection and response.

★ KEY TERMS

Authentication, 334	Hacker, 338	Public key encryption (PKE), 336
Authorization, 334	Hactivist, 338	Script kiddies or script
Backdoor program, 338	Hoaxes, 339	bunnies, 338
Biometrics, 335	Identify theft, 334	Smart card, 335
Black-hat hacker, 338	Information security, 330	Sniffer, 339
Content filtering, 336	Information security plan, 331	Social engineering, 331
Cracker, 338	Information security policy, 331	Spam, 336
Cyberterrorist, 338	Insider, 330	Spoofing, 339
Denial-of-service attack	Intrusion detection software	Spyware, 339
(DoS), 338	(IDS), 333	Token, 335
Distributed denial-of-service	Malicious code, 339	Trojan-horse virus, 338
attack (DDoS), 338	Packet tampering, 339	Virus, 338
Encryption, 336	Phishing, 334	White-hat hacker, 338
Elevation of privilege, 339	Polymorphic virus and	Worm, 338
Firewall, 331, 336	worm, 338	

★ CLOSING CASE ONE

Thinking Like the Enemy

David and Barry Kaufman, the founders of the Intense School, recently added several security courses, including the five-day "Professional Hacking Boot Camp" and "Social Engineering in Two Days."

Information technology departments must know how to protect organizational information. Therefore, organizations must teach their IT personnel how to protect their systems, especially in light of the many new government regulations, such as the Health Insurance Portability and Accountability Act (HIPAA), that demand secure systems. The concept of sending IT professionals to a hacking school seems counterintuitive; it is somewhat similar to sending accountants to an Embezzling 101 course. The Intense School does not strive to breed the next generation of hackers, however, but to teach its students how to be "ethical" hackers: to use their skills to build better locks, and to understand the minds of those who would attempt to crack them.

The main philosophy of the security courses at the Intense School is simply "To know thy enemy." In fact, one of the teachers at the Intense School is none other than Kevin Mitnick, the famous hacker who was imprisoned from 1995 to 2000. Teaching security from the hacker's perspective, as Mitnick does, is more difficult than teaching hacking itself: A hacker just needs to know one way into a system, David Kaufman notes, but a security professional needs to know *all* of the system's vulnerabilities. The two courses analyze those vulnerabilities from different perspectives.

The hacking course, which costs $3,500, teaches ways to protect against the mischief typically associated with hackers: worming through computer systems through vulnerabilities that are susceptible to technical, or computer-based, attacks. Mitnick's $1,950 social engineering course, by contrast, teaches the more frightening art of worming through the vulnerabilities of the people using and maintaining systems—getting passwords and access through duplicity, not technology. People that take this class, or read Mitnick's book, *The Art of Deception,* never again think of passwords or the trash bin the same way.

So how does the Intense School teach hacking? With sessions on dumpster diving (the unsavory practice of looking for passwords and other bits of information on discarded papers), with field trips to case target systems, and with practice runs at the company's in-house "target range," a network of computers set up to thwart and educate students.

One feature of the Intense School that raises a few questions is that the school does not check on morals at the door: Anyone paying the tuition can attend the school. Given the potential danger that an unchecked graduate of a hacking school could represent, it is surprising that the FBI does not collect the names of the graduates. But perhaps it gets them any how—several governmental agencies have sent students to the school.[10]

Questions

1. How could an organization benefit from attending one of the courses offered at the Intense School?

2. What are the two primary lines of security defense and how can organizational employees use the information taught by the Intense School when drafting an information security plan?

3. Determine the differences between the two primary courses offered at the Intense School, "Professional Hacking Boot Camp" and "Social Engineering in Two Days." Which course is more important for organizational employees to attend?

4. If your employer sent you to take a course at the Intense School, which one would you choose and why?

5. What are the ethical dilemmas involved with having such a course offered by a private company?

★ CLOSING CASE TWO

Hacker Hunters

Hacker hunters are the new breed of crime-fighter. They employ the same methodology used to fight organized crime in the 1980s—informants and the cyberworld equivalent of wiretaps. Daniel Larking, a 20-year veteran who runs the FBI's Internet Crime Complaint Center, taps online service providers to help track down criminal hackers. Leads supplied by the FBI and eBay helped Romanian police round up 11 members of a gang that set up fake eBay accounts and auctioned off cell phones, laptops, and cameras they never intended to deliver.

On October 26, 2004, the FBI unleashed Operation Firewall, targeting the ShadowCrew, a gang whose members were schooled in identity theft, bank account pillage, and selling illegal goods on the Internet. ShadowCrew's 4,000 gang members lived in a dozen countries and across the United States. For months, agents had been watching their every move through a clandestine gateway into their Web site, shadowcrew.com. One member turned informant called a group meeting, ensuring the members would be at home on their computers during a certain time. At 9 p.m. the Secret Service issued orders to move in on the gang. The move was synchronized around the globe to prevent gang members from warning each other via instant messages. Twenty-eight gang members in eight states and six countries were arrested, most still at their computers. Authorities seized dozens of computers and found 1.7 million credit card numbers and more than 18 million e-mail accounts.

ShadowCrew's Operations

The alleged ringleaders of ShadowCrew included Andres Mantovani, 23, a part-time community college student in Arizona, and David Appleyard, 45, a former New Jersey mortgage broker. Mantovani and Appleyard allegedly were administrators in charge of running the Web site and recruiting members. The site created a marketplace for over 4,000 gang members who bought and sold hot information and merchandise. The Web site was open for business 24 hours a day, but since most of the members held jobs, the busiest time was from 10 p.m. to 2 a.m. on Sundays. Hundreds of gang members would meet online to trade credit card information, passports, and even equipment to make fake identity documents. Platinum credit cards cost more than gold ones and discounts were offered for package deals. One member known as "Scarface" sold 115,695 stolen credit card numbers in a single trade. Overall, the gang made more than $4 million in credit card purchases over two years. ShadowCrew was equivalent to an eBay for the underworld. The site even posted crime tips on how to use stolen credit cards and fake IDs at big retailers.

The gang stole credit card numbers and other valuable information through clever tricks. One of the favorites was sending millions of phishing e-mails—messages that appeared to be from legitimate companies such as Yahoo!— designed to steal passwords and credit card numbers. The gang also hacked into corporate databases to steal account data. According to sources familiar with the investigation, the gang cracked the networks of 12 unidentified companies that were not even aware their systems had been breached.

Police Operations

Brian Nagel, an assistant director at the Secret Service, coordinated the effort to track the ShadowCrew. Allies included Britain's National High-Tech Crimes unit, the Royal Canadian Mounted Police, and the Bulgarian Interior Ministry. Authorities turned one of the high-ranking members of the gang into a snitch and had the man help the Secret Service set up a new electronic doorway for ShadowCrew members to enter their Web site. The snitch spread the word that the new gateway was a more secure way to the Web site. It was the first-ever tap of a private computer network. "We became shadowcrew.com," Nagel said. Mantovani and Appleyard were slated for trail in late 2005. Authorities anticipated using case evidence to make additional arrests.[11]

Questions

1. What types of technology could big retailers use to prevent identity thieves from purchasing merchandise?
2. What can organizations do to protect themselves from hackers looking to steal account data?
3. Authorities frequently tap online service providers to track down hackers. Do you think it is ethical for authorities to tap an online service provider and read people's e-mail? Why or why not?
4. Do you think it was ethical for authorities to use one of the high-ranking officials to trap other gang members? Why or why not?
5. In a team, research the Internet and find the best ways to protect yourself from identity theft.

1. **Firewall Decisions**

   You are the CEO of Inverness Investments, a medium-sized venture capital firm that specializes in investing in high-tech companies. The company receives over 30,000 e-mail messages per year. On average, there are two viruses and three successful hackings against the company each year, which result in losses to the company of about $250,000. Currently, the company has antivirus software installed but does not have any firewalls.

   Your CIO is suggesting implementing 10 firewalls for a total cost of $80,000. The estimated life of each firewall is about three years. The chances of hackers breaking into the system with the firewalls installed are about 3 percent. Annual maintenance costs on the firewalls is estimated around $15,000. Create an argument for or against supporting your CIO's recommendation to purchase the firewalls.

2. **Drafting an Information Security Plan**

   Making The Grade is a nonprofit organization that helps students learn how to achieve better grades in school. The organization has 40 offices in 25 states and over 2,000 employees. The company is currently building a Web site to offer its services online. You have recently been hired by the CIO as the director of information security. Your first assignment is to develop a document discussing the importance of creating information security polices and an information security plan. Be sure to include the following:

   ■ The importance of educating employees on information security.

   ■ A few samples of employee information security policies.

   ■ Other major areas the information security plan should address.

   ■ Signs the company should look for to determine if the new site is being hacked.

   ■ The major types of attacks the company should expect to experience.

3. **Discussing the Three Areas of Security**

   Great Granola Inc. is a small business operating out of northern California. The company specializes in selling unique homemade granola, and its primary sales vehicle is through its Web site. The company is growing exponentially and expects its revenues to triple this year to $12 million. The company also expects to hire 60 additional employees to support its growing number of customers. Joan Martin, the CEO, is aware that if her competitors discover the recipe for her granola, or who her primary customers are, it could easily ruin her business. Joan has hired you to draft a document discussing the different areas of information security, along with your recommendations for providing a secure e-business environment.

4. **College Security**

   Computer and online security is a growing concern for businesses of all sizes. Computer security issues range from viruses to automated Internet attacks to outright theft, the result of which is lost information and lost time. Security issues pop up in news articles daily, and most business owners understand the need to secure their businesses. Your college is no different from any other business when it comes to information security. Draft a document identifying the questions you should ask your college's CIO to ensure information security across your campus.

B7

Ethics

1. Summarize the guidelines for creating an information privacy policy.
2. Identify the differences between an ethical computer use policy and an acceptable use policy.
3. Describe the relationship between an e-mail privacy policy and an Internet use policy.
4. Explain the effects of spam on an organization.
5. Summarize the different monitoring technologies and explain the importance of an employee monitoring policy.

Introduction

The core units introduced **ethics,** which are the principles and standards that guide our behavior toward other people. Technology has created many new ethical dilemmas in our electronic society. The following are a few important concepts and terms related to ethical issues stemming from advances in technology:

- **Intellectual property**—intangible creative work that is embodied in physical form.
- **Copyright**—the legal protection afforded an expression of an idea, such as a song, video game, and some types of proprietary documents.
- **Fair use doctrine**—in certain situations, it is legal to use copyrighted material.
- **Pirated software**—the unauthorized use, duplication, distribution, or sale of copyrighted software.
- **Counterfeit software**—software that is manufactured to look like the real thing and sold as such.

The core units also introduced **privacy,** which is the right to be left alone when you want to be, to have control over your own personal possessions, and not to be observed without your consent. Privacy is related to **confidentiality,** which is the assurance that messages and information are available only to those who are authorized to view them. This plug-in takes a detailed look at **ePolicies**—policies and procedures that address the ethical use of computers and Internet usage in the business environment. These ePolicies typically address information privacy and confidentiality issues and include the following:

- Ethical computer use policy.
- Information privacy policy.
- Acceptable use policy.
- E-mail privacy policy.
- Internet use policy.
- Anti-spam policy.

Ethics

Individuals form the only ethical component of an IT system. They determine how they use IT, and how they are affected by IT. How individuals behave toward each other, how they handle information and technology, are largely influenced by their ethics. Ethical dilemmas usually arise not in simple, clear-cut situations but out of a clash between competing goals, responsibilities, and loyalties. Ethical decisions are complex judgments that balance rewards against responsibilities. Inevitably, the decision process is influenced by uncertainty about the magnitude of the outcome, by the estimate of the importance of the situation, by the perception of conflicting "right reactions," when there is more than one socially acceptable "correct" decision. Figure B7.1 contains examples of ethically questionable or unacceptable uses of information technology.

People make arguments for or against—justify or condemn—the behaviors in Figure B7.1. Unfortunately, there are few hard and fast rules for always determining what is and is not ethical. Knowing the law will not always help because what is legal might not always be ethical, and what might be ethical is not always legal. For example, Joe Reidenberg received an offer for cell phone service from AT&T Wireless. The offer revealed that AT&T Wireless had used Equifax, a credit reporting agency, to identify Joe Reidenberg as a potential customer. Overall, this strategy seemed like good business. Equifax could generate additional revenue by selling information it already owned and AT&T Wireless could identify target markets, thereby increasing response rates to its marketing campaigns. Unfortunately, by law, credit information cannot be used to sell anything. The Fair Credit Reporting Act (FCRA) forbids repurposing credit information except when the information is used for "a firm offer of credit or insurance." In other words, the only product that can be sold based on credit information is credit. A spokesman for Equifax stated that "as long as AT&T Wireless (or any company for that matter) is offering the cell phone service on a

Examples of Questionable Information Technology Use
Individuals copy, use, and distribute software.
Employees search organizational databases for sensitive corporate and personal information.
Organizations collect, buy, and use information without checking the validity or accuracy of the information.
Individuals create and spread viruses that cause trouble for those using and maintaining IT systems.
Individuals hack into computer systems to steal proprietary information.
Employees destroy or steal proprietary organization information such as schematics, sketches, customer lists, and reports.

FIGURE B7.1

Ethically Questionable or Unacceptable Information Technology Use

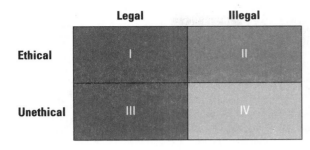

	Legal	Illegal
Ethical	I	II
Unethical	III	IV

FIGURE B7.2

Acting Ethically and Legally Are Not Always the Same

credit basis, such as allowing the use of the service before the consumer has to pay, it is in compliance with the FCRA."[1] But is it ethical?

This is a good example of the ethical dilemmas facing many organizations today; because technology is so new and pervasive in unexpected ways, the ethics surrounding information have not been all worked out. Figure B7.2 displays the four quadrants of ethical and legal behavior. The ideal goal for organizations is to make decisions within quadrant I that are both legal and ethical.

INFORMATION HAS NO ETHICS

Jerry Rode, CIO of Saab Cars USA, realized he had a public relations fiasco on his hands when he received an e-mail from an irate customer. Saab had hired four Internet marketing companies to distribute electronic information about Saab's new models to its customers. Saab specified that the marketing campaign be *opt-in,* implying that it would contact only the people who had agreed to receive promotions and marketing material via e-mail. Unfortunately, one of the marketing companies apparently had a different definition of opt-in and was e-mailing all customers regardless of their opt-in decision.

Rode fired the errant marketing company and immediately developed a formal policy for the use of customer information. "The customer doesn't see ad agencies and contracted marketing firms. They see Saab USA spamming them," Rode said. "Finger-pointing after the fact won't make your customers feel better."[2]

Information has no ethics. Information does not care how it is used. It will not stop itself from spamming customers, sharing itself if it is sensitive or personal, or revealing details to third parties. Information cannot delete or preserve itself. Therefore, it falls on the shoulders of those who lord over the information to develop ethical guidelines on how to manage it. Figure B7.3 provides an overview of some of the important laws that individuals must follow when they are attempting to manage and protect information.

FIGURE B7.3

Established Information-Related Laws

Established Information-Related Laws	
Privacy Act—1974	Restricts what information the federal government can collect; allows people to access and correct information on themselves; requires procedures to protect the security of personal information; and forbids the disclosure of name-linked information without permission.
Family Education Rights and Privacy Act—1974	Regulates access to personal education records by government agencies and other third parties and ensures the right of students to see their own records.
Cable Communications Act—1984	Requires written or electronic consent from viewers before cable TV providers can release viewing choices or other personally identifiable information.
Electronic Communications Privacy Act—1986	Allows the reading of communications by a firm and says that employees have no right to privacy when using the companies' computers.
Computer Fraud and Abuse Act—1986	Prohibits unauthorized access to computers used for financial institutions, the U.S. government, or interstate and international trade.

(Continued)

Established Information-Related Laws	
The Bork Bill (officially known as the Video Privacy Protection Act)—1988	Prohibits the use of video rental information on customers for any purpose other than that of marketing goods and services directly to the customer.
Communications Assistance for Law Enforcement Act—1994	Requires that telecommunications equipment be designed so that authorized government agents are able to intercept all wired and wireless communications being sent or received by any subscriber. The act also requires that subscriber call-identifying information be transmitted to a government when and if required.
Freedom of Information Act—1967, 1975, 1994, and 1998	Allows any person to examine government records unless it would cause an invasion of privacy. It was amended in 1974 to apply to the FBI, and again in 1994 to allow citizens to monitor government activities and information gathering, and once again in 1998 to allow access to government information on the Internet.
Health Insurance Portability and Accountability Act (HIPAA)—1996	Requires that the health care industry formulate and implement regulations to keep patient information confidential.
Identity Theft and Assumption Deterrence Act—1998	Strengthened the criminal laws governing identity theft making it a federal crime to use or transfer identification belonging to another. It also established a central federal service for victims.
USA Patriot Act—2001 and 2003	Allows law enforcement to get access to almost any information, including library records, video rentals, bookstore purchases, and business records when investigating any act of terrorist or clandestine intelligence activities. In 2003, Patriot II broadened the original law.
Homeland Security Act—2002	Provided new authority to government agencies to mine data on individuals and groups including e-mails and Web site visits; put limits on the information available under the Freedom of Information Act; and gave new powers to government agencies to declare national health emergencies.
Sarbanes-Oxley Act—2002	Sought to protect investors by improving the accuracy and reliability of corporate disclosures and requires companies to (1) implement extensive and detailed policies to prevent illegal activity within the company, and (2) to respond in a timely manner to investigate illegal activity.
Fair and Accurate Credit Transactions Act—2003	Included provisions for the prevention of identity theft including consumers' right to get a credit report free each year, requiring merchants to leave all but the last five digits of a credit card number off a receipt, and requiring lenders and credit agencies to take action even before a victim knows a crime has occurred when they notice any circumstances that might indicate identity theft.
CAN-Spam Act—2003	Sought to regulate interstate commerce by imposing limitations and penalties on businesses sending unsolicited e-mail to consumers. The law forbids deceptive subject lines, headers, return addresses, etc., as well as the harvesting of e-mail addresses from Web sites. It requires businesses that send spam to maintain a do-not-spam list and to include a postal mailing address in the message.

Developing Information Management Policies

Treating sensitive corporate information as a valuable resource is good management. Building a corporate culture based on ethical principles that employees can understand and implement is responsible management. In an effort to provide guidelines for ethical information management, *CIO* magazine (along with over 100 CIOs) developed six principles for ethical information management displayed in Figure B7.4.

To follow *CIO*'s six principles for ethical information management, a corporation should develop written policies establishing employee guidelines, personnel procedures, and organizational rules. These policies set employee expectations about the organization's practices and standards and protect the organization from misuse of computer systems and IT resources. If an organization's employees use computers at work, the organization should, at a minimum, implement ePolicies. *ePolicies* are policies and procedures that address the ethical use of computers and Internet usage in the business environment. ePolicies typically embody the following:

- Ethical computer use policy.
- Information privacy policy.
- Acceptable use policy.
- E-mail privacy policy.
- Internet use policy.
- Anti-spam policy.

ETHICAL COMPUTER USE POLICY

One of the essential steps in creating an ethical corporate culture is establishing an ethical computer use policy. An *ethical computer use policy* contains general principles to guide computer user behavior. For example, the ethical computer use policy might explicitly state that users should refrain from playing computer games during working hours. This policy ensures that the users know how to behave at work and that the organization has a published standard by which to deal with user infractions—for example, after appropriate warnings, terminating an employee who spends significant amounts of time playing computer games at work.

There are variations in how organizations expect their employees to use computers, but in any approach the overriding principle when seeking appropriate computer use should be informed consent. The users should be *informed* of the rules and, by agreeing to use the system on that basis, *consent* to abide by the rules.

An organization should make a conscientious effort to ensure that all users are aware of the policy through formal training and other means. If an organization were to have only one policy, it would want it to be an ethical computer use policy since it is the starting point and the umbrella for any other policies that the organization might establish.

CIO Magazine's Six Principles for Ethical Information Management

Six Principles for Ethical Information Management
1. Information is a valuable corporate asset like cash, facilities, or any other corporate asset and should be managed as such.
2. The CIO is steward of corporate information and is responsible for managing it over its life cycle—from its generation to its appropriate destruction.
3. The CIO is responsible for controlling access to and use of information, as determined by governmental regulation and corporate policy.
4. The CIO is responsible for preventing the inappropriate destruction of information.
5. The CIO is responsible for bringing technological knowledge to the development of information management practices and policies.
6. The CIO should partner with executive peers to develop and execute the organization's information management policies.

INFORMATION PRIVACY POLICY

Scott Thompson is the executive vice president of Inovant, the company Visa set up to handle its technology. Thompson errs on the side of caution in regard to Visa's information: He bans the use of Visa's customer information for anything outside its intended purpose—billing.

Visa's customer information details such things as what people are spending their money on, in which stores, on which days, and even at what time of day. Sales and marketing departments around the country no doubt are salivating at any prospect of gaining access to Thompson's databases. "They would love to refine the information into loyalty programs, target markets, or even partnerships with Visa. There are lots of creative people coming up with these ideas," Thompson says. "This whole area of information sharing is enormous and growing. For the marketers, the sky's the limit." Thompson, along with privacy specialists, developed a strict credit card information policy, which the company follows. The question now is can Thompson guarantee that some unethical use of his information will not occur? Many experts do not believe that he can.

In fact, in a large majority of cases, the unethical use of information happens not through the malicious scheming of a rogue marketer, but rather unintentionally. For example, information is collected and stored for some purpose, such as record keeping or billing. Then, a sales or marketing professional figures out another way to use it internally, share it with partners, or sell it to a trusted third party. The information is "unintentionally" used for new purposes. The classic example of this type of unintentional information reuse is the Social Security number, which started simply as a way to identify government retirement benefits and is now used as a sort of universal personal ID, found on everything from drivers' licenses to savings accounts.

An organization that wants to protect its information should develop an information privacy policy. An ***information privacy policy*** contains general principles regarding information privacy. Figure B7.5 highlights a few guidelines an organization can follow when creating an information privacy policy.

FIGURE B7.5

Organizational Guidelines for Creating an Information Privacy Policy

---

Creating An Information Privacy Policy

1. Adoption and implementation of a privacy policy. An organization engaged in online activities or e-business has a responsibility to adopt and implement a policy for protecting the privacy of personal information. Organizations should also take steps that foster the adoption and implementation of effective online privacy policies by the organizations with which they interact, for instance, by sharing best practices with business partners.

2. Notice and disclosure. An organization's privacy policy must be easy to find, read, and understand. The policy must clearly state:

- What information is being collected.
- The use of information being collected.
- Possible third-party distribution of that information.
- The choices available to an individual regarding collection, use, and distribution of the collected information,
- A statement of the organization's commitment to information security.
- What steps the organization takes to ensure information quality and access.

3. Choice and consent. Individuals must be given the opportunity to exercise choice regarding how personal information collected from them online may be used when such use is unrelated to the purpose for which the information was collected. At a minimum, individuals should be given the opportunity to opt out of such use.

4. Information security. Organizations creating, maintaining, using, or disseminating personal information should take appropriate measures to assure its reliability and should take reasonable precautions to protect it from loss, misuse, or alteration.

5. Information quality and access. Organizations should establish appropriate processes or mechanisms so that inaccuracies in material personal information, such as account or contact information, may be corrected. Other procedures to assure information quality may include use of reliable sources, collection methods, appropriate consumer access, and protection against accidental or unauthorized alteration.

Acceptable Use Policy Stipulations
1. Not using the service as part of violating any law.
2. Not attempting to break the security of any computer network or user.
3. Not posting commercial messages to groups without prior permission.
4. Not performing any nonrepudiation.
5. Not attempting to send junk e-mail or spam to anyone who does not want to receive it.
6. Not attempting to mail bomb a site. A *mail bomb* is sending a massive amount of e-mail to a specific person or system resulting in filling up the recipient's disk space, which, in some cases, may be too much for the server to handle and may cause the server to stop functioning.

ACCEPTABLE USE POLICY

An *acceptable use policy (AUP)* is a policy that a user must agree to follow in order to be provided access to a network or to the Internet. *Nonrepudiation* is a contractual stipulation to ensure that e-business participants do not deny (repudiate) their online actions. A nonrepudiation clause is typically contained in an AUP.

It is common practice for many businesses and educational facilities to require that employees or students sign an acceptable use policy before being granted a network ID. When signing up with an Internet service provider (ISP), each customer is typically presented with an AUP, which states that they agree to adhere to certain stipulations (see Figure B7.6).

E-MAIL PRIVACY POLICY

E-mail is so pervasive in organizations that it requires its own specific policy. In a recent survey, 80 percent of professional workers identified e-mail as their preferred means of corporate communications. Trends also show a dramatic increase in the adoption rate of instant messaging (IM) in the workplace. While e-mail and IM are terrific business communication tools, there are risks associated with using them.

For instance, a sent e-mail is stored on at least three or four different computers (see Figure B7.7). Simply deleting an e-mail from one computer does not delete it off the other computers. Companies can mitigate many of the risks of using electronic messaging systems by implementing and adhering to an e-mail privacy policy.[3]

One of the major problems with e-mail is the user's expectations of privacy. To a large extent, this exception is based on the false assumption that there exists e-mail privacy protection somehow analogous to that of U.S. first-class mail. This is simply not true. Generally, the organization that owns the e-mail system can operate the system as openly or as privately as it wishes. That means that if the organization wants to read everyone's e-mail, it can do so. If it chooses not to read any, that is allowable too. Hence, it is up to the organization to decide how much, if any, e-mail it is going to read. Then, when it decides, it must inform the users, so that they can consent to this level of intrusion. In other words, an *e-mail privacy policy* details the extent to which e-mail messages may be read by others.

Organizations are urged to have some kind of e-mail privacy policy and to publish it no matter what the degree of intrusion. Figure B7.8 displays a few of the key stipulations generally contained in an e-mail privacy policy.

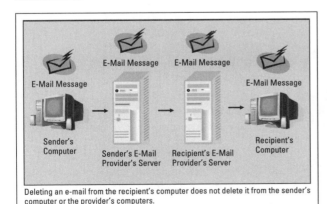

E-Mail Message · E-Mail Message · E-Mail Message · E-Mail Message

Sender's Computer → Sender's E-Mail Provider's Server → Recipient's E-Mail Provider's Server → Recipient's Computer

Deleting an e-mail from the recipient's computer does not delete it from the sender's computer or the provider's computers.

E-mail Privacy Policy Stipulations
1. The policy should be complementary to the ethical computer use policy.
2. It defines who legitimate e-mail users are.
3. It explains the backup procedure so users will know that at some point, even if a message is deleted from their computer, it will still be on the backup tapes.
4. It describes the legitimate grounds for reading someone's e-mail and the process required before such action can be taken.
5. It informs that the organization has no control of e-mail once it is transmitted outside the organization.
6. It explains what will happen if the user severs his or her connection with the organization.
7. It asks employees to be careful when making organizational files and documents available to others.

INTERNET USE POLICY

Similar to e-mail, the Internet has some unique aspects that make it a good candidate for its own policy. These include the large amounts of computing resources that Internet users can expend, thus making it essential that such use be legitimate. In addition, the Internet contains numerous materials that some might feel are offensive and, hence, some regulation might be required in this area. An *Internet use policy* contains general principles to guide the proper use of the Internet. Figure B7.9 displays a few important stipulations that might be included in an Internet use policy.

ANTI-SPAM POLICY

Chief technology officer (CTO) of the law firm Fenwick and West, Matt Kesner reduced incoming spam by 99 percent and found himself a corporate hero. Before the spam reduction, the law firm's partners (whose time is worth $350 to $600 an hour) found themselves spending hours each day sifting through 300 to 500 spam messages. The spam blocking engineered by Kesner traps between 5,000 and 7,000 messages a day.[4]

Spam is unsolicited e-mail. An *anti-spam policy* simply states that e-mail users will not send unsolicited e-mails (or spam). Spam plagues all levels of employees within an organization from receptionists to CEOs. Estimates indicate that spam accounts for 40 percent to 60 percent of most organizations' e-mail traffic. Ferris Research says spam cost U.S. businesses over $14 billion in 2005, and Nucleus Research stated that companies forfeit $874 per employee annually in lost productivity from spam alone. Spam clogs e-mail systems and siphons IT resources away from legitimate business projects.[5]

Internet Use Policy Stipulations
1. The policy should describe available Internet services because not all Internet sites allow users to access all services.
2. The policy should define the organization's position on the purpose of Internet access and what restrictions, if any, are placed on that access.
3. The policy should complement the ethical computer use policy.
4. The policy should describe user responsibility for citing sources, properly handling offensive material, and protecting the organization's good name.
5. The policy should clearly state the ramifications if the policy is violated.

Spam Prevention Tips

- **Disguise e-mail addresses posted in a public electronic place.** When posting an e-mail address in a public place, disguise the address through simple means such as replacing "jsmith@domain.com" with "jsmith at domain dot com." This prevents spam from recognizing the e-mail address.

- **Opt-out of member directories that may place an e-mail address online.** Choose not to participate in any activities that place e-mail addresses online. If an e-mail address is placed online be sure it is disguised in some way.

- **Use a filter.** Many ISPs and free e-mail services now provide spam filtering. While filters are not perfect, they can cut down tremendously on the amount of spam a user receives.

It is difficult to write anti-spam policies, laws, or software because there is no such thing as a universal litmus test for spam. One person's spam is another person's newsletter. End users have to be involved in deciding what spam is because what is unwanted can vary widely not just from one company to the next, but from one person to the next. What looks like spam to the rest of the world could be essential business communications for certain employees.

John Zarb, CIO of Libbey, a manufacturer of glassware, china, and flatware, tested Guenivere (a virus and subject-line filter) and SpamAssassin (an open source spam filter). He had to shut them off after 10 days because they were rejecting important legitimate e-mails. As Zarb quickly discovered, once an organization starts filtering e-mail, it runs the risk of blocking legitimate e-mails because they look like spam. Avoiding an unacceptable level of "false positives" requires a delicate balancing act. The IT team tweaked the spam filters and today, the filters block about 70 percent of Libbey's spam, and Zarb says the "false positive" rate is far lower but not zero. Figure B7.10 presents a few methods an organization can follow to prevent spam.

Ethics in the Workplace

Concern is growing among employees that infractions of corporate policies—even accidental ones—will be a cause for disciplinary action. The Whitehouse.gov Internet site displays the U.S. president's official Web site and updates on bill signings and new policies. Whitehouse.com, however, leads to a trashy site that capitalizes on its famous name. A simple mistype from .gov to .com could potentially cost someone her or his job if the company has a termination policy for viewing illicit Web sites. Monitoring employees is one of the largest issues facing CIOs when they are developing information management policies.

The question of whether to monitor what employees do on company time with corporate resources has been largely decided by legal precedents that are already holding businesses financially responsible for their employees' actions. Increasingly, employee monitoring is not a choice; it is a risk-management obligation.

A recent survey of workplace monitoring and surveillance practices by the American Management Association (AMA) and the ePolicy Institute showed the degree to which companies are turning to monitoring:

- 82 percent of the study's 1,627 respondents acknowledged conducting some form of electronic monitoring or physical surveillance.

- 63 percent of the companies stated that they monitor Internet connections.

- 47 percent acknowledged storing and reviewing employee e-mail messages.[6]

MONITORING TECHNOLOGIES

Many employees use their company's high-speed Internet access to shop, browse, and surf the Web. Fifty-nine percent of all 2005 Web purchases in the United States were made from the workplace, according to ComScore Networks. Vault.com determined that 47 percent of employees spend at least half an hour a day surfing the Web.[7]

This research indicates that managers should monitor what their employees are doing with their Web access. Most managers do not want their employees conducting personal business during working hours. For these reasons many organizations have increasingly taken the Big Brother approach to Web monitoring with software that tracks Internet usage and even allows the boss to read employees' e-mail. Figure B7.11 highlights a few reasons the effects of employee monitoring are worse than the lost productivity from employee Web surfing.

This is the thinking at SAS Institute, a private software company consistently ranked in the top 10 on many "Best Places to Work" surveys. SAS does not monitor its employees' Web usage. The company asks its employees to use company resources responsibly, but does not mind if they occasionally check sports scores or use the Web for shopping.

Many management gurus advocate that organizations whose corporate cultures are based on trust are more successful than those whose corporate cultures are based on distrust. Before an organization implements monitoring technology it should ask itself, "What does this say about how the organization feels about its employees?" If the organization really does not trust its employees, then perhaps it should find new ones. If an organization does trust its employees, then it might want to treat them accordingly. An organization that follows its employees' every keystroke is unwittingly undermining the relationships with its employees.[8]

Information technology monitoring is tracking people's activities by such measures as number of keystrokes, error rate, and number of transactions processed. Figure B7.12 displays different types of monitoring technologies currently available.

Employee Monitoring Policies

The best path for an organization planning to engage in employee monitoring is open communication surrounding the issue. A recent survey discovered that communication about monitoring issues is weak for most organizations. One in five companies did not even have an acceptable use policy and one in four companies did not have an Internet use policy.

Companies that did have policies usually tucked them into the rarely probed recesses of the employee handbook, and then the policies tended to be of the vague and legal jargon variety: "XYZ company reserves the right to monitor or review any information

Employee Monitoring Effects
1. Employee absenteeism is on the rise, almost doubling in 2004 to 21 percent. The lesson here might be that more employees are missing work to take care of personal business. Perhaps losing a few minutes here or there—or even a couple of hours—is cheaper than losing entire days.
2. Studies indicate that electronic monitoring results in lower job satisfaction, in part because people begin to believe the quantity of their work is more important than the quality.
3. Electronic monitoring also induces what psychologists call "psychological reactance": the tendency to rebel against constraints. If you tell your employees they cannot shop, they cannot use corporate networks for personal business, and they cannot make personal phone calls, then their desire to do all these things will likely increase.

FIGURE B7.11

Employee Monitoring Effects

Common Monitoring Technologies	
Key logger, or key trapper, software	A program that, when installed on a computer, records every keystroke and mouse click.
Hardware key logger	A hardware device that captures keystrokes on their journey from the keyboard to the motherboard.
Cookie	A small file deposited on a hard drive by a Web site containing information about customers and their Web activities. Cookies allow Web sites to record the comings and goings of customers, usually without their knowledge or consent.
Adware	Software that generates ads that install themselves on a computer when a person downloads some other program from the Internet.
Spyware (sneakware or stealthware)	Software that comes hidden in free downloadable software and tracks online movements, mines the information stored on a computer, or uses a computer's CPU and storage for some task the user knows nothing about.
Web log	Consists of one line of information for every visitor to a Web site and is usually stored on a Web server.
Clickstream	Records information about a customer during a Web surfing session such as what Web sites were visited, how long the visit was, what ads were viewed, and what was purchased.

stored or transmitted on its equipment." Reserving the right to monitor is materially different from clearly stating that the company does monitor, listing what is tracked, describing what is looked for, and detailing the consequences for violations.

An organization must formulate the right monitoring policies and put them into practice. *Employee monitoring policies* explicitly state how, when, and where the company monitors its employees. CSOs that are explicit about what the company does in the way of monitoring and the reasons for it, along with actively educating their employees about what unacceptable behavior looks like, will find that employees not only acclimate quite quickly to a policy, but also reduce the CSO's burden by policing themselves. Figure B7.13 displays several common stipulations an organization can follow when creating an employee monitoring policy.

Employee Monitoring Policy Stipulations
1. Be as specific as possible.
2. Always enforce the policy.
3. Enforce the policy in the same way for everyone.
4. Expressly communicate that the company reserves the right to monitor all employees.
5. Specifically state when monitoring will be performed.
6. Specifically state what will be monitored (e-mail, IM, Internet, network activity, etc.).
7. Describe the types of information that will be collected.
8. State the consequences for violating the policy.
9. State all provisions that allow for updates to the policy.
10. Specify the scope and manner of monitoring for any information system.
11. When appropriate, obtain a written receipt acknowledging that each party has received, read, and understood the monitoring policies.

A dvances in technology have made ethics a concern for many organizations. Consider how easy it is for an employee to e-mail large amounts of confidential information, change electronic communications, or destroy massive amounts of important company information all within seconds. Electronic information about customers, partners, and employees has become one of corporate America's most valuable assets. However, the line between the proper and improper use of this asset is at best blurry. Should an employer be able to search employee files without employee consent? Should a company be able to sell customer information without informing the customer of its intent? What is a responsible approach to document deletion?

The law provides guidelines in many of these areas, but how a company chooses to act within the confines of the law is up to the judgment of its officers. Since CIOs are responsible for the technology that collects, maintains, and destroys corporate information, they sit smack in the middle of this potential ethical quagmire.

One way an organization can begin dealing with ethical issues is to create a corporate culture that encourages ethical considerations and discourages dubious information dealings. Not only is an ethical culture an excellent idea overall, but it also acts as a precaution, helping prevent customer problems from escalating into front-page news stories. The establishment of and adherence to well-defined rules and policies will help organizations create an ethical corporate culture. These policies include:

- Ethical computer use policy.
- Information privacy policy.
- Acceptable use policy.
- E-mail privacy policy.
- Internet use policy.
- Anti-spam policy.
- Employee monitoring policy.

Acceptable use policy
  (AUP), 350
Adware, 354
Anti-spam policy, 351
Clickstream, 354
Confidentiality, 344
Cookie, 354
Copyright, 344
Counterfeit software, 344
E-mail privacy policy, 350
Employee monitoring policy, 354
ePolicies, 344, 348

Ethical computer use policy, 348
Ethics, 344
Fair use doctrine, 344
Hardware key logger, 354
Information privacy policy, 349
Information technology
  monitoring, 353
Intellectual property, 344
Internet use policy, 351
Key logger or key trapper
  software, 354
Mail bomb, 350

Nonrepudiation, 350
Opt-in, 346
Pirated software, 344
Privacy, 344
Spam, 351
Spyware (sneakware or
  stealthware), 354
Web log, 354

Sarbanes-Oxley: Where Information Technology, Finance, and Ethics Meet

The Sarbanes-Oxley Act (SOX) of 2002 was enacted in response to the high-profile Enron and WorldCom financial scandals to protect shareholders and the general public from accounting errors and fraudulent practices by organizations. One primary component of the Sarbanes-Oxley Act is the definition of which records are to be stored and for how long. For this reason, the legislation not only affects financial departments, but also IT departments whose job it is to store electronic records. The Sarbanes-Oxley Act states that all business records, including electronic records and electronic messages, must be saved for "not less than five years." The consequences for noncompliance are fines, imprisonment, or both. The following are the three rules of Sarbanes-Oxley that affect the management of electronic records.

1. The first rule deals with destruction, alteration, or falsification of records and states that persons who knowingly alter, destroy, mutilate, conceal, or falsify documents shall be fined or imprisoned for not more than 20 years or both.

2. The second rule defines the retention period for records storage. Best practices indicate that corporations securely store all business records using the same guidelines set for public accountants, which state that organizations shall maintain all audit or review work-papers for a period of five years from the end of the fiscal period in which the audit or review was concluded.

3. The third rule specifies all business records and communications that need to be stored, including electronic communications. IT departments are facing the challenge of creating and maintaining a corporate records archive in a cost-effective fashion that satisfies the requirements put forth by the legislation.

Essentially, any public organization that uses IT as part of its financial business processes will find that it must put in place IT controls in order to be compliant with the Sarbanes-Oxley Act. The following are a few practices you can follow to begin to ensure organizational compliance with the Sarbanes-Oxley Act.

■ Overhaul or upgrade your financial systems in order to meet regulatory requirements for more accurate, detailed, and speedy filings.

■ Examine the control processes within your IT department and apply best practices to comply with the act's goals. For example, segregation of duties within the systems development staff is a widely recognized best practice that helps prevent errors and outright fraud. The people who code program changes should be different from the people who test them, and a separate team should be responsible for changes in production environments.

■ Homegrown financial systems are fraught with potential information-integrity issues. Although leading ERP systems offer audit-trail functionality, customizations of these systems often bypass those controls. You must work with internal and external auditors to ensure that customizations are not overriding controls.

■ Work with your CIO, CEO, CFO, and corporate attorneys to create a document-retention-and-destruction policy that addresses what types of electronic documents should be saved, and for how long.

Ultimately, Sarbanes-Oxley compliance will require a great deal of work among all of your departments. Compliance starts with running IT as a business and strengthening IT internal controls.[9]

Questions

1. Define the relationship between ethics and the Sarbanes-Oxley Act.
2. Why is records management an area of concern for the entire organization?
3. What are two policies an organization can implement to achieve Sarbanes-Oxley compliance? Be sure to elaborate on how these policies can achieve compliance.
4. Identify the biggest roadblock for organizations that are attempting to achieve Sarbanes-Oxley compliance.
5. What types of information systems might facilitate SOX compliance?
6. How will electronic monitoring affect the morale and performance of employees in the workplace?
7. What do you think an unethical accountant or manager at Enron thought were the rewards and responsibilities associated with their job?

 CLOSING CASE TWO

Invading Your Privacy

Can your employer invade your privacy through monitoring technologies? Numerous lawsuits have been filed by employees who believe their employer was wrong to invade their privacy with monitoring technologies. Below are a few cases highlighting lawsuits over employee privacy and employer rights to monitor.

Smyth versus Pillsbury Company

An employee was terminated for sending inappropriate and unprofessional messages over the company's e-mail system. The company had repeatedly assured its employees that e-mail was confidential, that it would not be intercepted, and that it would not be used as a basis for discipline or discharge. Michael Smyth retrieved, from his home computer, e-mail sent from his supervisor over Pillsbury's e-mail system. Smyth allegedly responded with several comments concerning the sales management staff, including a threat to "kill the backstabbing bastards" and a reference to an upcoming holiday party as "the Jim Jones Kool-aid affair." Pillsbury intercepted the e-mail and terminated Smyth, who then sued the company for wrongful discharge and invasion of privacy.

The court dismissed the case in 1996, finding that Smyth did not have a reasonable expectation of privacy in the contents of his e-mail messages, despite Pillsbury's assurances, because the messages had been voluntarily communicated over the company's computer system to a second person. The court went on to find that, even if some reasonable expectation of privacy existed, that expectation was outweighed by Pillsbury's legitimate interest in preventing inappropriate or unprofessional communications over its e-mail system.

Bourke versus Nissan Motor Corporation

While training new employees on the e-mail system, a message sent by Bonita Bourke was randomly selected and reviewed by the company. The message turned out to be a personal e-mail of a sexual nature. Once Bourke's e-mail was discovered, the company decided to review the e-mails of the rest of Bourke's workgroup. As a result of this investigation, several other personal e-mails were discovered. Nissan gave the employees who had sent the personal messages written warnings for violating the company's e-mail policy.

The disciplined employees sued Nissan for invasion of privacy. The employees argued that although they signed a form acknowledging the company's policy that company-owned hardware

---

208

and software was restricted for company business use only, their expectation of privacy was reasonable because the company gave the plaintiffs passwords to access the computer system and told them to guard their passwords. However, a California court in 1993 held that this was not an objectively reasonable expectation of privacy because the plaintiffs knew that e-mail messages "were read from time to time by individuals other than the intended recipient."

McLaren versus Microsoft Corporation

The Texas Court of Appeals in 1999 dismissed an employee's claim that his employer's review and dissemination of e-mail stored in the employee's workplace personal computer constituted an invasion of privacy. The employee argued that he had a reasonable expectation of privacy because the e-mail was kept in a personal computer folder protected by a password. The court found this argument unconvincing because the e-mail was transmitted over his employer's network.

However, according to a news account of one case, a court held that an employer's use of a supervisor's password to review an employee's e-mail may have violated a Massachusetts state statute against interference with privacy. In that case, Burk Technology allowed employees to use the company's e-mail system to send personal messages, but prohibited "excessive chatting." To use the e-mail system, each employee used a password. The employer never informed employees that their messages would or could be monitored by supervisors or the company president. The president of the company reviewed the e-mails of two employees who had referred to him by various nicknames and discussed his extramarital affair. The two employees were fired by the company president, who claimed the terminations were for their excessive e-mail use and not because of the messages' content. The court denied the company's attempt to dismiss the suit and allowed the matter to be set for trial on the merits. The court focused on the fact that the employees were never informed that their e-mail could be monitored.

This case illustrates the importance of informing employees that their use of company equipment to send e-mail and to surf the Internet is subject to monitoring to prevent subsequent confusion, and a possible future defense, on the part of employees.[10]

Questions

1. Pick one of the above cases and create an argument on behalf of the employee.
2. Pick one of the above cases and create an argument against the employee.
3. Pick one of the above cases and create an argument on behalf of the employer's use of monitoring technologies.
4. Pick one of the above cases and create an argument against the employer's use of monitoring technologies.

★ MAKING BUSINESS DECISIONS

1. Information Privacy
   A study by the Annenberg Public Policy Center at the University of Pennsylvania shows that 95 percent of people who use the Internet at home think they should have a legal right to know everything about the information that Web sites collect from them. Research also shows that 57 percent of home Internet users incorrectly believe that when a Web site has an information privacy policy it will not share personal information with other Web sites or companies. In fact, the research found that after showing the users how companies track, extract, and share Web site information to make money, 85 percent found the methods unacceptable, even for a highly valued site. Write a short paper arguing for or against an organization's right to use and distribute personal information gathered from its Web site.

2. Acting Ethically

Describe how you would react to the following scenarios:

- A senior marketing manager informs you that one of her employees is looking for another job and she wants you to give her access to look through her e-mail.

- A vice president of sales informs you that he has made a deal to provide customer information to a strategic partner and he wants you to burn all of the customer information onto a CD.

- You start monitoring one of your employee's e-mail and discover that he is having an affair with one of the other employees in the office.

- You install a video surveillance system in your office and discover that employees are taking office supplies home with them.

3. Spying on E-Mail

Technology advances now allow individuals to monitor computers that they do not even have physical access to. New types of software can capture an individual's incoming and outgoing e-mail and then immediately forward that e-mail to another person. For example, if you are at work and your child is home from school and she receives an e-mail from John at 3:00 p.m., at 3:01 p.m. you will receive a copy of that e-mail sent to your e-mail address. A few minutes later, if she replies to John's e-mail, within seconds you will again receive a copy of what she sent to John. Describe two scenarios (other than the above) for the use of this type of software: (1) where the use would be ethical, (2) where the use would be unethical.

4. Stealing Software

The issue of pirated software is one that the software industry fights on a daily basis. The major centers of software piracy are in places like Russia and China where salaries and disposable income are comparatively low. People in developing and economically depressed countries will fall behind the industrialized world technologically if they cannot afford access to new generations of software. Considering this, is it reasonable to blame someone for using pirated software when it could potentially cost him or her two months' salary to purchase a legal copy? Create an argument for or against the following statement: "Individuals who are economically less fortunate should be allowed access to software free of charge in order to ensure that they are provided with an equal technological advantage."

19 Developing a 21st Century Organization

Developing Organizations

Organizations face changes more extensive and far reaching in their implications than anything since the modern industrial revolution occurred in the early 1900s. Technology is one of the primary forces driving these changes. Organizations that want to survive in the 21st century must recognize the immense power of technology, carry out required organizational changes in the face of it, and learn to operate in an entirely different way. Figure 19.1 displays a few examples of the way technology is changing the business arena.

21st Century Organization Trends

On the business side, 21st century organization trends are:

- Uncertainty in terms of future business scenarios and economic outlooks.
- Emphasis on strategic analysis for cost reduction and productivity enhancements.
- Focus on improved business resiliency via the application of enhanced security.

On the technology side, there has been a focus on improved business management of IT in order to extract the most value from existing resources and create alignment between business and IT priorities. Today's organizations focus on defending and safeguarding their existing market positions in addition to targeting new market growth. The four primary information technology areas where organizations are focusing are:

- IT infrastructures
- Security
- E-business
- Integration

INCREASED FOCUS ON IT INFRASTRUCTURE

A significant trend for the 21st century is to increase the focus on *IT infrastructure*—the hardware, software, and telecommunications equipment that, when combined, provide the underlying foundation to support the organization's goals. Organizations in the past underestimated the importance that IT infrastructures have on the many functional areas of an organization.

Industry	Business Changes Due to Technology
Travel	Travel site Expedia.com is now the biggest leisure-travel agency, with higher profit margins than even American Express. Thirteen percent of traditional travel agencies closed in 2002 because of their inability to compete with online travel.
Entertainment	The music industry has kept Napster and others from operating, but $35 billion annual online downloads are wrecking the traditional music business. U.S. music unit sales are down 20 percent since 2000. The next big entertainment industry to feel the effects of e-business will be the $67 billion movie business.
Electronics	Using the Internet to link suppliers and customers, Dell dictates industry profits. Its operating margins have risen from 7.3 percent in 2002 to 8 percent in 2003, even as it takes prices to levels where rivals cannot make money.
Financial services	Nearly every public e-finance company remaining makes money, with online mortgage service LendingTree growing 70 percent a year. Processing online mortgage applications is now 40 percent cheaper for customers.
Retail	Less than 5 percent of retail sales occur online. eBay was on track in 2003 to become one of the nation's top 15 retailers, and Amazon.com will join the top 40. Wal-Mart's e-business strategy is forcing rivals to make heavy investments in technology.
Automobiles	The cost of producing vehicles is down because of SCM and Web-based purchasing. eBay has become the leading U.S. used-car dealer, and most major car sites are profitable.
Education and training	Cisco saved $133 million in 2002 by moving training sessions to the Internet, and the University of Phoenix online college classes please investors.

FIGURE 19.1

Examples of How Technology Is Changing Business

In the early days of the Internet, the basic infrastructure in terms of protocols and standards was unsophisticated (and still is), but software companies managed to enhance the Internet and offer compelling applications for functional business areas. The original design for the Internet and the Web was for simple e-mail, document exchange, and the display of static content, not for sophisticated and dynamic business applications that require access to back-end systems and databases.

Organizations today are looking to Internet-based cross-functional systems such as CRM, SCM, and ERP to help drive their business success. The days of implementing independent functional systems are gone. Creating an effective organization requires a 360-degree view of all operations. For this reason, ownership of the IT infrastructure now becomes the responsibility of the entire organization and not just the individual users or functional department. This is primarily because the IT infrastructure has a dramatic influence on the strategic capabilities of an organization (see Figure 19.2).

INCREASED FOCUS ON SECURITY

With war and terrorist attacks in many people's minds, security is a hot topic. For businesses, too, security concerns are widespread. Increasingly opening up their networks and applications to customers, partners, and suppliers using an ever more diverse set of computing devices and networks, businesses can benefit from deploying the latest advances in security technologies. These benefits include fewer disruptions to organizational systems, increased productivity of employees,

FIGURE 19.2

The Position of the
Infrastructure within the
Organization

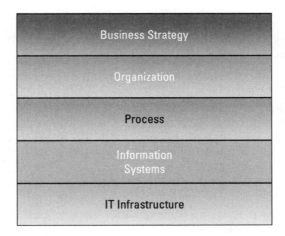

and greater advances in administration, authorization, and authentication techniques. For businesses it is important to have the appropriate levels of authentication, access control, and encryption in place, which help to ensure (1) that only authorized individuals can gain access to the network, (2) that they have access to only those applications for which they are entitled, and (3) that they cannot understand or alter information while in transit. Figure 19.3 displays a recent survey concerning both the level of physical security integration and the current security practices used by most organizations.

Security breaches not only inconvenience business users and their customers and partners, but can also cost millions of dollars in lost revenues or lost market capitalization. The business cost of inadequate security does not stop at inconvenience and loss of revenues or market valuation. It can even force a business out of existence. For example, in early 2002 British Internet service provider CloudNine Communications was the victim of a distributed denial-of-service (DDoS) attack that forced the company to close operations and to eventually transfer over 2,500 customers to a rival organization. While "disruptive technologies" can help a company to gain competitive advantage and market share (and avoid real business disruptions), lack of security can have the opposite effect, causing profitable companies to lose market share or even their entire business within hours or days of an attack.[28]

It is now more important than ever for an organization to have well-rehearsed and frequently updated processes and procedures to insure against a variety of adverse scenarios—Internet e-mail and denial-of-service attacks from worms and viruses, loss of communications, loss of documents, password and information theft, fire, flood, physical attacks on property, and even terrorist attacks.

FIGURE 19.3

Physical Security
Integration and Best
Security Practices

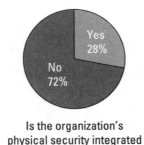

Is the organization's
physical security integrated
with IT security?

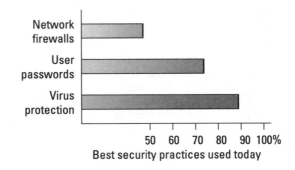

Best security practices used today

INCREASED FOCUS ON E-BUSINESS

Mobility and wireless are the new focus in e-business, and some upcoming trends are mobile commerce, telematics, electronic tagging, and RFID.

- *Mobile commerce (m-commerce)*—the ability to purchase goods and services through a wireless Internet-enabled device.
- *Telematics*—blending computers and wireless telecommunications technologies with the goal of efficiently conveying information over vast networks to improve business operations. The most notable example of telematics may be the Internet itself, since it depends on a number of computer networks connected globally through telecommunication devices.[29]
- *Electronic tagging*—a technique for identifying and tracking assets and individuals via technologies such as radio frequency identification and smart cards.
- *Radio frequency identification (RFID)*—technologies use active or passive tags in the form of chips or smart labels that can store unique identifiers and relay this information to electronic readers. Within the supply chain, RFID can enable greater efficiencies in business processes such as inventory, logistics, distribution, and asset management. On the mobile commerce side, RFID can enable new forms of e-business through mobile phones and smart cards. This can increase loyalty by streamlining purchases for the consumer. For example, RFID readers are being embedded in store shelving to help retailers, including Marks & Spencer and The Gap, to better manage their assets and inventories and understand customer behavior.[30]

These are all interesting subcategories within mobile business that open up new opportunities for mobility beyond simple employee applications. Electronic tagging and RFID are especially interesting because they extend wireless and mobile technologies not just to humans, but also to a wide range of objects such as consumer and industrial products. These products will gain intelligence via electronic product codes, which are a (potential) replacement for universal product code (UPC) bar codes, and via RFID tags with two-way communication capabilities.

Mobile employees will soon have the ability to leverage technology just as if they were in the office. Improvements in devices, applications, networks, and standards over the past few years have made this far more practical than it was when first introduced. The drivers for adoption are finally starting to outweigh the barriers. For example, major vendors such as IBM, Microsoft, Oracle, and Sybase are all playing a larger role and taking a greater interest in mobile business than they had previously. These vendors all have mature, proven offerings for enterprise mobility.

Mobile technology will help extend an organization out to its edges in areas such as sales force automation and enterprise operations. Benefits can include improved information accuracy, reduced costs, increased productivity, increased revenues, and improved customer service. Beyond being an additional channel for communications, mobile business will enable an organization to think about the powerful combination of business processes, e-business, and wireless communications.

INCREASED FOCUS ON INTEGRATION

Information technology has penetrated the heart of organizations and will stay there in the future. The IT industry is one of the most dynamic in the global economy. As a sector, it not only creates millions of high-level jobs, but also helps organizations to be more efficient and effective, which in turn stimulates innovation. The integration of business and technology has allowed organizations to increase their share of the global economy, transform the way they conduct business, and become more efficient and effective (see Figure 19.4).

FIGURE 19.4

The Integration of
Business and Technology

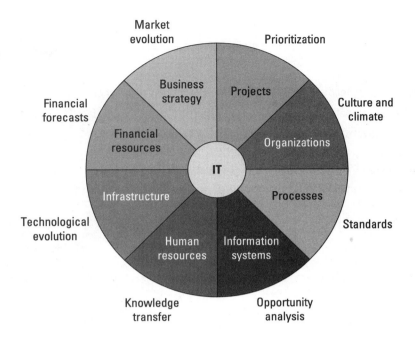

The past few years have produced a confluence of events that has reshaped the global economy. Around the world, free-market competition has flourished and a new globally interdependent financial system has emerged. Reflecting these changes, core business relationships and models are dramatically changing, including shifts from:

- Product-centricity to customer-centricity.
- Mass production to mass customization.
- The value in material things to the value of knowledge and intelligence.

In concert with these trends, a new series of business success factors and challenges has emerged that is helping to determine marketplace winners and losers:

- Organization agility, often supported by a "plug and play" IT infrastructure (with a flexible and adaptable applications architecture).
- A focus on core competencies and processes.
- A redefinition of the value chain.
- Instantaneous business response.
- The ability to scale resources and infrastructure across geographic boundaries.

These developments add up to an environment that is vastly more complex than even five years ago. This in turn has resulted in organizations increasingly embracing new business models. The new environment requires organizations to focus externally on their business processes and integration architectures. The virtually integrated business model will cause a sharp increase in the number of business partners and the closeness of integration between them.

Never before have IT investments played such a critical role in business success. As business strategies continue to evolve, the distinction between "the business" and IT will virtually disappear.

1. How might a hospital define its IT infrastructure when developing its 21st century strategy?

2. How might a hospital define security when developing its 21st century strategy?

3. How might a hospital define its e-business infrastructure when developing its 21st century strategy?

4. How might a hospital define its integrations when developing its 21st century strategy?

Chapter Nineteen Case: Creating a Clearer Picture for Public Broadcasting Service (PBS)

One of the leaders in the transformation of the broadcasting industry is André Mendes, chief technology integration officer, or CTIO, at Public Broadcasting Service (PBS). Mendes oversees the company's technology organization, a 50-person group created last year by melding PBS's IT and broadcast-engineering departments. The new CTIO position replaces the formerly separate jobs of CIO and CTO at the nonprofit television network.

Mendes encountered a few roadblocks during his first few months as CTIO including resistance from the broadcast engineering staff, his limited knowledge of broadcast engineering, and breaking down barriers between the two departments. Mendes managed through the change with finesse and now refers to it as a "bidirectional learning experience" for him and his staff. "Once you're in a new environment, you start asking a lot of questions," he says. "Every question requires the responder to think about the answer. That helped the process of evaluating why procedures and practices are done a certain way—and identifying possible improvements."

Michael Hunt, PBS's vice president of enterprise applications, states that Mendes broke down many barriers and offered his employees a way to address and respond to change. The united team is currently working on large, sophisticated projects that are improving the efficiency of PBS and its member stations. "Projects are getting bigger and bigger, with more and more collaboration, with a more global picture," says Marilyn Pierce, director of PBS digital assets, who came from the broadcast-engineering side of the company.

"The broadcast environment is becoming an IT environment," states Mendes in reference to the fact that as the worlds of broadcast and traditional information technologies converge, this uncovers new ways to improve quality of service and increase opportunities for innovation through new digitized formats, which replace traditional analog video. The primary drivers of this convergence are advances in digital technologies and the Internet. Though those changes are unique to the television industry, it is not the first—or last—time that welding together different technology organizations has been responsible for advances in technology. For instance, companies pursuing voice-over-IP (VOIP) initiatives are combining their IT and telecommunications groups, and other industries face similar integration challenges as everything from automobiles to appliances becomes increasingly technology dependent.

The integration of broadcast and information technologies is raising the visibility of technology as an organizational infrastructure enabler and a strategic partner for new business models. PBS is launching several projects that are revamping the way the company does business. One project allows producers to send program content digitally rather than on videotapes. In the past, PBS rejected and returned 60 percent of the video content because it did not contain key technical information such as the number of frames in a program to allow for seamless merging of programs. "From a supply chain standpoint, that was highly inefficient," Mendes says.

Another project is saving PBS tens of millions of dollars a year by transporting its programs to TV stations as e-mail files via TCP/IP over satellite. This delivery vehicle greatly improves quality by avoiding weather-related interference that can arise in transmitting programs by streaming signals over satellite. "The change in broadcast is similar to the transformation in the telecom industry as companies moved from switch circuitry to packet circuits," Mendes says. For PBS the business lines are blurring as the industry responds to technology changes, which is making the overall picture much clearer.[31]

Questions

1. Assess the impact to PBS's business if it failed to focus on IT infrastructures when determining its 21st century business strategy.

2. Assess the impact to PBS's business if it failed to focus on security when determining its 21st century business strategy.

3. Assess the impact to PBS's business if it failed to focus on e-business when determining its 21st century business strategy.

4. Assess the impact to PBS's business if it failed to focus on integrations when determining its 21st century business strategy.

B12

Emerging Trends and Technologies

1. Identify the trends that will have the greatest impact on future business.

2. Identify the technologies that will have the greatest impact on future business.

3. Explain why understanding trends and new technologies can help an organization prepare for the future.

Introduction

The core units brought out how important it is for organizations to anticipate and prepare for the future by studying emerging trends and new technologies. Having a broad view of emerging trends and new technologies as they relate to business can provide an organization with a valuable strategic advantage. Those organizations that can most effectively grasp the deep currents of technological evolution can use their knowledge to protect themselves against sudden and fatal technological obsolescence.

This plug-in identifies several emerging trends and new technologies that can help an organization prepare for future opportunities and challenges.

Reasons to Watch Trends

Organizations anticipate, forecast, and assess future events using a variety of rational, scientific methods including:

- *Trend analysis:* A trend is examined to identify its nature, causes, speed of development, and potential impacts.

- *Trend monitoring:* Trends viewed as particularly important in a specific community, industry, or sector are carefully monitored, watched, and reported to key decision makers.

- *Trend projection:* When numerical data are available, a trend can be plotted to display changes through time and into the future.

- *Computer simulation:* Complex systems, such as the U.S. economy, can be modeled by means of mathematical equations and different scenarios can be run against the model to determine "what if" analysis.

Top Reasons to Study Trends	
1. Generate ideas and identify opportunities	Find new ideas and innovations by studying trends and analyzing publications.
2. Identify early warning signals	Scan the environment for potential threats and risks.
3. Gain confidence	A solid foundation of awareness about trends can provide an organization with the confidence to take risks.
4. Beat the competition	Seeing what is coming before others can give an organization the lead time it requires to establish a foothold in the new market.
5. Understand a trend	Analyzing the details within a trend can help separate truly significant developments from rapidly appearing and disappearing fads.
6. Balance strategic goals	Thinking about the future is an antidote to a "profit now, worry later" mentality that can lead to trouble in the long term.
7. Understand the future of specific industries	Organizations must understand everything inside and outside their industry.
8. Prepare for the future	Any organization that wants to compete in this hyperchanging world needs to make every effort to forecast the future.

FIGURE B12.1

Top Reasons to Study Trends

■ **Historical analysis:** Historical events are studied to anticipate the outcome of current developments.

Foresight is one of the secret ingredients of business success. Foresight, however, is increasingly in short supply because almost everything in our world is changing at a faster pace than ever before. Many organizations have little idea what type of future they should prepare for in this world of hyperchange. Figure B12.1 displays the top reasons organizations should look to the future and study trends.[1]

Trends Shaping Our Future

According to the World Future Society, the following trends have the potential to change our world, our future, and our lives.[2]

■ The world's population will double in the next 40 years.
■ People in developed countries are living longer.
■ The growth in information industries is creating a knowledge-dependent global society.
■ The global economy is becoming more integrated.
■ The economy and society are dominated by technology.
■ The pace of technological innovation is increasing.
■ Time is becoming one of the world's most precious commodities.

THE WORLD'S POPULATION WILL DOUBLE IN THE NEXT 40 YEARS

The countries that are expected to have the largest increases in population between 2000 and 2050 are:

■ Palestinian Territory—217 percent increase.
■ Niger—205 percent increase.
■ Yemen—168 percent increase.

Expected Population
Decreases in Developed
and Industrialized Nations

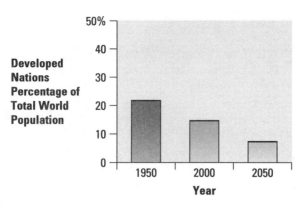

**Developed
Nations
Percentage of
Total World
Population**

- Angola—162 percent increase.
- Democratic Republic of the Congo—161 percent increase.
- Uganda—133 percent increase.

In contrast, developed and industrialized countries are expected to see fertility rates decrease below population replacement levels, leading to significant declines in population (see Figure B12.2).

Potential Business Impact

- Global agriculture will be required to supply as much food as has been produced during all of human history to meet human nutritional needs over the next 40 years.
- Developed nations will find that retirees will have to remain on the job to remain competitive and continue economic growth.
- Developed nations will begin to increase immigration limits.

PEOPLE IN DEVELOPED COUNTRIES ARE LIVING LONGER

New pharmaceuticals and medical technologies are making it possible to prevent and cure diseases that would have been fatal to past generations. This is one reason that each generation lives longer and remains healthier than the previous generation. On average, each generation in the United States lives three years longer than the previous. An 80-year-old in 1950 could expect to live 6.5 years longer today. Many developed countries are now experiencing life expectancy over 75 years for males and over 80 years for females (see Figure B12.3).

FIGURE B12.3

Rising Life Expectancy in
Developed Countries

Rising Life Expectancy in Developed Countries		
Country	Life Expectancy (Born 1950–1955)	Life Expectancy (Born 1995–2000)
United States	68.9	76.5
United Kingdom	69.2	77.2
Germany	67.5	77.3
France	66.5	78.1
Italy	66.0	78.2
Canada	69.1	78.5
Japan	63.9	80.5

Potential Business Impact

- Global demand for products and services for the elderly will grow quickly in the coming decades.
- The cost of health care is destined to skyrocket.
- Pharmaceutical companies will be pushed for advances in geriatric medicine.

THE GROWTH IN INFORMATION INDUSTRIES IS CREATING A KNOWLEDGE-DEPENDENT GLOBAL SOCIETY

Estimates indicate that 90 percent of American management personnel will be knowledge workers by 2008. Estimates for knowledge workers in Europe and Japan are not far behind. A typical large organization in 2010 will have fewer than half the management levels of its counterpart in 1990, and about one-third the number of managers. Soon, large organizations will be composed of specialists who rely on information from co-workers, customers, and suppliers to guide their actions. Employees will gain new power as they are provided with the authority to make decisions based on the information they acquire.

Potential Business Impact

- Top managers must be computer-literate to retain their jobs and achieve success.
- Knowledge workers are generally higher paid and their proliferation is increasing overall prosperity.
- Entry-level and unskilled positions are requiring a growing level of education.
- Information now flows from front-office workers to higher management for analysis. Thus, in the future, fewer midlevel managers will be required, flattening the corporate pyramid.
- Downsizing, restructuring, reorganization, outsourcing, and layoffs will continue as typical large organizations struggle to reinvent and restructure themselves for greater flexibility.

THE GLOBAL ECONOMY IS BECOMING MORE INTEGRATED

International outsourcing is on the rise as organizations refuse to pay high salaries for activities that do not contribute directly to the bottom line. The European Union has relaxed its borders and capital controls making it easier for companies to outsource support functions throughout the continent.

The Internet is one of the primary tools enabling our global economy. Internet users numbered 1 billion in 2005 and are anticipated to grow to 3 billion by 2010. One of the primary reasons for the increase in Internet use is the increase in connectivity technology. China's Internet users are growing by 6 percent each month, to 111 million in 2005. India's Internet users reached 50 million in 2005 (see Figure B12.4 for India's statistics). The increase in Internet use is increasing revenues for e-businesses.

Potential Business Impact

- Demand for personnel in distant countries will increase the need for foreign-language training, employee incentives suited to other cultures, and many other aspects of performing business globally.
- The growth of e-business and the use of the Internet to shop globally for raw materials and supplies will reduce the cost of doing business.
- The Internet will continue to enable small companies to compete with worldwide giants with relatively little investment.
- Internet-based operations require sophisticated knowledge workers and thus people with the right technical skills will be heavily recruited over the next 15 years.

FIGURE B12.4

Growth of Internet Users in India

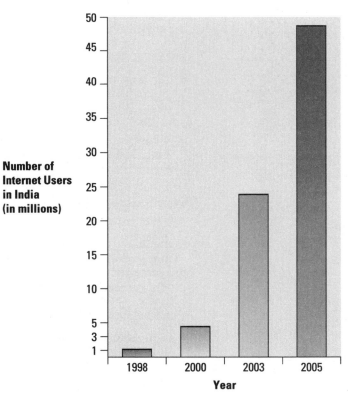

THE ECONOMY AND SOCIETY ARE DOMINATED BY TECHNOLOGY

Computers are becoming a part of our environment. Mundane commercial and service jobs, environmentally dangerous jobs, standard assembly jobs, and even the repair of inaccessible equipment such as space stations will be increasingly performed by robots. Personal robots will appear in the home by 2010. By 2009, artificial intelligence and expert systems will help most companies and government agencies assimilate data and solve problems beyond the range of today's computers including energy prospecting, automotive diagnostics, insurance underwriting, and law enforcement.

Superconductors operating at economically viable temperatures are expected to be in commercial use by 2015. Products eventually will include supercomputers the size of a three-pound coffee can, electronic motors 75 percent smaller and lighter than those in use today, and power plants.

Potential Business Impact

- New technologies provide dozens of new opportunities to create businesses and jobs.
- Automation will continue to decrease the cost of products and services, making it possible to reduce prices while improving profits.
- The Internet is expected to push prices of most products to the commodity level.
- The demand for scientists, engineers, and technicians will continue to grow.

PACE OF TECHNOLOGICAL INNOVATION IS INCREASING

Technology is advancing at a phenomenal pace. Medical knowledge is doubling every eight years. Half of what students learn in their freshman year of college about innovative technology is obsolete, revised, or taken for granted by their senior year. In fact, all of today's technical knowledge will represent only 1 percent of the knowledge that will be available in 2050.

Potential Business Impact

- The time to get products and services to market is being shortened by technology. Products must capture their market quickly before the competition can copy them. During the 1940s the average time to get a product to market was 40 weeks. Today, a product's entire life cycle seldom lasts 40 weeks.
- Industries will face tighter competition based on new technologies. Those who adopt state-of-the-art technology first will prosper, while those who ignore it eventually will fail.

TIME IS BECOMING ONE OF THE WORLD'S MOST PRECIOUS COMMODITIES

In the United States, workers today spend around 10 percent more time on the job than they did a decade ago. European executives and nonunionized workers face the same trend. This high-pressure environment is increasing the need for any product or service that saves time or simplifies life.

Potential Business Impact

- Companies must take an active role in helping their employees balance their time at work with their family lives and need for leisure.
- Stress-related problems affecting employee morale and wellness will continue to grow.

- As time for shopping continues to evaporate, Internet and mail-order marketers will have a growing advantage over traditional stores.

Technologies Shaping Our Future

The following technologies are changing our world, our future, and our lives.[3]

- Digital ink
- Digital paper
- Teleliving
- Alternative energy sources
- Autonomic computing

FIGURE B12.5

Digital Ink

DIGITAL INK

Digital ink (or *electronic ink*) refers to technology that digitally represents handwriting in its natural form (see Figure B12.5). E Ink Corporation, headquartered in Cambridge, Massachusetts, has developed a proprietary technology called electronic ink, which provides significant advantages over other display technologies. E Ink was founded in 1997 to advance electronic ink, develop applications, and create markets for displays based on this unique technology.

Potential Business Impact

- Digital ink has broad usage in many applications, from point-of-sale signs in retail stores, to next generation displays in mobile devices and PDAs, to thin, portable electronic books and newspapers. E Ink has collaborated with various companies like Lucent Technologies to produce reusable paper with digital ink.

- The ultimate dream of E Ink is *RadioPaper,* a dynamic high-resolution electronic display that combines a paperlike reading experience with the ability to access information anytime, anywhere. RadioPaper will be thin and flexible and could be used to create an electronic book or newspaper with real pages.

DIGITAL PAPER

Digital paper (or *electronic paper*) is any paper that is optimized for any type of digital printing. In some ways, digital paper is produced much like a sheet of paper. It comes from a pulp and the finished product has the flexibility to be rolled into scrolls of "paper." However, the major difference between paper produced from a tree and paper produced in a laboratory is that information on a digital paper sheet can be altered thousands of times and not degrade over time (see Figure B12.6). Digital paper offers excellent resolution and high contrast under a wide range of viewing angles, requires no external power to retain its image, is extremely lightweight, costs less, and is remarkably flexible, unlike computer displays.

Macy's department store was the first company to experiment by placing digital paper signs in the children's section at a New Jersey store. As the company spends more than $250,000 a week changing its in-store signs, such renewable signage could prove highly desirable. A networked programmable sign will run for two years on three AA batteries (see Figure B12.7).[4]

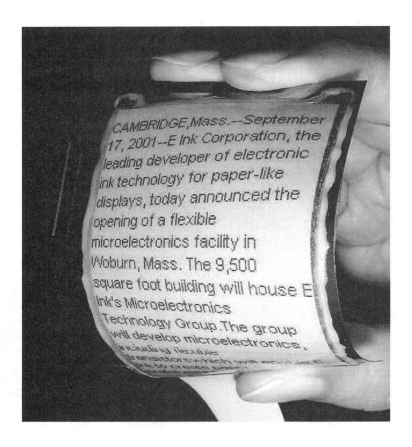

Date	Technology
April 1996	MIT's Media Lab starts work on electronic paper prototype.
April 1997	E Ink is founded to commercialize MIT's electronic paper displays.
May 1999	E Ink debuts Immedia electronic paper display products.
November 2000	E Ink and Lucent Technologies demonstrate first flexible electronic products.
December 2000	Gyricon Media is spun off from Xerox PARC.
February 2001	E Ink teams with Philips Components to develop a high-resolution display for smart handhelds.
March 2001	Gyricon introduces digital paper technology.
June 2001	Macy's is scheduled to test digital paper for in-store signage use.
Late 2001	E Ink/Philips handheld prototype is delivered.
2004/2005	E Ink electronic paper handheld devices becomes available to users.
Mid-2000s	Possible debut of E Ink's RadioPaper wireless electronic publishing technology.

As a laboratory prototype, digital ink and digital paper have been around for some time with demonstration of the technologies often leading to wild predictions about e-books and e-newspapers (see Figure B12.8).

Potential Business Impact

- Digital paper is driving a new wave of innovation in the content distribution field. Paperlike displays will replace newspapers, magazines, and books since they will be almost as manageable as paper and allow display resolution close to print.
- The concept of a reusable paper product is an environmentally sound idea considering that a major portion of the world's paper goes to printing newspapers, magazines, pamphlets, and so on.

TELELIVING

Lifestyle changes will emerge as computers develop capabilities that are more sophisticated. *Teleliving* refers to using information devices and the Internet to conduct all aspects of life seamlessly. This can include such things as shopping, working, learning, playing, healing, and praying. Even today, homes, autos, and work environments are wired into intelligent networks that interact with one another. Each year, 4 billion chips are embedded in everything from coffeemakers to Cadillacs.

Potential Business Impact

- In the future, people will move through a constant stream of information summoned at the touch of a finger. They will interact with life-size images, data, and text in homes and offices. The days of hunching over a computer will be gone.
- The *virtual assistant (VA)* will be a small program stored on a PC or portable device that monitors e-mails, faxes, messages, and phone calls. Virtual assistants will help individuals solve problems in the same way a real assistant would. In time, the VA will take over routine tasks such as writing a letter, retrieving a file, and making a phone·call.
- Robotic salespeople will take on human appearances and have the ability to perform all tasks associated with a sales job.

ALTERNATIVE ENERGY SOURCES

By the end of the decade wind, geothermal, hydroelectric, solar, and other alternative energy sources will increase from their present level of 10 percent of all energy use to about 30 percent. Worldwide wind-power generating capacity grew by 6,500 megawatts in 2003, the fastest rate of growth yet recorded and 50 percent more than the previous year (see Figure B12.9). Nuclear plants will supply 16 percent of the energy in Russia and Eastern Europe by 2010. New sources of carbon fuels are frequently being discovered and more-powerful extraction methods are being developed, thereby keeping supply up and costs down.

Potential Business Impact

- China, Asia, India, South America, and Russia are modernizing their economies, which increasingly use large amounts of energy.
- The cost of alternative energy sources is dropping with technical advances. This growing competition from other energy sources will help limit the price of oil.
- The imminent deregulation of the energy industry is expected to create a huge spurt of innovative entrepreneurship, fostering a wide variety of new energy sources.
- Oil will remain the world's most important energy resource. However, in two or three decades a declining reliance on oil will help reduce air and water pollution. By 2060, a costly but pollution-free hydrogen economy may become possible.

FIGURE B12.9

Wind Power—An Alternative Energy Source

AUTONOMIC COMPUTING

Autonomic computing is a self-managing computing model named after, and patterned on, the human body's autonomic nervous system. Autonomic computing is one of the building blocks of widespread computing, an anticipated future computing model in which small—even invisible—computers will be all around us, communicating through increasingly interconnected networks. Many industry leaders, including IBM, HP, Sun, and Microsoft, are researching various components of autonomic computing. However, autonomic computing is not an overnight revolution in which systemwide, self-managing environments suddenly appear. As described in Figure B12.10, autonomic computing is a gradual evolution that delivers new technologies that are adopted and implemented at various stages and levels.[5]

Potential Business Impact

- The complex IT infrastructures of the future will require more computer automation than ever before. Autonomic computing will be used in a variety of areas that include security, storage, network management, and new redundancy and fail-over capabilities.
- Autonomic computers will continuously seek out ways to optimize computing. In the autonomic environment, computers will monitor components and fine-tune workflows to achieve system performance goals.
- Autonomic computers will be able to "self-heal." In the event of a component failure, an autonomic computer will be able to diagnose the failure and develop a workaround that allows the computer to continue with its functions.

Level	Technologies Implemented
Level 1: Basic	The starting point where most systems are today, this level represents manual computing in which all system elements are managed independently by an extensive, highly skilled IT staff. The staff sets up, monitors, and eventually replaces system elements.
Level 2: Managed	Systems management technologies can be used to collect and consolidate information from disparate systems onto fewer consoles, reducing administrative time. There is greater system awareness and improved productivity.
Level 3: Predictive	The system monitors and correlates data to recognize patterns and recommends actions that are approved and initiated by the IT staff. This reduces the dependency on deep skills and enables faster and better decision making.
Level 4: Adaptive	In addition to monitoring and correlating data, the system takes action based on the information, thereby enhancing IT agility and resiliency with minimal human interaction.
Level 5: Autonomic	Fully integrated systems and components are dynamically managed by business rules and policies, enabling IT staff to focus on meeting business needs with true business agility and resiliency.

■ Autonomic computers will be able to "self-protect." Protection for computing resources primarily takes the form of fighting off invasive viruses and security intrusion attempts.

Organizations that can think ahead will be prepared to take advantage of all the new opportunities that rapid social and technological progress is creating. Trends shaping our future include:

- The world's population will double in the next 40 years.
- People in developed countries are living longer.
- The growth in information industries is creating a knowledge-dependent global society.
- The global economy is becoming more integrated.
- The economy and society are dominated by technology.
- The pace of technological innovation is increasing.
- Time is becoming one of the world's most precious commodities.

Technologies shaping our future include:

- Digital ink
- Digital paper
- Teleliving
- Alternative energy sources
- Autonomic computing

Autonomic computing,
   438
Computer simulation, 430
Digital ink (or electronic
   ink), 435

Digital paper (or electronic
   paper), 435
Historical analysis, 431
RadioPaper, 435
Teleliving, 437

Trend analysis, 430
Trend monitoring, 430
Trend projection, 430
Virtual assistant (VA), 437

Autonomic Railways

Canadian Pacific Railway (CPR), based in Calgary, Alberta, Canada, is one of the largest railway systems in North America. With more than 14,400 miles of rail line in Canada and the United States, this $2.6 billion (US) transportation company serves virtually every major industry, from the resource-based industries of the West to the manufacturing bases and consumer markets in central Canada and the northern United States.

Shippers expect fast, reliable services and on-time delivery of goods. As a result, CPR designed many programs—from improving asset management, to strengthening service reliability, to accounting for fluctuating costs—to help it respond to market forces with agility and ease. Val King, manager of IT security for CPR, explains that security management is an essential element in the delivery of these on demand services. King said, "We must protect our operations from technology attacks, while providing our customers easy, reliable access to information and services online."

The goal of the company's IT security team is simple: minimize risk while optimizing user satisfaction. Yet the team's greatest challenges are lack of resources and tight budgets. "We had to look to technology to help us accomplish our goals," explained King. CPR collaborated with IBM to deliver solutions that are both automated (they can control a defined process without human intervention) and autonomic (they can sense and respond to conditions in accordance with business policies). As a result, IT employees can deliver consistent, reliable service levels at reduced costs since they collaborated with IBM using autonomic computing resources such as Tivoli Risk Manager, Tivoli Access Manager, Tivoli Identity Manager, and Tivoli Decision Support. "The automation of processes through the intelligent self-managing features of Tivoli software can help companies respond to threats more quickly," King said. "The benefit is that organizations can strengthen the resiliency of their environments even as the number of security events increases."

CPR is realizing measurable results from its implementation of Tivoli Security Management solutions and King sees the already-realized benefits as only the "tip of the iceberg." Some of the notable ROI from CPR's investment in Tivoli Security Management solutions include:

1. **Improved productivity**—The IT security team spends less time managing security incidents with Tivoli Risk Manager. The IT staff also expects to spend less time on reporting because data from the various security monitors will be integrated.

2. **Reduced costs**—The application development team estimates that a centralized security model helps accelerate development time. The help desk organization reports a reduction in user calls, due to the password-reset capabilities of Tivoli Identity Manager.

3. **Increased business resiliency**—Using Tivoli Risk Manager, Tivoli Enterprise Console, Tivoli Decision Support, and Tripwire, a data integrity assurance solution from Tripwire, Inc., CPR tests show that if an attack shuts down a service, administrators can get systems back online much faster.

4. **Improved audit compliance**—Before the implementation of Tivoli Access Manager for e-business, security staff would need to look at each system or application to see if it properly applied security policy. Now, security policies are consistent enterprisewide.[6]

Questions

1. Which of the trends shaping our future discussed in this plug-in will have the greatest impact on CPR's business?
2. Which of the trends will have the least impact on CPR's business?
3. How are the functions of autonomic computing providing CPR with a competitive advantage?
4. How can CPR take advantage of other technological advances to improve security?

★ CLOSING CASE TWO

Wireless Progression

Progressive Corporation is the fourth-largest automobile insurer in the United States with more than 8 million policyholders and net premiums of $6.1 billion. Progressive offers wireless Web access to holders of its auto insurance policies, a move that analysts have said fits the company's reputation as a technology leader in the insurance industry and its emphasis on customer service.

Customers can use their Web-enabled phones to get price quotes, report claims, locate nearby independent agents by ZIP code, and access real-time account information through the company's Web site. Progressive also has the ability to push time-sensitive data to policyholders via wireless connections, instantly delivering information about an auto-recall notice to a customer's cell phone.

As a cost-saving measure, and in keeping with a corporate tradition of internal development, Ohio-based Progressive decided to build its own wireless applications. Policyholders simply have to type Progressive's Web address into their phones or connect to the site through search engines that specialize in wireless e-business.

Stephen Williams, president of the Insurance Institute of Indiana, a nonprofit trade association that represents insurers in that state, said it's "not uncommon for Progressive to be on the cutting edge with its use of technology." If Progressive is starting to take advantage of the wireless Web, other companies could follow its lead, he added. Jeffrey Kagan, an Atlanta-based wireless technology analyst, called Progressive "the Nordstrom's of insurance because of its emphasis on customer service." The addition of wireless access to its Web site "is a simple but smart way to use technology" to further improve the company's service, Kagan said. Progressive.com leads the insurance industry in consumer-friendly innovations. It was the first auto insurance Web site (1995), first to offer online quoting and comparison rates (1996), first to offer instantaneous online purchase of an auto policy (1997), and first to offer after-the-sale service (1998).

The progressive.com Web site leads the insurance industry in consumer-friendly innovations and functionality. Progressive.com was recognized as one of the "top 10 Web sites that work" by *InfoWeek Magazine* and was named to the Smart Business 50 by *Smart Business Magazine* for successful use of the Internet to enhance and expand its business.[7]

Questions

1. Which of the trends shaping our future discussed in this plug-in will have the greatest impact on Progressive's business?

2. Which of the trends will have the least impact on Progressive's business?

3. What other forms of advanced technology would you expect Progressive to deploy in the near future?

★ MAKING BUSINESS DECISIONS

1. Identifying and Following Trends
   What's Hot.com is a new business that specializes in helping companies identify and follow significant trends in their industries. You have recently been hired as a new business analyst and your first task is to highlight current trends in the e-business industry. Using the Internet and any other resources you have available, highlight five significant trends not discussed in this text. Prepare a PowerPoint presentation that lists the trends and discusses the potential business impacts for each trend.

2. Reading the Ink on the Wall
   iPublish.com is an e-book-only imprint publisher. While large publishers find that e-books are not selling as expected, iPublish.com continues to report positive growth. However, iPublish.com feels threatened by digital ink and digital paper inventions that seem to be revolutionizing the publishing environment and endangering the global paper industry. You have been hired by iPublish.com to develop a strategy to embrace this new technology. Create a detailed report listing the reasons iPublish.com needs to support these two new technologies.

3. **Pen Pal**

StyleUs is a digital pen that writes on ordinary paper printed with a unique dot pattern almost invisible to the naked eye. A tiny camera in the pen registers the pen's movement across a printed grid and stores it as a series of map coordinates. These coordinates correspond to the exact location of the page that is being written on. The dot pattern makes up a huge map of tiny distinctive squares, so small portions of it can also be given specific functions, such as "send," "store," or "synchronize." When a mark is made in the send box with the digital pen, it is instructed to send the stored sequence of map coordinates, which are translated into an image. The result is an exact copy of the handwriting displayed on the computer, mobile phone, or received as a fax anywhere in the world.

Analyze this new technology and identify how it might affect the digital ink or digital paper market. Be sure to include a Porter's Five Forces analysis of the market.

4. **Less Is More**

Your organization is teetering on the edge of systems chaos. Your systems administrator is stressed beyond tolerance by too many systems, too many applications, too few resources, and too little time. The scope, frequency, and diversity of demand are causing greater risk than anyone dares to admit. Automating (and reducing complexity) the operating environment is critical for your business to survive. Research autonomic computing and write a report discussing how this technology can help an organization gain control over its systems.

5. **Fly Pentop Computer**

BusinessED specializes in creating new and innovative software for education in the business market. Danny Henningson, founder and president of BusinessED, is interested in developing educational products using digital paper and digital ink. Danny has hired you as the vice president of research and development and is excited to hear your ideas for new products. Your first assignment is to study the Fly Pentop computer (www.flypentop.com) and decide how you can apply this type of technology to the business arena.

6. **Alternative Energy**

With energy costs on the rise, many U.S. homes are turning to homegrown energy solutions. Your friend Cole Lazarus has decided to start a business offering such solutions. Cole would like your help developing his business. Begin by researching the Internet and find different ways that you could design a home with its own energy sources. Create a document listing the different sources along with advantages and disadvantages of each source.

B13

Strategic Outsourcing

1. Explain the business benefits and challenges of outsourcing.
2. Identify the three primary outsourcing options.
3. Summarize a list of leading offshore outsourcing countries.
4. Summarize a list of up-and-coming offshore outsourcing countries.
5. Summarize a list of rookie offshore outsourcing countries.
6. Describe the future trend of multisourcing and how it can support a business need for outsourcing.

Introduction

The core units introduced the concept of *outsourcing,* an arrangement by which one organization provides a service or services for another organization that chooses not to perform them in-house. Typically, the outsourced process or function is a noncore business activity; what is outsourced can range from high-volume, repetitive processes such as electronic transaction processing to more customized services such as a help desk.

This plug-in describes outsourcing as a strategic mechanism that aligns technology initiatives and business goals, manages technology operations in a difficult business environment, and reduces operating costs. Often, companies begin the process by outsourcing nonessential business operations, which may include applications, assets, people, and other resources. As organizations realize the benefits of outsourcing, they extend this approach to other business functions or processes.

Yet outsourcing carries risks: loss of control, inflexibility, and geopolitical uncertainty. Not all functions and processes can or should be outsourced, at least not without careful analysis of the advantages and disadvantages.

The Outsourcing Phenomenon

The outsourcing market has experienced strong growth over the last several years because of businesses' need to focus on core competencies, Web implementation initiatives, consolidation across industries, and a tight labor pool. The outsourcing of noncore, transaction-based processes has gained significant momentum over the last few years as organizations have become more comfortable with the concept of outsourcing and its advantages.

Organizations elect to outsource for a variety of reasons. Some of these reasons are tactical, while others are strategic. In the past, outsourcing was often used tactically, as a quick-fix, short-term solution to a particular need or problem that did not form part of an overall business strategy. In recent years, many companies have begun to use strategic outsourcing where an organization works with suppliers in order to make a significant improvement in business performance.

No one would seriously expect an oil company to outsource its exploration and refining functions; pharmaceutical companies probably would not outsource their research and development; and few, if any, major automakers would consider outsourcing their production planning or marketing campaigns. These activities are core to their businesses and often the means for differentiation in the marketplace and a source of competitive advantage. Businesses outsource their noncore functions, such as payroll and IT. By outsourcing IT, most organizations can cut costs, improve service, and focus on their core business. According to research firm IDC, the worldwide IT outsourcing market will reach $230 billion by 2009.[1]

Best Buy Co. Inc. is the number one U.S. specialty retailer for consumer electronics, personal computers, entertainment software, and appliances. Best Buy needed to find a strategic IT partner that could help the company leverage its IT functions in order to meet its business objectives. Best Buy further wanted to integrate its disparate enterprise systems and minimize its operating expenses. Best Buy outsourced these functions to Accenture, a global management consulting, technology services, and outsourcing company. The comprehensive outsourcing relationship that drove Best Buy's transformation produced spectacular results that were measurable in every key area of its business, such as a 20 percent increase in key category revenue that translated into a $25 million profit improvement.[2]

According to PricewaterhouseCoopers' survey of CEOs from 452 of the fastest growing U.S. companies, "Businesses that outsource are growing faster, larger, and more profitably than those that do not. In addition, most of those involved in outsourcing say they are saving money and are highly satisfied with their outsourcing service providers." Figure B13.1 lists common areas for outsourcing opportunities across industries.[3]

The drivers behind the rapid growth of the outsourcing industry include the following:

- **Globalization:** As markets open worldwide, competition heats up. Companies may engage outsourcing service providers to deliver international services.

- **The Internet:** Barriers to entry, such as lack of capital, are dramatically reduced in the world of e-business. New competitors enter the market daily.

Industry	Outsourcing Opportunities
Banking and finance	Check and electronic payment processing, credit report issuance, delinquency management, securities, and trades processing
Insurance	Claims reporting and investigation, policy administration, check processing, risk assessment
Telecommunications	Invoice and bill production, transaction processing
Health care	Electronic data interchange, database management, accounting
Transportation	Ticket and order processing
Government	Loan processing, Medicaid processing
Retail	Electronic payment processing

FIGURE B13.1

Outsourcing Opportunities

- **Growing economy and low unemployment rate:** Building a competitive workforce is much harder and more expensive.
- **Technology:** Technology is advancing at such an accelerated rate that companies often lack the resources, workforce, or expertise to keep up.
- **Deregulation:** As private industries such as telecommunications and energy deregulate, markets open and competition increases.

OUTSOURCING BENEFITS

The many benefits associated with outsourcing include:

- Increased quality and efficiency of a process, service, or function.
- Reduced operating expenses.
- Focusing resources on core profit-generating competencies.
- Reduced exposure to risks involved with large capital investments.
- Access to outsourcing service provider's economies of scale.
- Access to outsourcing services provider's expertise and best-in-class practices.
- Access to advanced technologies.
- Increased flexibility with the ability to respond quickly to changing market demands.
- Avoiding costly outlay of capital funds.
- Reduced head count and associated overhead expense.
- Reduced frustration and expense related to hiring and retaining employees in an exceptionally tight job market.
- Reduced time to market for products or services.

Outsourcing Options

In the early 1990s, British Petroleum (BP) began looking at IT outsourcing as a way to radically reduce costs and gain more flexible and higher quality IT resources that directly improve the overall business. Over the past decade, all companies within the global BP Group have incorporated outsourcing initiatives in their business plans. BP's information technology costs were reduced by 40 percent globally over the first three years of the outsourcing engagement and have continued at a 10 percent reduction year after year, leading to hundreds of millions of dollars in savings to BP.

Information technology outsourcing enables organizations to keep up with market and technology advances—with less strain on human and financial resources and more assurance that the IT infrastructure will keep pace with evolving business priorities (see Figure B13.2). Planning, deploying, and managing IT environments is both a tactical and a strategic challenge that must take into account a company's organizational, industrial, and technological concerns. There are three different forms of outsourcing options:

1. **Onshore outsourcing** is the process of engaging another company within the same country for services.
2. **Nearshore outsourcing** refers to contracting an outsourcing arrangement with a company in a nearby country. Often this country will share a border with the native country.
3. **Offshore outsourcing** is using organizations from developing countries to write code and develop systems. In offshore outsourcing the country is geographically far away.

FIGURE B13.2

Outsourcing Models and Cost Savings

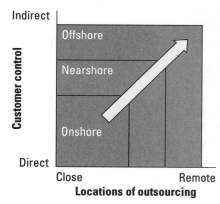

For many companies, certain IT services, such as application development, maintenance, and help desk support, fall within the category of functions that are ideal for outsourcing, including offshore outsourcing.

OFFSHORE OUTSOURCING

Since the mid-1990s, major U.S. companies have been sending significant portions of their software development work offshore—primarily to vendors in India, but also to vendors in China, Eastern Europe (including Russia), Ireland, Israel, and the Philippines. The big selling point for offshore outsourcing to these countries is "inexpensive good work." A programmer who earns as much as $63,000 per year in the United States is paid as little as $5,000 per year overseas (see Figure B13.3). Companies can easily realize cost savings of 30 percent to 50 percent through offshore outsourcing and still get the same, if not better, quality of service.[4]

Developed and developing countries throughout Europe and Asia offer some IT outsourcing services, but most are hampered to some degree by language, telecommunications infrastructure, or regulatory barriers. The first and largest offshore marketplace is India, whose English-speaking and technologically advanced population have built its IT services business into a $4 billion industry. Infosys, NIIT, Satyam, TCS, and Wipro are among the biggest Indian outsourcing service providers, each with a significant presence in the United States. There are currently three categories of outsourcing countries (see Figure B13.4):

1. The leaders—countries that are leading the outsourcing industry.
2. The up-and-comers—countries that are beginning to emerge as solid outsourcing options.
3. The rookies—countries that are just entering the outsourcing industry.[5]

Country	Salary Range Per Year
China	$ 5,000–$9,000
India	6,000–10,000
Philippines	6,500–11,000
Russia	7,000–13,000
Ireland	21,000–28,000
Canada	25,000–50,000
United States	60,000–90,000

FIGURE B13.3

Typical Salary Ranges for Computer Programmers

FIGURE B13.4

Categories of Outsourcing Countries

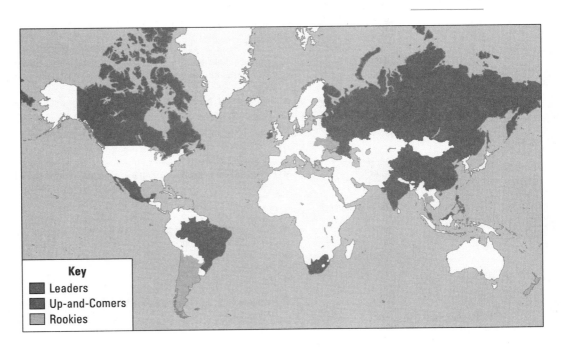

Key
- Leaders
- Up-and-Comers
- Rookies

The Leaders

The following countries are leaders in the outsourcing industry:

- Canada
- India
- Ireland
- Israel
- Philippines

CANADA

Expertise	■ Software development/maintenance, contact centers, technical support.
Major Customers	■ Allmerica, Agilent.
Advantages	■ Though labor costs are high, geographic proximity and cultural affinity with the United States make it highly desirable. ■ Contact center turnover is low.
Disadvantage	■ High cost of labor pool, but still less expensive than outsourcing in the United States.

INDIA

Expertise	■ Software development/maintenance, contact centers, financial processing.
Major Customers	■ Citigroup, GE Capital, American Express.
Advantages	■ India is the leader in business process and IT services outsourcing. ■ Two million English-proficient speakers graduate every year from more than 1,000 colleges that offer information technology education. ■ Strong history of software development. ■ Highly skilled labor pool. ■ Favorable cost structure.
Disadvantages	■ Political instability. ■ Labor costs are rising as demand for IT workers begins to exceed supply. ■ High turnover, particularly in contact centers, is becoming an issue.

IRELAND

Expertise	■ European shared-services centers, software development, contact centers.
Major Customers	■ Intel, Dell, Microsoft.
Advantages	■ Reputation for producing highly skilled IT professionals. ■ Strong cultural affinity with the United States. ■ Low political or financial risk. ■ Solid telecommunications infrastructure. ■ Strong educational system.
Disadvantage	■ High cost of IT salaries, however, labor costs are still lower than in the United States.

ISRAEL

Expertise	■ Software development/maintenance, packaged software implementation, application integration, security, e-business.
Major Customers	■ Merrill Lynch, Shaw Industries.
Advantages	■ Highly skilled workforce including scientists and engineers from Eastern Europe and Russia. ■ Excellent educational system. ■ Hotbed for IT innovation.
Disadvantages	■ Political instability. ■ Employee safety is a cause for concern. ■ High cost of IT salaries.

PHILIPPINES

Expertise	■ Accounting, finance, contact centers, human resources.
Major Customers	■ Procter & Gamble, American International Group, Citigroup.
Advantages	■ The population boasts a high percentage of English speakers with American accents. ■ Culture dictates aim-to-please attitude. ■ Estimated 15,000 technology students graduate from universities annually.
Disadvantages	■ Filipinos are not nearly as strong in software development and maintenance as other outsourcing countries. ■ Political instability.

The Up-and-Comers

The following countries are up-and-coming in the outsourcing industry:

■ Brazil

■ China

■ Malaysia

■ Mexico

■ Russia

■ South Africa

BRAZIL

Expertise	■ Software development/maintenance.
Major Customers	■ General Electric, Goodyear, Xerox.
Advantages	■ Big cost savings from a large supply of IT labor. ■ Brazil is Latin America's largest economy with a strong industrial base. ■ Brazil's national focus is on growing small and midsize businesses, including IT services. ■ Affinity with U.S. culture including minimal time zone differences.
Disadvantage	■ Remains on priority watch list of International Intellectual Property Alliance for copyright infractions.

CHINA

Expertise	■ Transaction processing, low-end software development/maintenance.
Major Customers	■ HSBC Bank, Microsoft.
Advantages	■ Large pool of educated IT workers with broad skill sets. ■ Government provides strong support for IT outsourcing industry. ■ Telecommunications infrastructure is improving. ■ Entry into World Trade Organization winning confidence of foreign investors. ■ Government has established 15 national software industrial parks.
Disadvantages	■ English proficiency low. ■ Workers lack knowledge of Western business culture. ■ Workers lack project management skills. ■ Intellectual property protections weak. ■ Piracy. ■ Red tape and corruption from a highly bureaucratic government.

MALAYSIA

Expertise	■ Wireless applications.
Major Customers	■ IBM, Shell, DHL, Motorola, Electronic Data Systems Corporation.
Advantages	■ Good business environment with strong government support for IT and communications industries. ■ Workforce has strong global exposure. ■ World-class telecommunications infrastructure. ■ Over half of the 250,000 students in higher education major in scientific or technical disciplines.
Disadvantages	■ Labor costs higher than India. ■ Few suppliers, which limits business choices. ■ Shortage of skilled IT talent.

MEXICO

Expertise	■ Software development, contact centers.
Major Customers	■ AOL Time Warner, General Motors, IBM.
Advantages	■ Solid telecommunications infrastructure. ■ Shares cultural affinity and time zones with the United States. ■ Second-largest U.S. trading partner. ■ Programmers highly proficient on latest technologies, including Sun's J2EE and Microsoft's .NET.
Disadvantages	■ English proficiency low. ■ Government corruption.

RUSSIA

Expertise	■ Web design, complex software development, aerospace engineering.
Major Customer	■ Boeing.
Advantages	■ Large number of highly skilled workers with degrees in science, engineering, and math. ■ Strong venue for research and development. ■ Programmers have skills for both cutting-edge projects and working with legacy applications. ■ European-based companies benefit from historic cultural affinity and geographic proximity.
Disadvantages	■ English proficiency not as widespread as in India or the Philippines, making contact centers impractical. ■ Government corruption and red tape. ■ Copyright piracy. ■ Outsourcing industry is fragmented and many firms have 20 programmers or less, making them unattractive to companies with large IT projects. ■ Telecommunications infrastructure needs work.

SOUTH AFRICA

Expertise	■ Contact centers, e-business, software development, IT security.
Major Customers	■ AIG, Old Mutual, Sage Life, Swissair.
Advantages	■ Time zone compatibility with Europe. ■ English is a native language. ■ Solid telecommunications infrastructure.
Disadvantages	■ Small pool of IT skilled workers. ■ IT talent tends to emigrate. ■ Crime.

The Rookies

The following countries are just beginning to offer outsourcing and are considered rookies in the industry:

- Argentina
- Chile
- Costa Rica
- New Zealand
- Thailand
- Ukraine

ARGENTINA

Expertise	■ Software development/maintenance, contact centers.
Major Customers	■ BankOne, Citibank, Principal Financial Group.
Advantages	■ Low costs resulting from an economic collapse in 2001. ■ Economy began to rebound in 2003, growing more than 8 percent, but unemployment remains high. ■ Large labor pool, including solid base of engineering talent.
Disadvantages	■ Country has yet to reach agreement with creditors on restructuring debt. ■ Foreign investors are cautious.

CHILE

Expertise	■ Software development/maintenance.
Major Customer	■ Compaq.
Advantages	■ Large highly skilled pool of IT talent. ■ State-of-the-art telecommunications infrastructure. ■ Good satellite connectivity and digital network. ■ Government actively supports business process and software development sectors. ■ Government plans to begin offering English classes to technical workers.
Disadvantages	■ English proficiency lacking. ■ Slightly higher costs than neighboring countries.

COSTA RICA

Expertise	■ Contact centers, e-business.
Major Customer	■ Unisys.
Advantages	■ Business-friendly environment. ■ Highly skilled pool of engineering talent. ■ Well-educated workforce. ■ Favorable cost structure. ■ English and Spanish widely spoken.
Disadvantage	■ Relatively small labor supply.

NEW ZEALAND

Expertise	■ Contact centers, e-business, Web hosting, Web design.
Major Customers	■ IBM, Microsoft, Cisco.
Advantages	■ Stable political and economic environment. ■ Well-established telecommunications infrastructure. ■ Thriving contact center industry. ■ Limited supply of domestic labor. To meet demand, the government has eased visa restrictions allowing entry of workers from countries such as Bangladesh.
Disadvantage	■ New Zealand cannot compete on costs with India and the Philippines.

THAILAND

Expertise	■ Software development/maintenance.
Major Customers	■ Dell, Glovia, Sungard.
Advantages	■ Reasonable telecommunications infrastructure. ■ Cost structure is slightly lower than Malaysia.
Disadvantages	■ Demand for skilled IT labor exceeds supply. ■ Population is not as educated as in neighboring countries. ■ English is not widely spoken.

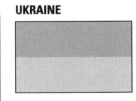

Expertise	■ Software development, Web site development.
Major Customers	■ Sears, Roebuck and Company, Target Corporation.
Advantages	■ History of training highly educated scientists and engineers. (The Soviet Union based the majority of its space and aviation technology work here.) ■ Information technology outsourcing growth predicted to double over the next couple of years.
Disadvantages	■ Unstable political climate. ■ Fears that the country is drifting away from democracy and pro-Western stance.

In summary, many countries are racing to participate in the outsourcing phenomenon. When an organization outsources, it needs to analyze all of its options and weigh all of the advantages and disadvantages. When faced with an outsourcing decision, be sure to evaluate the countries on such things as geopolitical risk, English proficiency, and salary cost (see Figure B13.5).

THE CHALLENGES OF OUTSOURCING

There are several challenges in outsourcing. These arguments are valid and should be considered when a company is thinking about outsourcing. Many challenges can be avoided with proper research on the outsourcing service provider. Some challenges of outsourcing include:

■ **Contract length**—Most of the outsourced IT contracts are for a relatively long time period (several years). This is because of the high cost of transferring assets and employees as well as maintaining technological investment. The long time period of the contract causes three particular problems:

1. Difficulties in getting out of a contract if the outsourcing service provider turns out to be unsuitable.

2. Problems in foreseeing what the business will need over the next 5 or 10 years (typical contract lengths), hence creating difficulties in establishing an appropriate contract.

3. Problems in reforming an internal IT department after the contract period is finished.

■ **Competitive edge**—Effective and innovative use of IT can give an organization a competitive edge over its rivals. A competitive business advantage provided by an internal IT department that understands the organization and is committed to its goals can be lost in an outsourced arrangement. In an outsourced arrangement, IT staff are striving to achieve the goals and objectives of the outsourcing service provider, which may conflict with those of the organization.

■ **Confidentiality**—In some organizations, the information stored in the computer systems is central to the enterprise's success or survival, such as information about pricing policies, product mixing formulas, or sales analysis. Some companies decide against outsourcing for fear of placing confidential information in the hands of the outsourcing service provider, particularly if the provider offers services to companies competing in the same marketplace. Although the organization usually dismisses this threat, claiming it is covered by confidentiality clauses in a contract, the organization must assess the potential risk and costs of a confidentiality breach in determining the net benefits of an outsourcing agreement.

THE LEADERS			
Country	Geopolitical Risk	English Proficiency	Average Programmer Salary
Canada	Low	Good	> $12K
India	Moderate	Good	$4K–$12K
Ireland	Low	Good	> $12K
Israel	Moderate	Good	> $12K
Philippines	Moderate	Good	$4K–$12K

THE UP-AND-COMERS			
Country	Geopolitical Risk	English Proficiency	Average Programmer Salary
Brazil	Moderate	Poor	$4K–$12K
China	Low	Poor	$4K–$12K
Malaysia	Low	Fair	$4K–$12K
Mexico	Moderate	Poor	> $12K
Russia	Moderate	Poor	$4K–$12K
South Africa	Moderate	Good	> $12K

THE ROOKIES			
Country	Geopolitical Risk	English Proficiency	Average Programmer Salary
Argentina	Moderate	Fair	$4K–$12K
Chile	Low	Poor	< $4K
Costa Rica	Moderate	Good	$4K–$12K
New Zealand	Low	Good	> $12K
Thailand	Low	Poor	$4K–$12K
Ukraine	Moderate	Poor	$4K–$12K

- **Scope definition**—Most IT projects suffer from problems associated with defining the scope of the system. The same problem afflicts outsourcing arrangements. Many difficulties result from contractual misunderstandings between the organization and the outsourcing service provider. In such circumstances, the organization believes that the service required is within the contract scope while the service provider is sure it is outside the scope and so is subject to extra fees.

Future Trends

Companies are getting smarter about outsourcing and about aligning efficiency with core business priorities. As businesses become increasingly networked (for instance, via the Internet)—global, commoditized, 24×7, and collaborative—outsourcing is becoming less of a cost-saving strategy and more an overall context for business.

Outsourcing is rapidly approaching commodity status, and this will transform the outsourcing value equation from high margins and vendor control into a classic buyers' market with competition driving down margins, adding features and services, and increasing buyer choices. U.S. companies should consider Mexico and Canada for nearshore outsourcing since those countries often provide very competitive pricing. Vendors in these countries can be viable alternatives, such as IBM Global Services (Mexico and Canada), Softtek (Mexico), CGI (Canada), and Keane (Canada).[6]

Companies should look for value-based pricing rather than the lowest possible price. The emerging trend of companies using reverse auction bidding to select offshore vendors is a dangerous one—it could result in low prices, but also low value and low customer satisfaction.

MULTISOURCING

For many years, outsourcing has predominantly been a means to manage and optimize businesses' ever-growing IT infrastructures and ensure return on IT investments—or at a minimum, more cost-effective operations. As businesses move to Internet-based models, speed and skill have become more important than cost efficiencies, giving way to a "utility" service provider model called multisourcing. *Multisourcing* is a combination of professional services, mission-critical support, remote management, and hosting services that are offered to customers in any combination needed. Like the general contractor model, multisourcing brings together a wide set of specialized IT service providers, or "subcontractors," under one point of accountability. The goal of multisourcing is to integrate a collection of IT services into one stable and cost-effective system. Therefore, multisourcing helps companies achieve the advantages of a best-of-breed strategy.

A multisourcing service provider can offer a seamless, inexpensive migration path to whatever delivery model makes sense at that time. For instance, HR processes are outsourced to one best-of-breed outsourcing service provider. Logistics are outsourced to another. IT development and maintenance to another. Although multisourcing mitigates the risk of choosing a single outsourcing service provider, additional resources and time are required to manage multiple service providers.

Outsourcing IT services and business functions is becoming an increasingly common global practice among organizations looking for competitive advantage. The guiding principle is that noncore and critical activities of an enterprise can be handed over to companies with expertise in those activities, thereby freeing internal resources to focus on enhancing the added-value of the organization's core business.

Outsourcing is no longer a simple matter of cutting costs and improving service levels. As more companies consider the benefits of outsourcing their IT functions and their business processes, they will find new ways to create business value. Companies that succeed will find innovative solutions to help drive costs down, select only the problem areas to outsource, and more important, learn to use outsourcing as a strategic weapon.

Companies continue to outsource at an increasing rate, despite reports of organizations disappointed and disillusioned by the process. The ultimate goal is multisourcing, combining professional services, mission-critical support, remote management, and hosting services.

★ KEY TERMS

Multisourcing, 455	Offshore outsourcing, 446	Outsourcing, 444
Nearshore outsourcing, 446	Onshore outsourcing, 446	

★ CLOSING CASE ONE

Mobil Travel Guide

For the past 45 years, the *Mobil Travel Guide* has been providing information on destinations, route planning, resorts, accommodations, restaurant reviews, and other travel-related subjects for people traveling in the United States and Canada. Print versions of the *Mobil Travel Guide* are created and updated annually at the company's Park Ridge, Illinois, headquarters, and are sold at most major booksellers and other publishing outlets.

Mobil Travel Guide, a well-known name in the travel industry, wanted to leverage its brand recognition by providing a highly responsive, real-time online service for leisure travelers that include customized travel planning, an around-the-clock customer service center, and a variety of privileges and rewards at a linked network of hotels and restaurants.

Mobil's existing online solution offered only a limited amount of static Web content that ran on just four servers, which were unable to process the site's considerable traffic, resulting in downtime for customers. Mobil needed a more robust solution that would provide real-time services such as route planning and fast access to the company's vast travel information database. The solution also had to be flexible and resilient enough to handle seasonal usage fluctuations, including anticipated spikes during the summertime and over major holidays. Mobil Travel Guide's internal goals also created a challenge for any solution. The site was expected to grow rapidly, but the company did not want to invest in an infrastructure capable of supporting its vision for the Web site.

Instead of using stand-alone Web, application, and database servers, Mobil Travel Guide decided to outsource all these functions to IBM. Because IBM delivers e-business infrastructure capacity as a utility, Mobil Travel Guide pays only for the processing, storage, and networking capacity it needs and can scale its virtual infrastructure up to meet demand spikes.

By avoiding up-front capital investment without sacrificing scalability, reliability, or flexibility, Mobil Travel Guide is positioned for success. The company can optimize its spending by scaling its infrastructure dynamically to meet demands and channeling resources toward generating new business and revenue. "Otherwise, we would have to buy enough infrastructure to handle the biggest day we could imagine, but typically it would sit unused. Now, we can take advantage of any market sweet spot we find, because we can scale with minimal lead time and capital dollars," explained Paul Mercurio, chief information officer for Mobil Travel Guide.

What is more, this capability moves portions of the Web-serving workload from Mobil Travel Guide's site onto servers located at strategic network points, so end users get faster responses even while Mobil Travel Guide lowers its per-transaction costs. "Because our service level ramps up or down dynamically in response to peaks and valleys in demand, we pay only for the capacity we need at any given moment in time," Mercurio said.

The on-demand delivery has already benefited Mobil Travel Guide in an unexpected way. After initially setting a committed capacity level that was too high, the company was able to leverage the flexibility of its IBM solution to "right-size" its capacity by reducing its contracted capacity level.

By outsourcing the solution to IBM, Mobil anticipates it will save about 35 percent in overall maintenance and software costs, while deploying an excellent e-business infrastructure solution that guarantees high availability, rapid scalability, and easy management of usage fluctuations.[7]

Questions

1. What are the main reasons Mobil Travel Guide used an outsourcing option?
2. What other areas would you recommend Mobil Travel Guide outsource?
3. What advantages and disadvantages would offshore outsourcing or nearshore outsourcing have for Mobil Travel Guide?
4. List the countries where Mobil could outsource its *Travel Guide.*

★ CLOSING CASE TWO

Outsourcing Brew

Coors Brewing Company, the third-largest brewer in the United States, manufactures and markets more than a dozen varieties of beer and malt beverages in 30 markets around the world. In a rapidly consolidating industry, Coors had a choice: keep growing or be acquired. To create the optimal conditions for growth, the company needed to improve access to information, consolidate systems, and reduce costs.

In less than a decade, Coors Brewing Company had more than doubled in size. Managing that growth became increasingly difficult for the company's internal IT staff. The company wanted to maintain responsibility for the technologies directly related to making and selling beer. Therefore, Coors was looking for a partner with deep industry expertise, mature application experience, and global reach to help revitalize its technology to support its business goals—including bringing new acquisitions online quickly.

The company decided to outsource its day-to-day management of its technical operations, conversion of legacy applications, and systems. Coors outsourced these functions to EDS in order to create a globally integrated enterprise solution, helping to optimize the supply chain from beginning to end. EDS is an experienced outsourcing services company with more than 130,000 employees and 2003 revenues of $21.5 billion, ranked 80th on the Fortune 500.

EDS offered Coors an infrastructure "on demand." Coors avoids a huge up-front investment in infrastructure, but is able to access increased capacity when business volumes increase. Now IT costs are predictable, and additional infrastructure is instantly available when the company needs it. Coors also controls costs by using EDS's Best ShoreSM Services, which enables Coors to reduce the cost of applications management by as much as 40 percent through a combination of offshore, nearshore, and local service centers and personnel.

EDS's solutions at Coors deliver much more than lower costs and increased reliability. As EDS assumed control of Coors's help desk, staff increased service levels while identifying patterns that let Coors focus training where it was most needed and kept the company aware of where potential problems lay. Standardizing the company's desktop environment has allowed Coors to get rid of many obsolete applications.

EDS is much more than an information technology outsourcing service provider; it is Coors's business partner. "They work with us on project management and root-cause analysis, which have helped us to add a lot of discipline in our organization," said CIO Virginia Guthrie. With a modernized and efficient information environment taking shape, EDS and Coors have ambitious plans for the future, from improving manufacturing processes to enhancing Coors's global presence. Guthrie said, "What we really want here is for this partnership to be a poster child for how outsourcing partnerships should work."

With the help of EDS, Coors was able to:

- Within just 60 days, reduce cost of application maintenance by 70 percent.
- Save more than $1.2 million on project resources related to SAP implementation.
- Reduce applications in use by 48 percent.
- Work to retire 70 percent of legacy systems.[8]

Questions

1. Describe an alternative approach that Coors could have used instead of outsourcing to EDS.
2. What would be the advantages of offshore outsourcing the Coors IT department?
3. What are some other reasons Coors outsourced its information technology functions that were not mentioned in the case?
4. Describe some of the factors causing Coors to be "forced" to outsource its information technology functions.

★ MAKING BUSINESS DECISIONS

1. Sports Sourcing

Sierra Sports Network launched its Web site SierraSports.com in 2001. With a huge influx of new visitors expected this football season, it is critical that SierraSports.com attracts, retains, and handles its Web traffic. It needs an overhaul of its existing Web site. Since Sierra Sports Network does not have the in-house skills to support the needed changes, it must look at outsourcing its Web development. Some of the company's needs are working with an outsourcing service provider who is proficient in English, has a solid telecommunications infrastructure, and operates in a similar time zone. List the outsourcing countries that could assist Sierra Sports for Web development needs, in addition to the advantages that each country could give to the company.

2. **Ops.com**

Contact center Ops.com provides information to those who are involved in real-time customer service. Contact centers have emerged as *the* critical link between a company and its customers. The growth in contact centers has resulted in a strong demand for Ops.com's services; so much that it now needs to outsource part of its operation. One main reason for the move to an outsourcing service provider is its need to develop a new service to collect information, such as account numbers, via an automated attendant and tie it back to a database. Ops.com can tap the database information to give callers automated access to more information, such as account balances, and create priority queuing for their most important customers. Describe the advantages that outsourcing would give Ops.com and list the outsourcing options along with a recommendation of prospective countries that have the resources available to be considered.

3. **The Travel Store**

In 2004, The Travel Store faced a dilemma. The retailer had tripled in size over a three-year period to $1 billion in sales, but it had done so despite operational deficiencies. The company's inability to evolve its business processes as it grew was causing problems. Within a year, sales and profits fell below expectations, and its stock price plummeted from approximately $10 a share to less than $2 a share. The Travel Store is determined to take quick and decisive action to restore profitability and improve its credibility in the marketplace. One of its top priorities is to overhaul its inventory management system in an effort to create optimal levels of inventory to support sales demand. This would prevent higher volume stores from running out of key sale items while also ensuring that lower sales stores would not be burdened with excess inventory that could only be moved at closeout prices. The company would like to outsource this function but is worried about the challenges of transferring the responsibility of this important business function, as well as the issues surrounding confidentiality, and scope definition. Make a list of the competitive advantages outsourcing could give to The Travel Store, along with recommendations for addressing the company's outsourcing concerns.

4. **Software Solutions**

Founded in 2003, Gabster Software provides innovative search software, Web site demographics, and testing software. All serve as part of its desktop and enterprise resource planning solutions for government, corporate, educational, and consumer markets. Web site publishers, digital media publishers, content managers, document managers, business users, consumers, software companies, and consulting services companies use the Gabster's solutions. The company is currently thinking about offshore outsourcing its call center functions, e-business strategies, and its application development. Describe how Gabster could use multisourcing along with the potential advantages it might receive.